Let Freedom Ring

Let Freedom Ring

Michael L. MesMer

ISBN : 1-4196-5736-4

To order additional copies, please contact us.
BookSurge, LLC
www.booksurge.com
1-866-308-6235
orders@booksurge.com

Let Freedom Ring

CONTENTS

INSPIRATION

I wrote an essay review titled "I Have a Dream," inspired from an autobiography written by Dr. Martin Luther King, Jr. Dr. King was a man who lived his dreams, and his autobiography is a masterpiece of eloquent words that can move a person to reach new heights. Reading about the life and trials of Dr. King helped me to go after my dream of writing this book. "I have a dream" — now live it!

PREFACE

Welcome to *Let Freedom Ring*. The very words mean so much to so many different people who live in the land of opportunity known as America. This book could have been written in hundreds of different styles and with much more detail and in-depth history. However, this book was written by an average American, born and raised in the heartland of Kansas, molded into a young man on the farm, and who raised his right hand and swore an oath of honor to protect the Constitution of the United States against all enemies, both foreign and domestic. Hopefully, I will amuse you with my personal views on several subjects, ranging from life on the farm to our Founding Fathers, and on a more serious note, sharing my thoughts and views on the events of 9/11 and the war in Iraq.

INTRODUCTION
"MY COUNTRY"

My country was bought at a price by men and women who paid for it with their lives. "Let freedom ring!" they shouted. "Give me liberty or give me death," another said. It was a war won with the heart for a new land—a new land of milk and honey, rich with adventure, waiting and ready to build character in the lives of the men and women who set out to conquer her. My country is a land of independence with several symbols of justice. First, there is a flag that originally bore thirteen stars with red and white stripes. "Old Glory" was her name, and she inspired a song that cries out these precious words: "Oh, say does that Star-Spangled Banner yet wave – O'er the land of the free and the home of the brave." ("Old Glory" was a nickname given by Captain William Driver in 1824 to the Star-Spangled Banner flag. In 1814, it inspired Francis Scott Key to write our National Anthem.)

The flag represents our unity while the bald eagle is a symbol of our freedom. To be able to soar on the wings of eagles, free and independent from any unjust rule or tyranny, was the foundation of the making of my country. Another symbol came in the form of pen and ink. Thomas Jefferson wrote what is probably the single most important document aside from the Holy Bible: The Declaration of Independence, which transformed my country from a mere thirteen colonies into the beginning of a great nation. It might have taken men's lives, muskets and cannon fire to create this nation, but as Mr. Shakespeare stated, "The pen is mightier than the sword,"

Jefferson proved this as he penned the famous words, "Freedom, Liberty, and Justice for all."

This book reflects how our nation began on the foundations of godly principles and deeply rooted Christian values. Just as Thomas Jefferson expressed his deep emotional feelings while writing the Declaration of Independence, we as a nation were once in search of *our* independence. Now that we have it, however, we have turned it into an independence of greed, impurity, and selfishness. The rest of the material for this book comes from the conviction that God Himself is in control of everything. It was in fact the divine plan of God, expressed through our Founding Fathers and through the Holy Bible, that we became what our hearts truly wanted to be—FREE.

In memory of my mother, Josephine Jean Marie Rosencutter, the mother of six children, an artist and green-thumb, and a woman who loved her kids more than anything on God's earth. To Brad "Deaner" Dennis, the 5-horsemen, we ran for you with all of our hearts Brad, thank you for helping me to see the true meaning of life. And to Mike Beal Fairfield High School, Langdon, Kansas, thanks Mr. Beal for believing in me, the "Duck Call" will sound again!

WHO AM I?

Who am I? First, I will tell who I am not. I am not one of the first men who set foot on this continent, enduring a long and treacherous journey across an unforgiving monster of a sea to become a free nation. Those were men who had prayers of becoming free from the rule of tyranny at the hands of their king. Those were men who had to fight their very brothers and fellow countrymen from whom they had fled in the first place. I am not one of the men who survived the first winter in the new country and welcomed the spring air with an ax in one hand and a shovel in the other. Their hard work, sweat, and tears were expended over the building of a homestead, a place to call their own, a new nation of people. No, I never lived on the edge of the wild frontier or battled with the natives or even took part in the first Thanksgiving.

Before long the prayers and dreams of these first men became reality, and new colonies emerged and grew into a nation that would soon cry out words like "liberty and justice for all." I never knew the little boy who could not tell a lie and became our first commander in chief, leading his men into glorious battle. I was not there to lay my head to rest in Valley Forge, cold, hungry, and tired, nor did I cross the Delaware in a courageous effort to shout the battle cry. I never knew the men who declared victory to their general, the man who became our first president and Founding Father who took office in Philadelphia after the end of the American Revolution.

I did not sign the Declaration of Independence or sign my "John Hancock" to the Bill of Rights. I did not help write the Constitution, let alone be sent on a peace journey to France to end a war—the war that started it all—a war that until that day no other country, nation, or empire had fought in order to create a true democracy designed for the *people*, by the *people,* and was the *people.* I did not salute the flag on June 14, 1775, when the men of the 1st became the official Army of the United States. I did not have the honor of seeing the sun set on July 4, 1776, the first day of a new beginning. I was not there the day Thomas Jefferson signed the Louisiana Purchase treaty and sent out Lewis and Clark to explore the great West.

As America grew and changed, it soon became a comparatively far cry from the early settlements of Roanoke, Jamestown, and Plymouth Rock. From wooden forts for protection to the stones of independence that shaped the new cities of America and gave a life breath to all who would embrace her, America was ready—ready to cultivate a generation of people all her own.

America was becoming a country of wealth and prosperity where men and women could build as big as their dreams would carry them. Unfortunately, some of those dreams resulted in enslaving men, women, and children from a different country. I was not there the night many cried out to be set free, nor was I there to see the man who stood up to fight in response to those cries. My ears did not hear Abraham Lincoln when he gave the Gettysburg Address or when he presented the Emancipation Proclamation. I did not fight in a war where brothers were divided by blue and gray uniforms, and I never walked the battlegrounds with Generals' Grant, Lee, or Jackson.

I did not move out on a horse riding in the 1st Cavalry Regiment to wage a war on Native Americans. I was not present with the "Son of the Morning Star" as his troops advanced upon some of my own flesh and blood at the Battle of Little Big Horn. I never served in the ranks of the soldiers who hunted down a great leader, Geronimo, who soared on the wings of eagles and will be a legend forever. I did not follow Chief Nez Perce in pursuit of a promised land, and neither did I cry my eyes dry on the Trail of Tears. The first Americans—natives, warriors, brothers, and hunters of the great buffalo—were unjustly removed from their native lands. I pray that God may one day give Mother Earth back to them, and if not literally, then perhaps in the afterlife.

As the sands in the hourglass ran down and the 1800's passed into the 1900's, I never heard the sounds of the first Model T's nor did I fly in the first airplanes. I did not enlist in the United States Army as America witnessed its first World War, shipping her young men off to battle. I never served in the Navy and stood portside to see the sun set on the sandy beaches of Hawaii. I did not know any of the men who died on the USS Arizona, nor did I storm the beaches of Normandy in the world's largest allied combined force to ever set sail. I was not there when brave Marines raised the flag over Iwo Jima nor faced the harsh winters of Korea. I never went on dangerous patrols in the dense jungles of Vietnam only to face an unwelcome homecoming. And last but not least, I was not part of the largest ground force/air assault operation of Desert Storm/Shield.

No, I was not yet created when God helped shape the face of America. As I look back on the history of America, I am truly thankful for the spirit of the men and women who gave their lives to see justice served, to have liberty, and to be free. The very words of our National Anthem, penned by Francis Scott Key in 1814, "And the rockets' red glare, the bombs bursting in air, gave proof through the night that our flag was still there..." have lived on from that battle through many other battles so that we can still sing, "Oh, say does that star-spangled banner yet wave, O'er the land of the free and the home of the brave?"

Now that you know who I am *not*, the question remains— Who am I? First of all, I will tell you that "I am an AMERICAN," free and able to choose my own destiny. The sky is the limit and my own lack of desire is all that stands in the way of pursuing dreams, goals, and ambitions of living the richest life that America has to offer. The words that are printed on these pages are just one aspect of my own dreams, goals, and ambitions of writing a book. I am the little red-headed boy who was picked on throughout grade school yet I made it past puberty, survived adolescence, and conquered high school. I am the class leader and student class president who served his fellow classmates with leadership, team work, and setting a high example. I am the cross-country state champion who dedicated his entire senior year to a fallen classmate. We ran for you, Brad "Deaner" Dennis, and we called ourselves the "Five Horsemen."

I am the impressionable young man who learned the value of hard work while digging postholes during a hot, dry, Kansas summer. I moved on from bucking hay bales and scooping out grain bins to lacing up combat boots and sounding off with "Yes, Sir!" You see, I am also a patriot who volunteered to serve his country, pick up and bear arms, and swore an oath to God and country to defend the Constitution of the United States against all enemies both foreign and domestic.

I am a soldier living a life of sacrifice to go and fight for freedom and possibly die for it as well. Like my brothers before me who took a stand against the evil forces of the world in order to ensure a life of freedom and justice for all, I too am ready to take a stand to help preserve that freedom, that justice for all, no matter what the cost. I am the sergeant responsible for the lives of seven soldiers who served under me. They looked to me for the answers, and when it was time to move out, they were ready to *"follow me."* Also I am a husband and father who must make the ultimate sacrifice, leaving my wife and son at home while I deploy overseas with only the grace of God to bring me back. All this and much more describes who I am. "To each his own" can be said about anyone, for everyone has his or her own stories about life.

Who am I now? I am a man who has lived life for thirty-two years, and God has been good to me thus far. As I was thinking just the other day, I believe in my heart that there is a reason for my writing this book. Like I said, everyone has his or her own stories about life. This book is my story, and it shows that I have a deep, heartfelt conviction to look into the reasons why we have allowed ourselves to stray from Christian values in our culture and in our government. Not that we, America, have altogether abandoned our values. NO, but as time moves on, I feel that more and more we are slipping farther and farther away from those values.

I took into account a lot of different things as to why I am the person who I am. I find that both the way I was raised to know God and how to treat others, as well as living the principles of the Bible, have helped me to maintain the values of honesty, integrity, patience, justice, mercy, faithfulness, and the like. It seems simple enough to try to live your life with standards like "love, joy, peace, patience, kindness, goodness, gentleness, and self-control"—all of which can be found in the Bible in the book of Galatians. I cannot help but wonder that if more people chose to adhere to these principles that we would not have some of the social problems we do have. I have always considered myself to be a nice person, someone who can get along well with others, and who would give the shirt off my back to help out someone in need. Maybe the ability to live by these principles is a gift from God, and perhaps I hold the same core values as that of our Founding Fathers, who valued a man by the way he conducted himself in society, the way in which a man held steadfastly to godly values, and the way in which a man wanted nothing more than to see his country maintain the principles that shaped it from the very beginning.

That is another reason I feel it necessary to write this book. Shame on me if I hold my feelings back or if I shrink back with the attitude of "Who cares?" I do care and I hope that you care, too. If I never thought it important to share with others my concerns, regardless of what they might think, then the whole idea of having a dream and living it would be a wasted effort on my part. I do have a dream and I am living it. I will strive to continue to be who I am and make a contribution not only with my life, but also to the lives of others in my community and to my country.

Just remember—this is who I am. The only reason I am who I am, have what I have, and am able to live where I live is because of the sacrifice, determination, and patriotic pursuits of our Founding Fathers. They went to their graves fighting for freedom so that you and I could live in peace and harmony and live life to the fullest, something that is known as the American Dream. All of this came about from men like George Washington and Benjamin Franklin, who helped create these United States of America, "Land that I love, from the mountains to the prairies and to the oceans white with foam." Was their dream and sacrifice not for you and for me, for our children and grandchildren and those still to come? Was their sacrifice not also for those without freedom, to be able to start a new life and to prosper so that all in all we can go on to say, "God bless America, My home sweet home?"

In a rather lengthy conclusion, my thoughts take me back to when I was young, very young in fact, and not yet realizing what life was all about. As a young boy I remember singing a song in pre-school which was probably the first song I ever memorized, excluding my ABC's. The song title was "America" (or "My Country 'tis of Thee") and at the time I could not comprehend the true meaning behind the message of the words. I do remember thinking, however, about how the Pilgrims were meeting with the Native Americans, or Indians as I called them back then, but I didn't understand what it meant when the song read "where my fathers died" or "from every mountainside." At that age I think we sometimes take words literally. I had no real father in my life, and I had no understanding of my father's dying and no concept of every mountainside when I lived in the middle of Kansas and had never seen a mountain—let alone an ocean white with foam. The words were meaningless in my mind and soon I was off to other endeavors. Now that I am thirty something and have lived a while, traveled around the world several times, and have a better understanding of life, I have noticed something that has greatly drawn my attention. In fact, it is one of the main reasons for writing this book. As I look back and study our nation's history, about our birth and the very true principals on which we developed our constitutional foundations, I see one constant variable to the beginning and end of all matters big and small. I see it in the patriotic songs, the beginning of our First Continental Congress, our printed money, and probably most importantly from the very mouths of the men who set all of this into motion in the first place. What is it? Look at this simple little phrase — "In God We Trust."

IN GOD WE TRUST

Those four little words have so much power that they helped to create this nation to be what it is today. Nevertheless, there are so many people — *Americans* — who are against them. They are quick to spit out of their mouths, "What about my rights; I have my rights you know," and yet they are determined to leave God out of their lives and the life of their country. I fully understand that we as a distinct people have the absolute right to choose to worship a god, or *the* God, or whatever religion we choose that best fits our lifestyle. One thing that boggles my mind and my conscience, however, is the fact that too many times the same people who are in such an *uproar* over the separation of church and state, the Pledge of Allegiance, and the simple phrase "In God We Trust" are only thinking of themselves. They are not thinking of the true meaning and history behind the delicate pages of our nation's beginning. If only they would stop and listen to the words coming out of their mouths, maybe they would realize that our nation's history is so much more in-depth spiritually, and the vast sum of the moral foundations of our nation's documents were derived from none other than inspiration from the Holy Bible.

I think that our Founding Fathers knew what they were doing, and if we also look at our relatively young system of government, we will find that we basically have created one of the most powerful systems of government in history and in the least amount of time. In terms of comparing the United States to other countries with a formed, organized style of government, we are but a "babe in the woods," especially when compared to Egypt which has had various styles of government and has been a living, breathing dynasty for some 5,000 years ("The Story of America," Readers Digest Inc. 1975). Compare that 5,000 years to our history making date of July 4, 1776, and you cannot convince me that God was not involved in the founding of

America. After 5,000 years, Egypt should have been the first to land on the moon, but in just a little over two hundred years we have become the single most prosperous nation ever organized on the face of this earth.

At the same time I am reminded that we are not perfect by any means and never will be. I would love to sit down with Mr. Jefferson, Benjamin Franklin, and General Washington and ask each one if they truly believed that God had in some way or another put His hand into the melting pot and blessed this land into becoming a great nation. It was Jefferson himself who said these words when confronting the issue of defending a great cause such as freedom: "I have sworn upon the altar of God, eternal hostility against every form of tyranny over the mind of man." (*America's God and Country Encyclopedia of Quotations,* p. 323). A man doesn't just say he swears upon the altar of God if in fact he doesn't mean it sincerely. Remember that Thomas Jefferson was a man passionate about assuring a God-given liberty to every man. It is reflected in his penmanship of the Declaration of Independence, when Jefferson writes, "They are endowed by their creator..." and at the closing again he states, "...for the support of this Declaration, with a firm reliance on the Protection of divine Providence...." (America's God and Country Encyclopedia of Quotations, p. 322).

I am a man who believes that God had everything to do with helping our forefathers shape the face of America. Are we perfect? No, not at all, and we never will be, just as I stated before—but shame on us if we fail to give credit where credit is due. The very words from the fourth stanza of "My Country 'Tis of Thee," tell us "Our fathers' God, to Thee, author of liberty, to Thee we sing..." It is obvious that our fathers before us gave credit and praise to God as the "Author of Liberty," and as the song continues we go on to sing, "Long may our land be bright with freedom's holy light; Protect us by Thy might, great God, our King." Although many may say, "God Bless America," do we mean it in our hearts? "Long may our land be bright..." Well, it had been bright long before Thomas Edison invented the light bulb, and it is still running strong today. I think what the song writer meant, however, was that our "brightness" would come from our reliance on the fact that God is the center of our government. "Protect us by thy holy might..." is what they cried out. Protect us from an unjust king, unjust taxes, and religious contradictions so that we can be free to live, prosper, and grow. I think shortly after the Revolutionary War, we forgot about "Thy Great God" and ran after prosperity and self growth, which in turn has led to a majority of selfish, greedy, money-hungry "KINGS" of today. No, not everyone who is prosperous fits into this category, but one only has to look around to see how greed and money and the like have hurt other people. If we are going to be "KINGS" then why not take it to heart in everything that America stands for and "crown thy good with brotherhood from sea to shining sea?" Then we can sing and shout "America! America! God shed His grace on thee..."

Do you agree with what you are reading? Just look at one aspect of the selfish, greedy, money-hungry "kings" of Enron. They too were protected under the same God-given liberty and justice as the very employees who lost, in most cases, every penny they had invested in the company. The same liberty, the same justice, and the same freedoms protected them, yet they made a conscious choice to be deceitful and murder the hopes, dreams, and ambitions of hundreds of fellow Americans—the same Americans that more than likely sang the same song I did growing up, "My country 'tis of thee, sweet land of liberty, of thee I sing." Unfortunately, though, their sweet dreams in the land of liberty were crushed.

Hundreds of lives were crushed by the "kings" of Enron as they built huge mansions in Florida, because Florida law prohibits the courts from liquidating personal property for lawsuit purposes. The "kings" will wake up each morning rejoicing in the land of opportunity, thankful that they are living "high on the hog," while their former employees wake up to another day of job hunting and rebuilding their lost fortunes. (Note: Since the writing of the above statement, some top

Enron executives have been prosecuted.) Of course it took the Enron debacle to happen before the government started its crackdown on corrupt CEO's, so perhaps justice will be served. My point is that we are all responsible for our own actions good, bad, and ugly. The above mentioned "kings" of Enron are only a drop in the bucket compared to "The Fleecing of America," as Tom Brokaw would say, that goes on daily here in the land of opportunity. We have all at one point in our lives sung a patriotic song, taken an oath of office, an oath to protect life or the Constitution, and/or sworn an oath to "tell the truth, the whole truth, and nothing but the truth so help me God," with the sole intentions of doing the right things. For those of us who have upheld our oaths—Bravo! But to those who have not, just look at what our foundation was built on and ask yourselves this question: Do I truly understand what I am saying when I say, "God bless America," or "I swear to tell the whole truth so help me God?" Even this simple statement, "I am proud to be an American," has often been overstated to the point that it seems to have lost its true meaning. Take a minute or two and look at yourself in the mirror, and see if you can live up to the words that are coming out of your mouth.

I know that when I, Michael L. MesMer, stood in front of the flag of the United States of America and swore an oath to defend this great nation so help me God, I meant it! Therefore, for the past thirteen years I have faithfully served my country, my fellow comrades, my commander in chief, my family, and yes, all of the citizens of this country so that freedom will live to see another day. All in all, I do not participate in trying to scam my way in this life, trying to get around the "system." I do not participate in a "lock out" or go on strike just because I feel I should be compensated more for the high risk service that I perform. I defend the rights of freedom so that professional athletes can complain about swinging a bat or throwing a ball for millions of dollars, and then complain because one player/athlete gets a million more than the other. I am not berating professional athletes, for I myself am a professional soldier; however, I find it extremely amazing that although I don't swing a bat or throw a ball for a million dollar contract, I am willing to die, lose my very life if necessary, for the same freedom as the individuals doing the complaining. In addition, I do it for around thirty to forty thousand dollars a year. It is not about the money for me. I am just one of many Americans who understand the cost of freedom. Freedom was paid for with the lives of men and women who died protecting the very words that describe what should be one of the most important foundations in the lives of all Americans—"I pledge allegiance to the flag of the United States of America and to the republic for which it stands. One nation, under God, indivisible, with liberty and justice for all." We are One Nation, pledging an allegiance to fight for freedom no matter where it is. Whether it is from the shipyards of Boston or the streets of Philadelphia, we, like Paul Revere who shouted, "The red coats are coming!" will ride on to say "Let's roll!" As one nation under God, fighting for liberty and justice for all, we will go the distance from Afghanistan to Iraq and to the next battlefield. We will not stop until justice is served. Why? So that in the end we can all still have the right to sing "Let Freedom Ring!!" [Note: I wrote the above passage in early 2004 while standing up the 2nd Stryker Brigade Combat Team. At that time Pat Tillman and his brother were assigned to the 2nd Ranger Battalion here at Fort Lewis, Washington. I was unaware that Pat had left the NFL in order to serve with his brother as a U.S. Army Ranger. I meant what I said above about certain professional athletes complaining about million dollar contracts, and it even goes on further when you have such role models who do outrageous things for fame and/or fortune. Pat Tillman was a true patriot, the kind who did in fact give up millions to go and possibly die serving his country, giving the ultimate sacrifice in order for others to live in peace. In light of his death, I will add a new chapter in this book—"The Patriot"—in honor of Pat Tillman.]

From George to George

No other American historical figure of the caliber of our first president and commander in chief, General George Washington, has had such an impact on the founding of a new country. His face can be seen by millions of Americans, stretching from the all-mighty one dollar bill to the magnificent Mount Rushmore in scenic South Dakota. As one of the original Founding Fathers, George Washington has been crowned "**THE FATHER OF HIS COUNTRY.**" He lead the men of the 1st Continental Army into battle against British forces, faced great adversity against man and nature, and sparked the torch of liberty with a victory in 1781 at Yorktown over Lord Cornwallis in the last battle of the Revolutionary War. It can be confidently said that Washington is one of the most honored men in American history (E.D. Hirsch, Jr. *A First Dictionary of Cultural Literacy*).

From the time I was old enough to go to school and start learning about our American heritage, I heard the unforgettable story of a little boy who "could not tell a lie" and who chopped down his father's cherry tree. Little did I know that that little boy was the man who took a small step to see others achieve bigger dreams—dreams that would one day lead to the moon and provide Neil Armstrong with the opportunity to say, "That's one small step for man, one giant leap for mankind." Well, in a matter of speaking, Washington took a giant leap for all mankind when he took on a matter bigger than himself: the foundation of creating equality for the greater good of others so that a single nation could breathe freedom, prosper from the hand of God, and declare on its own that "all men are created equal" and are therefore justified in fighting for a cause so great that it literally changed the face of a nation and the world forever.

General George Washington, a decorated war hero, left the battlefield to serve as our first president. Can you imagine one day being face to face with the icy waters of the Delaware, rowing to meet your enemy to do battle, and the next day you are faced with leading a new country comprised of a vast mixture of cultures and economic expenditures? The British still wanted their hands to be entangled in the faraway land they had just lost, the war debt, Native American uprisings, land expansion, free trade, states' rights, creating a Constitution, big government vs. small states, and on and on and on. These are just some of the trials and tribulations that Washington faced as the new president. Like he said in his first inaugural address on April 30, 1789, "The foundation of our national policy will be laid in the pure and immutable principles of private morality...the propitious smile of Heaven can never be expected on a nation that disregards the eternal rules of order and right which Heaven itself has ordained..." (*America's God and Country Encyclopedia of Quotations*, p. 652). Washington clearly understood that the creation of a new country, a miraculous birth so to speak, did not come about by the hands of man alone. The smile of Heaven was in fact the hands of God allowing what just took place to happen so that you and I would be afforded the opportunity to live in the land of "milk and honey."

To further illustrate this notion of a God-given right to liberty, Washington went on to say, "A nation that disregards the eternal rules of order and right which Heaven itself has ordained..." and any nation that wants to have peace and the strength to fight for peace must rely on the fact that God gives the right to build and destroy as He sees fit. Just look at how our first drafted government documents were written—they all had a tendency to give thanks to our Sovereign Lord and Savior. It is black and white in our Constitution, our court systems, our opening sessions of Congress—i.e., the ever living praise to God, our Creator. If it so *black* and *white* as I see it to be, then this question remains to be answered: Why is there a civil battle going on to remove the godly principles that were laid out in the foundations of our beginning government that both Washington and Jefferson were so adamant about? Thomas Jefferson said this about our new nation: "Can the liberties of a nation be sure when we remove their only firm basis, a conviction in the minds of the people, that these liberties are a gift from God?" (*America's God and Country Encyclopedia of Quotations,* p. 323). What a stark contrast to what we as a people think and believe today!

Without a doubt in my mind, for every one person who still holds to the belief that God has blessed America and that our rights as citizens are a gift from Him, there are just as many others who think the opposite. They have a right to think and feel their own way, a right to believe in a Creator or not, but to hold these truths as one's own and deny the very institution from which they came is wrong. Today, in the year 2006, who in their rational minds can say and believe that their "rights" are theirs, and no one person or government has the ability to infringe upon those rights even when those rights are written in stone in our U.S. Constitution? We hear it all the time: someone claiming to have "my rights." Well, you do have your rights; however, do you really know and truly understand from where those rights came? The separation of church and state, the Ten Commandments in U.S. courthouses, the Pledge of Allegiance or Bill of Rights, or anything that resembles a heavenly being is slowly being eradicated from our system of self-government.

The fact that our rights came from men who knew and understood and believed that a higher power than themselves helped in creating an atmosphere in which freedom could be born is truly a remarkable thing—if you stop to really understand it, that is. An example of what I mean can be found in Title 36, Section 302, of U.S. Code, adopted by Congress July 30, 1956, which clearly states that our National Motto will be none other than, "In God We Trust." Now, I know that is post-American Revolution; however, that is the *spirit* of our government doing exactly what I have been trying to explain all along—acknowledging that a power greater than man blessed our nation and helped to create one of the greatest governments ever assembled. So to merely convey one's thoughts or attitudes, grievances or opinions, without looking into the matter leads me to think that some people are just blowing hot air. By looking into the matter, and even a little bit at that, then and only then—according to my understanding—can a man or woman say, "Yes, I have my rights" and "Yes, I know from whence those rights derived."

To be able look at Thomas Jefferson today and hear him say, "These liberties are a gift from God" would be incredible. To have him witness men and women screaming to have the name of God taken out of our pledge or a depiction of the Ten Commandments taken out of a courthouse just because someone chooses not to believe in God but at the same time feels it's his/her constitutional right to have those commandments removed for the common good of others would be a slap in the face to the liberties that Jefferson fought so hard to create. Well, now it is my turn to SCREAM!

Don't you see—these people who are so quick to demand that they have a constitutional right to take away a piece of artwork—a Biblical piece of artwork—and yet murder the very principles of what Jefferson, Washington, Adams, and the like worked so hard for is unreasonable. We must not forget that it was Washington and his men who nearly froze to death in Valley Forge, and all for the hope and prayers of our independence as a nation. George Washington, a man from Virginia who was born and raised in the New World, destined to bear arms for the people, go the distance and quite possibly die fighting for it, paved the way for all of America to witness independence break free from the hands of tyranny. As stated previously, Washington's face is displayed on the one dollar bill, which is passed through countless millions of American hands every single day. Just sit down some time and look at a one dollar bill and let it speak to you. What do you hear? I hear the sound of ONE.

One Nation Under God,

One Liberty and Justice for All,
One Land where my Fathers died,
One Sea to shining Sea,
One Grand Old Flag,
One Rockets' Red Glare,
One Swift Sword,
AND
One Home Sweet Home.
"GOD BLESS AMERICA"
"ONE NATION UNDER GOD"

George Washington was just ONE man, yet I believe that even the decision, many years after his death, to place his face on the one dollar bill was in a way divine. Almost everything starts with one thing or another, and he was the one man to represent the people as a new creation, helping to form what is probably the most profound body of government ever assembled. Just as the Father in Heaven sent his one and only son to deliver the world from evil, Washington was sent as a son to us all to deliver us from evil as well. The power of ONE—not so much one's own self strength but the power of hope and determination—is what can drive a man to go above and beyond the call of duty. The call of duty for George Washington has touched us all. There was a portrait painted of Washington with this epitaph written on it: "First in War. First in Peace. First in Defense of our Country." Yes, the power of ONE! And last but not least, think of all who have saved, invested, or won a *million* dollars. That large sum of a *million* dollars would be worth absolutely nothing at all if it were not for the all-mighty ONE DOLLAR BILL!!! Remember the POWER OF...ONE...!!!

The year was 1776 and a certain spirit was being born. Minute Men gathered at a moments notice, Congress convened and discussed the future of an independent nation, and an able-bodied Continental Army mustered together. The shot heard "round the world" was fired and America had a war on its hands. Likewise the year was 2001 and a certain calmness was in the air. Congressmen and women are by far veterans at politics, Minute Maid is a household name more popular than a history question regarding the identification of the Minute Men, and an able-bodied "Army of One" could be deployed war ready within ninety-six hours anywhere and at anytime. As for the latest shot heard round the world—it came in the form of a horrific event that was not only heard around the world within seconds after it happened but also caught the world off guard and forever changed the lives of millions.

At approximately 0600 hours West Coast time and 0900 East Coast time, terrorists willingly took their own lives along with the lives of some 3,000 innocent bystanders when they took control of two large commercial jet airliners and flew them into the World Trade Center's twin towers. Another jet plunged into the Pentagon killing yet more innocent people. All the while, brave citizens plotted together with the first true *patriot act* to foil the plans of yet another plane headed for another undisclosed target, now believed to have been the White House. Those men and women rose up against terrorists in the first true battle of the War against Terrorism and their battle cry was "Let's Roll!" The passengers of that flight, United Airlines flight 93, came to rest in a grassy field near Shanksville, Pennsylvania, far from their intended destination. Todd Beamer was the man who cried out "Let's Roll!" and if he were a man of uniform, then I could imagine that his brave efforts to fight his enemy face to face and hand to hand would have earned him some kind of a hero's medal. Nevertheless, no medal or award could ever replace the precious life of anyone who died on 9/11 as a result of America's most costly act of terror from the outside world. The patriotism of such men and women on that day and the days to follow can never be rewarded or recognized in such a way that it could bring total relief. We will forever hold their memories in our hearts with the continuing pledge to fight terror whenever and wherever it is.

President George W. Bush is by no means a Founding Father and neither has he been crowned as the Father of his Country, yet in the events I have just described, September 11, 2001 is the *revolution* of the twenty-first century and Bush is, so to speak, our "Father." Not that George Bush is fighting for independence as in '76, but he is fighting to preserve what our country has established as a land of opportunity to all who would embrace her. Remember, Freedom Is Not Free. Just ask any member of the Armed Forces who have served during any given operation. The cost of freedom sometimes costs the lives of men and women who are willing to fight for it. Thomas Jefferson said, "The tree of liberty must be refreshed from time to time with the blood of patriots and tyrants." (Quotes from Founding Fathers. www.dojgov.net/Liberty_Watch.htm.) That is why we have an outstanding military today, and that is why the military constantly trains with this motto: "Train as you would fight." George Bush and George Washington are just two men who happened to be in the position of leading a nation that must in all cases preserve the very nature of what this country was founded upon—"Liberty and Justice for All." On a lighter note, George Washington is the only U.S. president to have been chosen unanimously for the presidency. George W. Bush claimed victory in a tight race in the prolonged "battle of the ballot" in the year 2000. A lot has changed from 1776 to the year 2006 and with it an even greater responsibility for any president trying to govern over these United States. Bush Jr., as some would say since his father, George H. W. Bush, held the same office from 1988 to 1992, has in many ways an even greater task of leading a nation than Washington and even perhaps his father did. A native Texan, Bush comes from what a lot of Texans feel as the "greatest nation in the state," that nation being Texas itself. Anyway, Texas is impressive with its total land mass and its array of vast climate changes and intriguing terrain that can take you from "surf's up" in the morning to desert hiking in the afternoon and then to cap off the day you can catch the latest blues band on Sixth Street in downtown Austin. The Texas lifestyle is BIG and, as everybody knows, everything is Bigger and Better in Texas. Coming from the Lone Star State, Bush has taken up the biggest task of them all—leading the American people in a time of war.

To what war am I referring? It is certainly not the traditional war of the past, such as when Adolph Hitler decided to invade all of Europe and the Japanese bombed Pearl Harbor. Those events grabbed American hearts and subsequently Americans grabbed their guns. Those wars were justified and all of America pulled together as "One Nation under God," supporting the troops who in turn gave up their personal lives to be shipped overseas to a faraway place with no guarantee of a return trip home. The current war I am speaking of is by no means a conventional war. It is a war that is dirty and hateful, religious and meaningless, and it has at times no purpose other than to destroy what God created in the beginning—the world and everything in it, beautiful and plentiful, for the sole purpose of bringing life to man. Just like when George Washington had to make a decision to march north into modern-day Quebec in order to pursue British forces, George W. Bush had to make a decision to fight terrorism, in the deserts of Afghanistan or in the metropolis of Baghdad, Iraq. The point is that the decision was made in the best interests of the American people, whether the people liked it or not. General Washington could have decided against marching north and quite possibly have encouraged the British to keep a stronghold with fortified positions, ready to strike down the men of the Continental Army. Instead, he made a decision and lived by it, and in turn it strengthened the hopes of the people with a victory. George Bush, on the other hand, made a decision to crush down an evil tyrant who actively supported terror in his country and abroad, deprived his country for nearly thirty years of the simplest of common pleasures known to man, and even used chemical weapons on his own people. Was capturing Saddam Hussein a victory for us? By no means a victory for us but rather a victory for the people of Iraq, for the children who will now have better opportunities to succeed in life, and for the cause of humanity itself. I mean, what nation can sit by and passively allow another human being to rain down chemical agents on other living creatures and watch them die a horrific death? Hitler did that to thousands of Jews, and not only did the world react with a vengeance, but we still remember the atrocities to this very day. Saddam Hussein marched into Kuwait City only to take candy from a baby, so to speak, and U.S. forces were there to greet him. Just like Generals Eisenhower and Patton, who defeated Hitler's troops, General Norman H. Schwarzkopf stopped Saddam dead in his tracks in an effort to stomp out tyrants who persist to bully their way around the world. Is that the American way? Should it be? I don't really know, but if we as Americans don't lead the way to stop terror dead in its tracks, which nation(s) will? George Bush said in a speech addressing Osama Bin Laden and his terrorist network, "There's an old saying out west that goes...

"WANTED
DEAD OR ALIVE".

I honestly do not think the president was cracking a joke in light of the current events unfolding at that moment. No. I believe he was dead serious about bringing justice to the American people and to other nations who lost loved ones in the events of 9/11. The problem is that too often in today's society we want instant gratification as well as everything bigger, faster, and stronger. Nevertheless, the fact remains just as the Secretary of Defense stated, "Hunting down Osama and his terrorist network will take time..." The hunt for terrorists is not a "fly by the seat of your pants" operation, and it is not something that can be done in one term in the Oval Office. Nonetheless, when Bush does leave his post, it will take someone with an unyielding strength, a loyal patriotic determination, and the will to go against the grain in hunting down terrorists. May God bless his or her soul!

☙

I mentioned that this war is dirty and hateful. I am by no means a war professor with substantial credentials from a prestigious university. I have not spent countless hours of study and research, and I do not have a single hour of instruction or teaching that can qualify me to suggest that I know how to legally, rightfully, and even morally classify what kind of war this is. However, it does not take a rocket scientist to put two and two together to get an idea of what acts of terrorism do to a peaceful society. What I can tell you is this: unlike some people who *do* have prestigious credentials, I have walked in downtown Jerusalem. I have been to the West Bank. I have passed Palestinians in the street, and I have driven in both Cairo and Kuwait City. I have had the sands of Iraq blown into my face. To add to that, I have served in the infantry for over thirteen years, and I am proud to say that I work for the Commander in Chief. Therefore, I think I am entitled to say YES this war is dirty and hateful.

It is dirty in the way that we are fighting a ghost of an enemy who hides behind women and children, peers around the corner of buildings to shoot you in the back, captures innocent non-combatants, hangs burned American bodies as a spectacle of power and force, barbarically cuts the heads off of its captives, and hijacks commercial jetliners filled with innocent passengers with the sole purpose of flying them into skyscrapers. As for hateful—this enemy has a burning desire to kill *Americans.* Note that I said Americans and not people in general. To them we Americans are not human but are some other form of creature that deserves death because we set foot on "their" holy ground. They are hateful in the respect that the desire to kill Americans has erupted into such a state of evil that the plans for peace or the "Road Map to Peace" will probably never be achieved to the extent the White House desires. In Webster's Dictionary hate is described as: 1: intense hostility and aversion 2: extreme enmity and/or the abominate. In the eyes of extremists, anyone who is against them but stands for peace is an abomination to their so-called holy crusade, or jihad, a holy war that justifies the killing of the enemies of Allah.

That holy war, as it is called by some, brings me to the conclusion that this is also a religious war. For thousands upon thousands of years, war has been a way of life to the people of the Middle East. It is clearly documented in the Bible by both God and Jesus that the enemies of God will never rest until the complete fall of Zion has occurred. Thank God He promised to deliver us in His due time, but the point stands that rest has not actually fallen on the world like we wish it would. If you take Iraq alone, forgetting about Israel and the Palestinians and/or any other part of the world, you can see a distinct fact. Religion plays a strong role in the Arab world, so strong that people are killed because of what they do or do not believe. There are three basic religions in Iraq and not ONE of them can begin to stand the other. Although they may tolerate each other a little, and maybe for a short time, the fact remains that the Shiite Muslims hate the Sunni Muslims and the Sunni Muslims hate the Shiites and together they both hate the Kurds in the north. That would be something like if next Sunday a Baptist church from the South declared open season on a Church of Christ in Oklahoma. And frankly speaking, it makes NO sense to me whatsoever!

All in all, I know that this war is more than meets the eye. It is a plan to rid evil wherever evil exists, and it is more complicated than I choose to understand. In my opinion, this war is too complicated for anyone to understand fully; it should be looked at from the standpoint of GOOD vs. EVIL and then leave it at that. That sounds a little naive and, perhaps to some, an uneducated guess on the clarification of a war, but how else can anyone fit all of the little intricate pieces into just one frame of explanation? In my opinion, NO one can truly explain what or why this war is what it is. We as Americans have one view and an Iraqi citizen who was born and raised in Iraq and knows nothing else in his life has another. He doesn't walk in our shoes and we certainly don't walk in his. Perhaps his view on life is not the utopia that we as Americans often like to perceive that life should be. [Note: On the average, an American child has at least three times as many shoes as does a child from a Third World country. (This was deduced from a personal experience in Egypt.) My point about the shoes is this: we have all we want, need, and desire, but for many people in the Middle East buying a new pair of shoes is not a top priority for living life. Once as I stood in line at an Egyptian border crossing waiting to enter Israel, a man approached our line and started to offer a price for anyone of us who would sell him our shoes. Consequently, he walked away empty handed and barefooted.]

Last but not least, this war is meaningless to some! As the

world witnessed at pre-Iraq invasion rallies around the globe, many, many people everywhere felt that this war is meaningless. As one famous military general once said, "War is Hell." Now, not everyone has to like war, but war has been a part of civilizations from Mesopotamia to the Roman Empire and from Napoleon Bonaparte to Adolph Hitler. The true goal of any civilized nation is to avert war, but sometimes evil has to be uprooted, and then the act of war becomes inevitable.

Any time there is a war, men and women will die in the process, therefore I would not dare to say to those who lost their lives on 9/11, on the USS Cole, during Operation Enduring Freedom and Operation Iraqi Freedom, and/or any other campaign where lives have been lost in the absolute effort to preserve life, liberty, and the pursuit of happiness that this WAR, the War against Terrorism, is meaningless. To do so would be shameful. To do so would violate the idealism that I, a volunteer member of the United States Armed Forces, raised my right hand under oath to God and country, and swearing to protect the very nature of the principles of the Constitution of the United States of America, will at all cost put my life in harm's way to see justice done.

In conclusion, I have made some comparisons to our first president, George Washington, with our current president, George W. Bush. To my surprise I find that the State of the Union is in some ways the same. Both presidents were dealing with the fact that each had made a conscious decision to send young American soldiers into battle. Why? They sent them in the name of freedom and to protect what our first generation of *Patriots* fought so hard for—independence and the opportunity to live a life free from tyranny. Are all presidential decisions the right ones? No, but I would bet my last dollar that anyone who is willing to trade places with someone who lives in an oppressed state, not able to even taste the glory of what freedom has to offer and be subjected to a totalitarian style of leadership, might reconsider their views on just how bad they think our government is in making decisions to fight in a war that is clearly that—a war! George Washington had to battle a nation fresh off the war wagon with a victory over Great Britain, and I am sure he made decisions that were not at all popular with the local train of thought. George Bush has to battle with a nation that *is* the war wagon and where the only victory lies in knowing that he made the right decision. Regardless of whether the local populace likes or dislikes the decision, where is that great spirit of American pride that rolled up its sleeves and said with a mighty roar, "This we will defend?" John F. Kennedy said, with a profound sense of pride and enthusiasm, "Ask not what your country can do for you, but what you can do for your country." Have we lost it altogether? Have we lost that sense of American pride that looks first to helping others and then ourselves? I surely hope not! There is a motto that only some know and keep inside their hearts. It is a silent motto but in times of trouble it can be deployed as fast as a lightning bolt. Not everyone has the right to declare this motto and I barely have the breath to speak of it let alone be part of it myself. The motto is this:

"DE OPPRESSO LIBER"

It means "To Free the Oppressed." Are there oppressed people in the world in need of help, even when that help means fighting in a bloody battle? Yes, there are! Are we the first to rise up against evil and stop it in its tracks? NO, we are not! JFK made a decision that put evil in its place and prevented what could have been a horrible attack on American soil in the form of short-range missiles. (Goggle, "*The Cuban Missile Crisis,*"1962.) President Bill Clinton ordered special operations teams into Somalia in an attempt to bring relief to a whole nation of oppressed peoples. Ronald Reagan said, "Mr. Gorbachev, tear down this wall," and again that decision brought relief to many people. All in all, are we as Americans going to help support and defend the Constitution against all enemies, foreign and domestic, or are we only going to look out for Number One? Isn't it time that we stopped focusing on just ourselves and what we are entitled to and stand up to help others have the same? We live in one of the richest countries in the world and not just money-wise either. We as Americans do have "A Charge to Keep."* We must not forget that before us others made the charge to seek freedom, and we are the next generation to help keep that freedom free.

[* "A Charge To Keep" is an inscription on a painting that belongs to the president. A friend of George Bush's painted the scene that depicts an old, rugged cowboy, with a look of great determination on his face, riding his horse through rough ground and sagebrush. Yes, we do have a charge to keep and that charge means so much in a society today that is infected with pride, greed, sexual immorality, murder, rape, hostility, and terrorism. It is not easy to stand up for doing what's right because doing the right thing is not always easy.]

A DAY IN HISTORY

It was such a peaceful morning and very quiet at that. The sun was just about to crest over the top of Mount Rainier and shine down on the state of Washington. I was working security at a mental health hospital in Tacoma and had noted the time was approximately 0555 in the morning. My posted place of duty was the front desk to greet incoming employees and ensure their safety, as sometimes visitors to the hospital were not coming to seek help.

After my duty was complete at the front desk, I returned to the main entrance to continue morning operations when I heard a very distinct tone of voice coming from the break room. It was a TV reporter with breaking national news. "Wow, national news at 0600 hours," I quietly thought to myself as I went to the break room to watch the TV. Then I saw a very disturbing image on the TV screen. One of the World Trade Center towers was engulfed in heavy black smoke that was quickly filling the New York City skyline. As I watched, my total focus was on hearing what had caused such a freak thing, when out of nowhere and from within the camera's pan of view, a huge jet slammed straight into the side of the other twin tower. It was at that precise moment that I, and everyone else who was a witness to that second jet, whether on TV or from a downtown New York City café, knew that something had gone terribly wrong. My heart sank inside my chest and I felt numb, yet somewhat afraid. I was afraid to analyze what had just happened and was afraid for the people of New York City.

I immediately called my wife who was still in bed asleep like most of the people of the West Coast, and after I explained the bizarre incident, she couldn't believe what I was telling her. After I hung up the phone, a new update came across the TV screen: another jet had crashed into the Pentagon killing more Americans. Not too long after that yet another jet mysteriously crashed near Shanksville, Pennsylvania. All of this happened so quickly that it was hard to fully comprehend what was going on and I felt like I wanted desperately to do something, but all I could do was sit there and watch and listen to the TV. As I sat there in my break room preparing to end my shift and go home, I started to wonder about those passengers on all four flights. What had they prepared for that day? Was it just another routine day jumping on a flight headed back home or perhaps was it to go visit a long lost friend? What did they have planned for that day and who was waiting for them at the airport? What kind of prayers did they say, if any, that morning? Maybe some prayed as they always did and maybe some didn't pray at all. At the very moment that their eyes and ears encountered the evil plot to change the course of their flights, change the normalcy of their day, and ultimately change the course of history, however, it could be expected that many were praying for their very lives.

What does all this mean? What course of action will we take now? How will this change our lives? Who is in control? Only God knows what is to come but for now my prayer is for the leaders of our country to look into their hearts and find the strength they need from God to make the right choices. For Americans, I hope we can pull together as One Nation, Under God, for Liberty and Justice for All. [Note: I wrote this passage the day after 9/11. I sat all alone in my new house with just the radio playing. I cried a lot, felt angry at times, and wondered what was going to happen next.]

As I reflect back now five years after that terrible day, I realize that at that time we were in our own state of "shock and awe." How could this have happened to us, the United States of America? The big question, of course, was who to blame? Should we blame the FBI, the CIA, George W. Bush, Bill Clinton, or someone else? Maybe we just did not have the answer for whom to blame, but with everything that goes bump there has to be somebody or something at which to point a finger. A White House spokesperson said during the 9/11 commission something like, "We as an administration and/or America as a whole could not have imagined that any one person or organization would have dreamed up a plan of attack such as flying huge jets into the side of city skyscrapers." [Note: I just paraphrased what was said and in no way am I putting words into the mouth of anyone.] Regardless of what happens, and in any situation, there is always something or someone at fault. To try and pin the blame on one single person or organization other than the terrorists who did this is unthinkable. In my opinion you cannot just simply investigate something as big as 9/11 and come to the sole conclusion that it was definitely this or that person's fault. To say that George W. Bush should have done more to protect Americans from the 9/11 attacks is like saying that on June 14, 2011, there might be a huge tornado that hits the Central Plains states, so we better start preparing now. Our administration knew of the threat from Osama Bin Laden, but even if we had taken severe actions to target him prior to 9/11, it would not have prevented some kind of attack on American soil. The facts are that somewhere out there was a definite "PLAN," so to speak, in the making to attack an American interest, and it was just a matter of time before "it" happened. Remember that the twin towers were a target all along and "cells" were actively working in America long before September 2001. Yes, I believe that we could have been more aggressive about who entered our borders and for what reasons, yet if there is such a hatred toward America—and there is—then no amount of preparation could have totally defended against some kind of an attack. It is a sad fact that not only are there active terrorist cells in America that are linked to Al Qaeda ,but we also have groups of the KKK who think that white power is the only power. We have anti-government militias all over the United States. David Koresh and his Branch Davidian followers in Waco, Texas, is just an example, and there are many others. There are "Americans" who hate and in some ways are no different in their thinking than the terrorists who hate.

Enough of the blame game already! What we need now is for our leaders to stand up and fight for doing what is right. Yes, 9/11 became a day in history that has changed our world forever. The question is not so much what we are going to do about the past but rather what are we going to do for the future? Not only the future of America is at stake, but also the future of our children, the future of our fighting military, the future of our principles, and the future of our commitment to the American way of life. Last but not least, the future of our ability to continue to provide all Americans with this dream is at stake—the dream to live in a peaceful place filled with endless opportunities to succeed.

"LIFE IS LIKE A BOX OF CHOCOLATES"

The phrase above is familiar to most people, for it's from the hit movie "Forrest Gump" starring Tom Hanks as an all-around nice guy who had a different outlook on life. If I take a moment to sit down and ponder the thought, I sometimes wish that life were indeed like a box of chocolates. I mean, it's easy to just put back the chocolates that don't agree with your taste buds and carefully select another to suit your desires. You know what I mean—it never fails when you pick the chocolate that looks so inviting, the one that is round and rises to a shiny little swirl of chocolate that screams, "Pick me, pick me, I am the one you want!" So without hesitation you pluck that one out of its tray, and while caressing it between your thumb and index finger you take a nice little bite. One chew or maybe two and it's all over—peach coconut was not the chocolate that you wanted at all. No, you wanted a chocolate-covered cherry or a caramel or, even better, a chocolate-covered toffee. As you tell yourself this, you simply put back the half-eaten creamy and start the selection process all over again. It is kind of fun to pick and choose or mix and match the candies you want. It requires a minute amount of strength or effort on your part to lift your hand from the box to your mouth, chew, chew, and chew some more, and it's back to the tray for a second round. What if life were this easy, this simple, and this uncomplicated? All we would have to do is make a decision to just put back the bad ideas or mistakes and pick another one and still try again if that one doesn't work out either. I am sure that there are many people who would gladly put back some bad "chocolates" of life and reach for new ones.

In view of the most tragic events of September 11, 2001, I am positive that many Americans wish they could close their eyes, dream a little dream, and reopen their eyes to see a different view on life. Possibly this view could bring back a husband or wife, a child or friend, a police officer, soldier, or perhaps a firefighter. Instead we are stuck with only memories of our loved ones. There is a grave difference between the death of a single person, which occurs every single day, and the horrific deaths of thousands caused by a senseless evil.

America has definitely encountered a mass of death, destruction, pain, and suffering and a level of injustice that has pierced the hearts of thousands from the East Coast to the West Coast. How could this happen and why did it happen? This question is irrelevant in the sense that it did happen, and now we as Americans will have to deal with the situation for the rest of our lives. There is no putting it back—the chocolate that you thought you wanted. We have tasted the bad and even though the taste will linger in our mouths for a long period of time, we will overcome!

Someone might say that if God is so great and powerful, why did this have to happen, why the deaths of so many good and innocent lives? I cannot speak for God, for even the Bible says, "Man can not comprehend what God has done from the beginning to the end." It is true that man is not able to fully comprehend the mysteries of the Heavens, or if God really does exist, or even the precise distance from the surface of the Earth to the icy fields of Pluto. My point is that in some cases man will never know why or how something has happened but only that it does and that it did. As stated again from the Bible, "What God has done from the beginning to the end..." is a profound mystery indeed. One thing that is not a mystery, however, is the fact that history has been made, and it is history that will bear the scar of terrorism for a long, long time. Although we do not know the end, we know one thing for sure: as long as terrorists continue to plot death and destruction, finding them and hunting them down will never end. So you see, life is much harder and more complex than a box of chocolates, and we cannot simply change the nature of evil men. What we can and must do is move on and try to make ourselves and America better.

SECURITY

The dictionary defines security as 1: safety; 2: freedom from worry; 5: protection. YES, security comes in many different forms. Since the events of 9/11, however, the United States government has had to reinvent security. Not only the government but also American citizens have taken their own personal approaches to creating a more secure atmosphere for themselves and their families.

Speaking of security, I was employed by a private security agency at the Seattle-Tacoma international airport (SEA-TAC) prior to the federalization of all U.S. airports across the nation. On an average day it was not surprising to have some 1,500 to 2,000 passengers pass through my security station. At this point in my life I was already very familiar with working with different types of people, different attitudes, and of course with different types of stressors—waiting in long lines, not knowing what to expect next, dumping and inspecting my personal belongings, just to name a few. Besides, after spending a few years in the military, I was comfortable with all of that. It had become second nature to me. I have been deployed to several foreign countries, including Egypt and Kuwait. Believe me when I say our bags were dumped both before and after and by both U.S. Customs and foreign customs agents subsequently then, one can only succumb to it. As for waiting in long lines, well, I have been doing that since kindergarten, and not knowing what to expect next, as sometimes things can and do change, is just a common part of life. I described all of that to prove a point, for what I am about to write was actually a shock to me. People seemed to be overly impatient and unforgiving when it came to their personal time management versus the exact time it takes to keep a nation secure. Plainly speaking, it does take time to ensure that all bags are properly screened and also that passengers undergo screening themselves for the common good and safety for everyone who wants to fly the "friendly skies." I have my own opinions and thoughts as to why so many people got fed up with how security issues were first handled after 9/11. Think about it for a minute. For many years we as Americans have been taught that we deserve service NOW and to always go after the bigger, better deal. We see it everywhere we look, from McDonald's to movie tickets. Why settle for just the normal burger and fries when you can "Super Size" it, or why stand in line at the movies when you can just *Fandango* it?

Following is a mere sample of all the attitudes that I encountered at SEA-TAC airport after 9/11. On one occasion a business traveler was outright furious at the fact that he had to remove his shoes in order for me to screen them for any potential explosive material. As he sat there untying his shoes, he made it quite clear to me and the passengers around him that, and I quote, "All of this should have been fixed on 9/12." WOW, America experienced its most devastating attack ever and this man expected it to have been fixed within a window of only twenty-four hours! My hat goes off to the flight crew who subdued Richard Reed, the infamous shoe bomber, before he carried out his plan to murder innocent lives aboard a jumbo jet bound for America by using the shoes that provided comfort for his feet. This business gentleman—not so gentle—was only one of several hundred people who didn't like the idea of removing their shoes in the name of national security. For the hundreds of passengers who didn't mind and even thanked me for asking them to remove their shoes, I salute you.

Another situation that I witnessed was a security procedure that is simple and thorough: the continuous baggage check where an agent randomly selects a bag, any bag, and performs a screen on it. All of this was done in the name of security— your security. I would often hear passengers complain and say things like, "Why are you picking my bag, do I look like I am dangerous?" or "Hey, do I look like a terrorist to you? This is ridiculous," and the all too familiar comment, "Come on, my plane leaves in twenty minutes and I am going to miss my flight!"

It didn't take long before I would simply smile and let the comments go in one ear and out the other. Besides, I had been trained under strict rules never to argue with passengers and to give them the respect they deserve. Of course, I had to keep my personal comments to myself and limit their disclosure within the pages of this book. In my response though, it goes like this: You are right. YOU do not look like a terrorist, and no, I did not pick YOUR bag specifically. I just picked a bag. As for YOUR plane's leaving in twenty minutes and will I please hurry up, I am sorry that I have to properly finish my job before I can give you back your bag. I took an oath to myself and to my country to help protect her, but I can clearly see that you do not find it worth the trouble by allowing me time to do my job in a way that ensures the safety of all passengers.

Well, I guess after years of living a certain lifestyle where we get what we want, so to speak, maybe those passengers had a right to be angry—or maybe not. Anyway, all of the Puget Sound news agencies broadcasted the many ways that travelers could prepare themselves for a successful trip to the airport and that passengers should arrive at least three hours prior to departure time. They even gave a list of prohibited items and firmly stressed that one must be patient while standing in line. Surely this would have prepared these people to expect some inconvenience. Then again, Be patient...Stand in long lines... Who wants to do that? I know it does not seem American to have to wait more than two minutes for anything, let alone have to wait three hours. Because this is the age of the super-information highway, I should not have to inconvenience myself by waiting in longer lines. Nevertheless, it is all in the name of SECURITY, right?

Time has gone by and as we recently reflected on what happened five years ago on September 11, 2001, I know that security has changed at all airports since it first took such monstrous steps in redefining itself. At the same time I hope we do not forget why we have gone through such changes. Also, I hope we can remember that our lives have changed! We must change the way we operate and do away with the mentality that things should be simple. If long lines means saved lives, then that is just fine with me. All in all, I believe that security is the responsibility of all Americans.

Perhaps we were overcome at first with such great emotions that long lines at airports or having to remove our shoes at security check points felt rather overboard. Some would even use the term "utterly ridiculous." We must remember, however, that our country is a baby in terms of the history of the world. We are not veterans in the practice of anti-terrorist tactics such as our allies the Israelis, who probably never step foot out of their doors without wondering if their day will be interrupted by an explosion of some sort. Americans should be able to feel safe going anywhere and at any time, but as you and I both know, times have changed and the practice of security must become a part of our daily lives.

THE COST OF FREEDOM

In the shaping of American stature, Patrick Henry said it best when he said, "Give me liberty or give me death." As Americans we have been face to face with both liberty and death, but no Americans before us were faced with the likes of the tragic events of 9/11. On that peaceful autumn morning, what appeared to be just another normal day turned into the worst attack on American soil since the birth of this blessed nation. Life is different now and will continue to be as nation rises against nation or certain individuals plot to carry out their evil attempts to destroy freedom. All in all, what *is* the cost of freedom that we as a people who were created to be equal must endure? The answer might possibly be time. That is correct—time. Time is a precious thing in a time-consuming world filled with all the luxuries to make life simply too easy. Just one aspect of time can be found waiting in a line at our nation's airports. Whether it is waiting for a tall white mocha or having your patience tried while waiting in a security line, we must accept that waiting in a line is now a national priority to ensure the safety of all who choose to fly the "friendly skies."

As a former pre-board screener at SEA-TAC International Airport, I am a firsthand witness to the sometimes chaotic and frustrating delays caused by the extended security measures put into place since 9/11. I myself am no stranger to imminent danger, long lines or enforced security measures. I have served my country proudly and in the most profound way, protecting the very nature of what Mr. Henry declared when he said, "Give me liberty or give me death." With my liberty I chose to face death in order to protect the people of the United States of

America. I did this at no cost to me other than my pride and a few drops of sweat. I question, however, why there are so many Americans who are angry with a cost that requires no more than a little bit of extra planning in order to show up at the airport an hour or two earlier, stand in line like everyone else, and be happy that the flight they are on prayerfully will not be their last. What about the small number of pilots who refused to follow FAA guidelines that require all persons to be screened prior to entry into the secure area of an airport? Such was the case in January 2002, when an American Airlines pilot boldly refused to allow a qualified pre-board screener to clear him using a hand-held metal detection device. The pilot was escorted from the security station by the Port of Seattle Police, returned later, and subsequently followed through with the security procedures. Also that year a pilot kicked a passenger off his plane because the pilot reportedly felt threatened by the passenger's Middle Eastern appearance. The passenger was in fact a Secret Service agent flying to meet up with his presidential party to provide security to President Bush. These are the same pilots who are captains and have taken an oath to provide the highest level of professionalism and personal safety for all passengers to feel confident to fly. There are other stories that reflect not only pilots but also passengers who are making it more difficult for the majority of "us" to go about our daily lives with a sense of peace. Only time will tell if we can adjust ourselves to this new way of living. I just pray that time is on our side.

THE TEN COMMANDMENTS

In the history of the world, the Bible tells all as some perceive to believe it. Although the Bible does not tell all of what life is about and how to live that life, for the many Christians and fellow believers out there, the Bible does hold the truths of God's eternal promises. So why include a chapter referring to the Ten Commandments? It is not literally the Ten Commandments that I want to focus on but rather the principle of a standard of living that should be the moral basis for all of us. I mean, I do not expect everyone to fall on their knees and declare to their neighbors—let alone the whole world—that they have been "born again." Nevertheless, since a portion of the material in this book covers how our nation was founded on divine principles, then the questions of where we are headed, what we have become, and what has happened to the "simple way of life," so to speak, are in every way worth looking into. Before I ever became involved in a church, I learned how to be good to others, to respect my parents, to never lie, and basically live the "Golden Rule" of doing unto others as you would have them do to you.

The earth, moon, stars, the galaxy, and all of the universe as we know it today is a splendid creation that has kept man guessing, wondering, and exploring since the dawn of time. The preeminent question that is continually asked is whether or not our universe and all the splendid oddities that go with it was created by a higher power or whether the power of evolution through science created our world? When I am laid to rest in my grave (and hopefully that will be when I am of a good old age) the above stated question regarding creationism versus evolution will still be a heated debate. Christians are quite certain that the almighty God did in fact create the earth and the heavens above while others believe the complete opposite. Some believe that our world came about from hot gases, exploding stars, and black holes, known as the big bang theory. Still there are others who really do not care one single little bit and think that whether a God or gods, wind and fire, or rain and snow created the earth, it is here and we should just enjoy it. What do I believe? The fact that I wake up every morning, breathing, thinking, and functioning with a body that is so complex, with external features and working internal parts unlike any other human being on the face of the planet, is a miracle that causes me to believe that God did in fact create me. Also, there are certain other things that have happened in my short thirty years of life that can only have one explanation, and that is God.

Let Freedom Ring is the title of this book and it means a lot of different things to many different people just like the Ten Commandments and the Bible mean a lot of different things to a lot of different people. The Ten Commandments come from the Old Testament yet they represent in themselves that God is our supreme power. Through God's son Jesus Christ, He gave us the freedom to choose. YES, that's right, the freedom to choose and make our own choices. Not one time in the New Testament does Jesus ever pressure us or hold our feet to the fire and make us worship Him. It is our freedom of choice to believe or not in the one whom God sent us or not to believe that there is either a God at all or that He sent any one in the first place. I do appreciate, however, that nearly two hundred or so years ago some men and women decided to make a choice, and that choice was to let freedom ring. That freedom was a belief that God sent His one and only son to die on a cross for us so that we could have a relationship with Him, and because of that men had it in their hearts to fight for a place to call home—a place of worship and a place of security, a place of new beginnings and of new hope. They also fought for a place of new birth that from the very start had God's name written all over it. Remember that it was Thomas Jefferson who said, "Can the liberties of a nation be sure when we remove their only firm basis, a conviction in the minds of the people, that these liberties are a gift from God?"

From the very start the only firm basis for starting a new government that would ensure that men would remain faithful — and not only to that government but also to the continuing efforts to see that holy justice remains holy for the sole good of its people — comes from the foundation of Scriptures. How else can you define the reasoning behind the laws and regulations of man brought out in the pages of the Constitution that are and can be directly linked to God's holy word? It is in there, it really is, if you will just look for yourself and find out. The people who founded America had a conviction to create a government that not only worked but also worked for the common good of others. In doing so the only logical manuscript available that could produce such evidence of that logic was the Bible. Not that King George himself didn't support religion and more than likely used the Bible during his reign as sovereign of Great Britain, but he did it in a way that was corrupt.

Why then did the Puritans leave England and why did the colonists want to separate themselves from their motherland? When Christopher Columbus spearheaded his voyage to find a new land and years later others followed, it was only a matter of time before America would be born. Many others followed after Columbus, and consequently, some of those people left their homelands because of either religious persecutions or simply because living under a king's rule could become quite unpleasant at times. Was I there when the Puritans made the decision to look for a new land to worship their God, free from a king's rule and free from a king's interference? No. Was I there when this nation gave birth to its Declaration of Independence under the guiding hand of God? No. I wasn't there when our Founding Fathers placed their hands on the Holy Bible and took an oath to God and decided to lead this country in a just and righteous way. If it were only about two hundred years ago that men believed that God helped them to become a free nation and to have liberty and justice for all, then why are we slowly suffocating these holy principles and taking God away from our government? If God were not important, not relevant, not in the least little bit true, then why is His name identified with our oaths of office and our sacred documents that are the foundation of our country? (I wish someone would explain this to me.) The very money we spend, save, invest, and some even kill for, has this inscription printed on it: In God We Trust.

$--In God We Trust--$

Who do we trust? Do we trust in ourselves, others, or even in our country? "Oh, I can spend my hard-earned money on whatever I choose. I can save it for a rainy day, a great vacation, buy a fancy car, and even spend it on the best colleges for my kids. It is *my* money, right? Boy, I sure do hate that our money says 'In God We Trust.' I suppose I should give my money back to the government. No, they have trouble enough just budgeting their own money, so I better just burn it in a hole out back in my yard and watch those greenbacks go up in smoke. But, man, it really does bother me that my money says 'In God We Trust' so maybe I will…" Get the picture yet? Or what about having Bibles in courtrooms where people swear to God to tell the truth? We would be better off swearing to tell the truth, the whole truth, and nothing but the truth so help me "Barney," the big purple whatever thing! What about the thousand or so people everyday who swear under oath to help defend the Constitution of the United States and become United States citizens? A judge swears them into citizenship in the United States under the hand of God, but since so many people these days are abruptly offended by our public display of anything referring to God, then maybe these people aren't really Americans? Heck, maybe we aren't Americans and we have been living a huge lie for the past two hundred years.

Excuse my language, but I am sick and tired of a bunch of crybabies fighting the very government that gives them freedom to live their lives in peace. Not only can they live in peace but also they can live here and choose not to worship any God! Our government does not force its citizens to worship one God or image, nor does our government come knocking on your door making sure you are in compliance with rules and regulations that are unjust. NO! That's why every single day the flag of the United States flies in all fifty states in our country, so that we as Americans won't forget where we came from. That is also why there is a separation of church and state, so that our government won't impose regulations on its citizens on how they choose to worship. I guess some have forgotten—or maybe they don't care—that men died for the flag and died for the cause of freedom.

Maybe putting on a façade and raising your right hand under oath to God or simply being born in America and sharing in all of our God-given rights is not good enough. Not good enough to let God be right where He has been from the very start. But you can bet your bottom dollar that as soon as one of these "Americans" has been trampled on by society and feels that in some fashion or another he or she is owed a monetary reimbursement, God has everything to do with it! But in the meantime—"Please, can you refrain from mentioning His name in public, and can we take that monument out of the courthouse, and by the way...I feel uncomfortable having my child pledge 'under God' but as far as the liberty and justice for all—I'll keep those."

So what is it that binds this country together? Is it Top Secret or is it too much of a touchy subject with a lot of "yeah-buts" to even mention it? GOD! There I said it! How hard was that, unless of course you choose not to believe in God, and that's perfectly okay because you do have the right not to believe. And I will not be the person who holds that choice against you. But don't consume yourself with trying to stop others from believing in God or seeing God in our style of government. If you do decide to wage a personal battle and seek to have your battleground be a court order trying to keep God out of our schools, courthouses, national monuments and the like, then I advise you to plan your course of action wisely. Study our American history and get inside the minds of our Founding Fathers and see for yourself if what they—George Washington, Thomas Jefferson, Benjamin Franklin, John Adams, and there are many more—did was a noble and holy thing or did they just create a government that has no foundation, no principles, and no moral standards which we as a society today should emulate? The noble thing that they accomplished was simple: The Founding Fathers recognized that the Almighty Creator who gives us life, liberty, and the pursuit of happiness was in fact the very one who enabled the above Founding Fathers to have the inspiration to create what "We the people, for the people, and by the people" have today. What we have today is "One nation under God with liberty and justice for all."[Note: I realize that in 1936 "under God" was added to the pledge of allegiance. Nevertheless, the principle is still the same.] How hard is that to understand? Isn't that the inspiration we need to be called patriots? Or has the definition of a patriot been watered down so much that we have succumbed to becoming crybabies fighting the very nature of what our government is? The fact as I see it is that we as Americans have lost our "Patriotic Spirit." We claim to have it, but only when it benefits us personally by some kind of capital gain. Our "Patriotic Spirit" is dead, and I would be ashamed to walk our nation's birthplace if Mr. Washington or Mr. Jefferson were to ever pay a visit from the past. Don't get me wrong. Our Founding Fathers had their moments of difficulty, and some of their decisions were not in the best interest of God or the people, and that is simply due to the fact that man is by no means perfect. Even as I write these words one day after remembering the fifth anniversary of 9/11, I realize we have lost our "Patriotic Spirit." Now some Americans still have it, but that is a rare blessing. What I mean is that it is rare that some people don't need to be reminded or told about their spirit, for they have it dwelling inside of them all the time. It is people like these who honor those who went before them and who fought hard to preserve the American way of life.

Twice daily the United States Army performs a time-honored tradition. At precisely 0630 every morning a bugle sounds out the tunes of "Reveille" and the flag of the United

States is raised. Then again at 1700 hours a bugle again sounds off with "To the Colors and Retreat" and the flag is lowered. As I stand at attention with a sharp, crisp salute, I often think about my freedom and how proud I am to be an American. Sometimes a tear wells up in the corner of my eye and I can feel a sense of great emotion overwhelm me. When was the last time the flag caused some kind of emotional response inside of you? If it hasn't, then go find your own "Patriotic Spirit" and believe in your heart that our spirit of freedom in fact comes from a higher power. And remember that in the beginning we pledged in our hearts that "In God We Trust" and we should strive to hold onto that motto.

In keeping with the spirit of this chapter, The Ten Commandments, in August 2003, a U.S. District Judge ordered Chief Justice Roy Moore of Alabama to remove a stone monument depicting the Ten Commandments from the state Supreme Court building, citing that it interfered with the Constitution's ban on government endorsement of religion. A group of lawyers who would pass the monument on their daily visits to the courthouse were presumably offended by what the monument stands for, a belief that the Ten Commandments represents the moral foundation of American law, as stated by Moore himself. On the contrary, the 11th U.S. Circuit Court of Appeals in Atlanta ruled that Mr. Moore had clearly violated the separation of church and state by displaying the monument in a public place.

Okay, let us pause for just one moment...Good. Now let us take an opportunity to see what our Founding Fathers had to say about the constitutional separation of church and state and the divine authority that gave them the inspiration to form the very foundations of the government that we now stand on.

Continental Congress

July 1, 1776

John Adams

"Before **God**, I believe the hour has come...All that I have, and all that I am, and all that I hope in this life, I am now ready here to stake upon it...I am for the Declaration.

It is my living sentiment, and by the blessing of **God** it shall be my dying sentiment.

Independence now, and Independence forever!"

July 3, 1776

John Adams

"The second day of July, 1776, will be the most memorable epoch in the history of America, to be celebrated by succeeding generations as the great anniversary festival, commemorated as the day of deliverance by solemn acts of devotion to **God Almighty** from one end of the Continent to the other, from this time forward forevermore."

Patrick Henry

"It cannot be emphasized too strongly or too often that this great nation was founded, not by religionists, but by Christians; not on religions, but on the Gospel of **Jesus Christ**.

For this very reason peoples of other faiths have been afforded asylum, prosperity, and freedom of worship here."

Chief Justice of the United States Supreme Court
John Jay

"Providence has given to our people the choice of their rulers, and it is the duty, as well as the privilege and interest of our Christian nation, to select and prefer

Christians for their rulers."

June 20, 1785

Religion vs. Civil Government

James Madison

"Religion is the basis and foundation of Government.

We have staked the whole future of American civilization, not upon the power of government, far from it. We have staked the future of all of our political institutions upon the capacity of mankind for self-government...to sustain ourselves according to the **Ten Commandments of God**."

United States Supreme Court 1789

"Proclaimed at the beginning of each session...

God save the United States and the Honorable Court."
United States Supreme Court
1980

"The Bible may constitutionally be used in an appropriate study of history, civilization, ethics, comparative religion, or the like."

(America's God and Country Encyclopedia of Quotations)

A lot can be said about the faith of our forefathers. Because of their faith, they gave to us the freedom to practice not only the religion of our choice but the law to which we bind together our fabric of society as one nation under God. Now who can argue with the fact that God did and does have everything to do with our being? Obviously, some do in fact have a problem seeing God or anything that resembles divinity intertwined with our system of "self rule." May I remind us that it is NOT our system of self-government—as if we created it yesterday— but rather it is a divine system of government created by men who had a profound relationship with God and the Bible and who took it upon themselves to ask the Almighty Creator to assist in developing this system of government that we now hold as our own. Just as Chief Justice Moore said, "Separation of church and state never was meant to separate God from our government. It was never meant to separate God from our law." Clearly his statement is a mirror image of what Patrick Henry said, and that is that religion (belief in God and the Bible) is the foundation of our government. Why is that so hard to comprehend? Even James Madison declared that we as a people ought to govern ourselves according to the Ten Commandments, although not in a literal sense as walking Bible thumpers. The point is that there is good reason to follow godly principles, and we are slowly destroying what has been handed down to us from generations past.

Is it not true that both the lawyers who initially complained and the judge who ordered Chief Justice Roy Moore to remove the monument themselves raised their hands upon the holy word of God and declared under oath to uphold the Constitution of the United States *so help them God?* Perhaps they either forgot that their left hands rested on the word of God and their right hands were raised in the presence of many declaring a holy oath, or maybe they merely took it for granted as a "right of passage," so to speak. It is indeed a right of passage to represent the people of this great nation—*Under God and with Liberty and Justice for all*—and to be our representatives to the courts, speaking with truth and power and justice. But, oh, America, woe to "us" that words are cheap and money talks. Right? Wrong! The word of God will stand the test of all tests, and it is man who will perish whether he chooses to believe in the one who created him or not. It is sad to read the words of past statesmen who created our government and to now bear witness to the changes that some want to make, which ultimately puts a scar on the face of the independence for which so many died.

On September 11, 1777, our government approved a motion that 20,000 Bibles be imported for the distribution to the peoples of this nation in an effort to share God's word. (*America's God and Country Encyclopedia of Quotations*). Not coincidently, at least to me, on September 11, 2001, our government again sought God's help when an attack on our very way of life brought to light the need for some kind of a spiritual awakening. How long will we deny that God is, has been, and will continue to be part of our government, now and forevermore?

The last example from the previous text that showed how our Founding Fathers and the government relied on God's word was dated 1980, far from the Revolutionary War time period. At that time Congress stated that the Bible is useful for appropriate study as history and a guide to ethics. Also they stated at the time that the Bible holds in its divine pages a gift that man can live by, and that gift clearly shows how to live as a peace-filled people, a kind-hearted nation, and a government that holds true to the motto that declares:

"We hold these truths to be self-evident, that all men are created equal. That they are endowed by their Creator with certain unalienable Rights, that among these are Life, Liberty, and the pursuit of Happiness...we mutually pledge to each other our Lives, our Fortunes, and our sacred Honor."

SAMUEL ADAMS

"We have this day restored the Sovereign to whom all men ought to be obedient. He reigns in heaven and from the rising to the setting of the sun, let his kingdom come."

(America's God and Country)

I know that in my lifetime, my *short* lifetime, that I have not always been an obedient servant to God and to the instructions in the Bible. I hope that with my pure intentions to mention such strong points of view that I would only create some kind of action or emotion in the hearts of those who read these pages in an attempt to encourage a patriotic devotion to a supreme being known as God. I derive this devotion from a deep personal conviction that wages war inside of me: the ever-present battle to remove godliness from our land. The Ten Commandments were used at a certain time and for a certain reason. Today, however, we can still gain valuable lessons not only from those commandments but also from the overall foundation of the Bible itself.

George Washington said, "It is impossible to rightly govern the world without God and the Bible...." (America's God and Country Encyclopedia of Quotations). I believe that this was as true a statement in the 1700's just as much as it is today in 2006. How else can we "Let Freedom Ring" and ensure to future Americans that this body of government will remain steadfast and loyal? Yes, the future of America was on Washington's heart when he said, "Let us unite, therefore, in imploring the Supreme Ruler of nations, to spread his holy protection over these United States; to turn the machinations of the wicked to the confirming of our constitutions; to enable us at all times to root out internal sedition, and put invasion to flight; to perpetuate to our country that prosperity, which His goodness has already conferred, and to verify the anticipation of this government being a safeguard to human rights..." (*America's God and Country*)

Washington knew that after he passed on, what he and the other Founding Fathers helped to create would have to endure the test of time. I think he anticipated it. I think he also prayed to the Lord that we, the United States, would not lose heart to seek after divine wisdom in leading the peoples of this great nation. Just one example, addressed earlier, is Chief Justice Roy Moore and the depiction of the Ten Commandments inside his courthouse. Remember that Washington said, "Let us unite...." Let us unite and not fight the very institutions that give us the right to choose, the right to be free, and the right to be independent. Was not Moore only following the examples already set forth in our governing body? Was he not expressing that the Supreme Ruler of nations is why he (Moore) had the ability to justly judge others' fates? I would like to say that I believe it to be true that it is impossible to rightly govern without God and the Bible. How else can we expect to know how to forgive? God forgave us, and we ought to forgive others as well. But how do we institute that forgiveness into a governing body of law? Well, by doing exactly what our first governing body did: "Unite...and implore the Supreme Ruler of nations...confirm our constitution... root out internal sedition...and verify the anticipation of this government being a safeguard to human rights..." How on earth can a man who only wants to serve his country, do the right and just thing, be ruled against by a higher level of law regarding the removing of something as simple as a stone monument? Tell me how that is confirming our Constitution! Is that an example of the efforts of this government to safeguard human rights? Oh, yes, the rights of those fellow Americans who raised their right hands and swore an oath to God to help support and defend the Constitution of the United States, so help them God. Who then turned right around and declared it unconstitutional to have the Ten Commandments publicly displayed for all to see. Shame on them, those individuals who took advantage of the system that allowed them to pursue their dreams, becoming lawyers, and then suffocating the dreams of other individuals by removing a reminder that our government was born on a belief in a higher power!

How I wish that George Washington could have presided on the ruling of Chief Justice Roy Moore. I cannot help but wonder if the body of government that enforced the ruling to remove the stone monument of the Ten Commandments won't go all the way and remove the metal clasp fixed to the five-hundred-and-fifty-five-foot tall Washington Monument that states:

"PRAISE BE TO GOD"

What about the tribute blocks engraved in the staircase along the way to the same monument? Some of them carry the following phrases:

"SEARCH THE SCRIPTURES"
"IN GOD WE TRUST"
"GOD AND OUR NATIVE LAND"
"MAY HEAVEN TO THIS UNION CONTINUE ITS BENEFICENCE"

I implore you, the American citizen, to take to heart these words, even if I am being repetitious. I would rather be a resounding gong with the right message than a vocal fool! I pray and hope that heaven itself will guard this nation, that in God we can trust, and that I can continue my freedom to search the Scriptures for myself. I hope that we, these United States of America, are not in jeopardy of losing the very God-given rights to continue to worship the Lord whenever and wherever we see fit. There have been some men in this world who understood the power of God and who were not afraid to declare His praises among the people. Abraham Lincoln was such a man. What if God had not blessed him in becoming our sixteenth president? What if he did not have on his heart the lessons learned four score and seven years prior to his address at Gettysburg? How might the course of this nation gone if it had not been for his deeply heartfelt convictions to reside in the comforts of God Almighty? Can you imagine if Lincoln had declared it unconstitutional to put an end to slavery? Or don't you think that God had something (or everything) to do with his becoming president at the precise time that he did? History tells us that he had many failures before making it into the White House. That is why God's timing is everything! Perhaps some of the most famous words ever to be spoken by a president after the likes of George Washington and Thomas Jefferson came from Mr. Abraham Lincoln. I leave you at this point with the following words spoken by the man who has been recognized as one of the greatest presidents of the United States:

"Our fathers brought forth on this continent, a new nation, conceived in Liberty, and dedicated to the proposition that all men are created equal...that this nation, under God, shall have a new birth of freedom—and that *government* of the people, by the people, for the people, shall not perish from the earth." (*The Great American History Fact Finder* Pam Cornelison and Ted Yanak, p. 575).

DR. PHIL AND SIMON COWELL

How on earth could Dr. Phil and Simon Cowell fit into a book titled *LetFreedom Ring*–a book written by an unknown author who writes short essays on various subjects including patriotic idealisms, inspirations from our Founding Fathers, and life on the farm? Easy—I simply admire both of these men for their integrity and honest desire to tell the truth.

I'll start with Dr. Phil who, next to Oprah, is in my opinion pretty much the only daytime talk show worth investing time in watching. Their shows both deal with everyday subjects that are family oriented and real. Everyone may not like watching the Dr. Phil show, but from the moment I first watched his show I had a strong and positive reaction to it. I sat up straight in my chair and thought to myself, Wow, here is a man who is humble, wise, and bold enough to tell individuals the truth about their lives no matter how much it hurts. Dr. Phil dares to go where no man has gone before and on national television to boot—looking someone straight in the eyes and telling that person the truth about any given situation in his or her life in order to help that person become better physically, mentally, and/or spiritually. He is a true testament not only to how a single person can care but also how a family as a unit of loving and caring individuals can be just that: a family that is directly involved with each other's lives. Most of all, I admire his approach in dealing with the NOW issues and the true facts that go along with them, that every individual must first start by looking at himself or herself, accepting responsibility, and then building a foundation that promotes peace and understanding.

Much of this book is centered around the foundation of our nation's birth, that foundation being godly and/or spiritual principles that shaped the lives of the men and women who sought a freedom that would in turn benefit all who embraced it. I believe that Dr. Phil represents the foundation to which I am referring: **Truth, Honesty, Spiritual and Godly principles, Morals and Standards, and Character.** I salute you, Dr. Phil, and I hope that your show will impact others in the same way it has impacted me!

From a doctor who helps people with their life situations to a British man who will tell you in a New York minute that you absolutely stink, and by stink I mean you couldn't hold a note to save your life, Simon Cowell has made it into the pages of my book. Does that matter to him? Not one little bit! With his reputation, like that of Dr. Phil, Simon is not afraid to look someone in the eyes and tell them, "Quite frankly, you suck." Now if Mr. Cowell were to read my book and then proceed to tell me that in fact it does suck, then of course I would be hurt, but hopefully his opinion would be followed up with some helpful and constructive criticisms. Maybe Simon comes across as harsh with his witty British humor, but the point I am making is that he will honestly tell someone the truth even if it hurts.

There are not enough people in the world today who actually tell the blunt truth. Instead, we like to beat around the bush, hide from conflict, or just plainly ignore a situation. An example is some of the "American Idol" contestants who simply ignore what the panel of experts had to say because they are living a life of utter denial. They do not want to subject themselves to wisdom from someone else's past. We, too, as Americans often ignore the wisdoms of the past. We think we know best when in fact our Founding Fathers knew that the only way to secure a solid foundation in the form of a democratic style of government was to follow the examples set forth by God's own word. [Are we too much of an independent people that we cannot see that without a basic foundation molded in truth and pressed upon our hearts as a real and powerful weapon for keeping alive all that we know to be true in the first place—OUR FREEDOM...?] It is in black and white and can be found in Colossians 3:12 and 13—"Clothe ourselves with **compassion, kindness, humility, gentleness, and patience.** Bear with each other and forgive whatever grievances you may have against each other. Forgive as the Lord has forgiven you." If we are willing to follow this admonition, then maybe we could understand that merely stating that we harbor truth because it sounds like a noble thing to say cannot compare to actually putting that truth into action. As Dr. Phil says time and time again, we first have to accept our responsibilities and work hard at building a foundation that truly does promote these noble characteristics.

Enough of the soapbox lecture! I tend to get carried away on subjects that I take to heart, so bear with me as I try hard to illustrate some simple facts, as *I* understand them to be, and articulate what I have been trying to prove all along. For the most part, we as a nation have lost our sensitivity to the moral standard of living found in the pages of the Bible. Okay, okay, I know what you are thinking: "So who is to say what moral standards should be anyway, and what about the First Amendment that says I have my rights?" Here we go again with this "my rights" thing. You do have both civil and personal rights that are actually *privileges* extended by our government. Privileges should not to be confused with prideful notions that I, man or woman, can do anything, say anything, and be anything I want, and no one is going to STOP me. What then is the value of a privilege if the privilege cannot at some point be taken away? [It defeats the whole idea that in some way we as a society have to uphold a certain unalienable cause to see that we faithfully adhere to the standards set forth in our civil codes.] Just as I stated earlier, the whole idea of a civil code has already been spelled out for us and it is in the pages of our Constitution and the pages of the Bible. In the last chapter of this book there are some famous quotes, and one of those quotes is from Bob Dylan who says that we have a degree of responsibility for our freedom. The same goes with our privileges as citizens of this great nation. We must uphold the values that were ingrained in both our Declaration of Independence and our Constitution or we will lose them. I will say it again: We Will Lose Them. If we are so quick to point out that we have our rights to do and say anything we want, justify immoral practices, and basically water down core family values for the sake of "the changing times," then where do we draw the boundary of our responsibilities? Our freedom is a privilege, a God-given privilege, that can be taken away if abused. These days with everyone's "rights," is it not our responsibility to fight for keeping the standard alive? Think about it, meditate on it, and I hope it will create a spark inside of you and show that I am not the only one who thinks and feels like this.

The theme for this chapter is the character of both Dr. Phil and "American Idol" icon Simon Cowell. The character traits that I admire about these men and have described in detail above is the ability to tell someone the honest to God truth even if the truth hurts. I know that I may have gotten carried away a bit, but passion is a powerful thing. Passion has created many marvelous and priceless artifacts and inventions that have caught man's attention over the past thousands of years. Take the Romans, for example. They had a tremendous amount of passion for life and love, and they had ambitions to rule the world. Before them, the Egyptians had passion so great that they created one of the Seven Wonders of the World: the Great Pyramid of Giza. Christopher Columbus had passion even when others did not and they chastised him for it. His passion, however, led to the leadership of our very own Founding Fathers who used their passion to create these United States of America. I, too, have passion, enough of it to share my thoughts and opinions about why I think we are losing our motivation to hold onto the very nature of our foundation.

If we continue to take God out of our system of government, not fully understanding what the separation of church and state means, then we will inevitably start to spiral out of control. It seems to me that we have already begun. It starts by removing something as simple as a stone monument from a courthouse where people are on trial for their lives, but you can bet they still put their hands on the holy word of God in the form of the Bible and swear by it. It continues by fighting to remove "Under God" or "In God We Trust" from our pledges and oaths. It goes on to fight for gay rights, not for the rights as a people or person—men have already died for that—but for the right to go against God's word, which says homosexuality is wrong. The person is still a person just like a bank robber is still a person, but the physical act of bank robbery is wrong. And it finishes with the watering down of our morals that says it is a sign of weakness to stand up for what is right, what is honest, and what is spiritual.

Last but not least is action defining appropriate action. What action will you take to see that our foundation is protected? What action will you take to see that what our forefathers died for will last lifetimes? And what action will you take to see justice done? My action comes from the passion to write what is on my heart. I can only express what I feel by expressing what I know. I know that we are the greatest nation on the face of the planet, yet we still have many faults and shortcomings. I know also that we stand for peace even in the face of war. I know that in America people can live free lives with roofs over their heads and food to eat. I know that I have the ability to dream a little dream and see that dream come alive, if I keep on trying and never give up. I know that I believe in God, that He gave me certain talents, and if I choose not to use those talents, then it's on me. I know that when I see the flag flying high it gives me a feeling of pride and true patriotism. I know that when I am in Iraq I hope that I can help bring the taste of freedom to the hearts of hungry people. And finally, I know that whatever life I live on this earth, I want to be remembered when I die as one who lived his dream.

All in all it comes down to one basic word: COMPROMISE. In a lot of ways we have compromised our religious freedom and turned it into what I call "American Religiosity"—having a form of religion but denying its true power. We have religion that is both watered down and turned into a mere spectacle of show rather than a true Bible-based Godly religion. Oh, we say we believe in God, but do we follow the Bible? No, we do not! Another example is totally denying God's standard and replacing that standard with the standard of man. Man has compromised God's principles so much that we are in a state of total acceptance of homosexual priests, ordained women, watered-down versions of Christianity, and a lack of true conviction to stand up and do the right thing. [Note: Women have played and do play an important role in God's Holy church, however, just as much as God says that certain "roles" are to be carried out by certain individuals, then I stand firm on my personal belief that a woman's role is not to lead an entire congregation.]

Religion is a very touchy subject with most people, but it is a subject worth discussing. How can one look at one scripture in the Bible, claim it must be followed and disregard all the rest? You do not have to look too hard to find and understand that the above-mentioned acts (homosexuality, select obedience, etc.) are against God's own words. Today's society is preaching a different, compromised version of what God intended his true word to be. Also, we have made great compromises in our moral standards along with the strength to enforce those standards.

Television is corrupting the minds of our children. In one aspect it portrays men as pigs only satisfied with beer, food, and sex, while women are regarded as objects of pleasure rather than wives, companions, and friends. Am I going against the grain? Yes, I am! Who, however, will be the one to make a change if not me? I cannot change the world, but I can at least make a change for my family and me. Am I saying we need to run around with Bibles in our hands, trying to convince the world they are wrong? No, not at all, but what I am trying to do is show that the foundation we started out on is not the foundation on which we currently are standing. Unless we drastically do something to make changes, our nation is not going to change by itself. I am one person among a million, a son to one mother and one father, a brother to my siblings, a husband to my wife, and a father to my son, a friend, a soldier, a mentor, a defender of freedom, and last but not least—

I AM AN AMERICAN

In conclusion to this chapter, although many interpretations of the Bible and of God's word have been debated over the sum of two thousand years, there is still no hard core evidence that God and His one and only Son do not exist. In fact, there is conclusive evidence that Jesus did walk the earth, and there are other artifacts that have been recovered that point to the fact that the Bible is as real as a man walking on the moon. If someone had said in 1849 that someday a man would step foot on that glowing ball in the sky known as the moon, no doubt there would have been a great debate over whether a man could ever get to the moon in the first place. Just as Abraham told the Israelites that God would deliver them into the Promised Land and that some day He would send a messiah to save His people, some laughed all the way to their graves while others had faith and believed. The point is—and has been throughout the pages of this book—that no matter what, man will always be suspicious of what he cannot see, hear, or touch. If it is not a tangible "thing," then it must not exist. Therefore, it must be true that we originally came about through a little sea creature called an amoeba. Do you want the truth? The truth is that someone bigger and stronger than man himself created our very existence—period!

THE GREAT COMMUNICATOR
THE 40th PRESIDENT OF
THE UNITED STATES OF AMERICA
PRESIDENT RONALD WILSON REAGAN
1911-2004

In grand retrospect regarding American liberties, Ronald Reagan not only continued to pave the way for Americans to live the "American Dream" but at the same time also upheld the core values in which our Founding Fathers so desperately believed in. They all believed in a free land where the common man can live and prosper without worry of unjust tyranny or the fear of oppression. It is with great respect and honor for one of America's most respected and admired dignitaries that I include a chapter in this book about President Ronald Reagan, who, in his own words "Has slipped the surly bonds of earth...to touch the face of God..." Mr. Reagan left us on June 5, 2004, at the graceful age of ninety-three years.

When I think about Ronald Reagan I remember a time in my life when I had no worries other than if I could somehow convince my mother to give me a cookie even though snack time was still hours away. I was just a kid in the 1980's yet I can clearly remember Governor Reagan raising his right hand as he accepted full responsibility as the supreme leader, commander in chief, and rightful president of the United States of America. I remember him debating against Walter Mondale and winning his second term in office. I remember how soft his voice was as it whispered out of the TV. Perhaps it was his tone of voice that caught the attention of the hearts of America.

I remember sitting in my fifth-grade classroom in Fort Scott, Kansas, on a mid-summer day when over the intercom came the voice of our school principal telling of the terrible accident of the space shuttle Columbia. Later that evening I recall listening to the president as he addressed the nation, sharing his deep sense of appreciation and admiration for the courage of the astronauts. His words, no matter what the occasion, seamed to always stick to our hearts and make us feel as if President Reagan actually had walked in our shoes. Ironically, this book features short stories about my life and the lives of other Americans, past presidents, true patriots, businessmen and actors, NFL football players, and soldiers. Ronald Reagan in some way or fashion played a part in all of the roles just described, and yet I feel as though he was a modern-day patriot and hero for all that he did. At the same time I had not thought of him for several years until Saturday, June 5, 2004, when I was out running some errands and heard the news of his death on the radio. I was shocked and saddened. I guess for some of us it is a testament to how busy we can become with our own lives that we forget the good others have done either for us directly or for the common good of a country, as did President Reagan. I think a lot of people would agree with me that Ronald Reagan did in fact deeply care about others, this country, his job as commander in chief, and most obviously, his cherished wife and partner, Nancy. In one of many speeches, he said, "I have the greatest love for this country," which is more evident in the good that he did than in the words that he spoke. It is with that kind of a heart that I brand former President Ronald Reagan as a "True Patriot," one who was willing to go above and beyond the call of duty and who went against the grain, against the norm, in order to prevail for the cause of freedom, justice, and love of country.

It has been said before that the true measure of a man lies not in what he says but rather in what he does. President Reagan did what he said and said what he did. He upheld the "Golden Rule" of doing unto others as you would have them do unto you. He led from the front, setting an example for all to follow, and he took responsibility for his actions. Through the good, the bad and the ugly, he accepted full responsibility for whatever did or did not happen under his watch. Some critics may differ in opinion; however, I believe that President Reagan portrayed a genuine, humble character that should be immolated to this day!

At one point in his run for the presidency, Mr. Reagan made a reference to being of the people, by the people, and for the people. I believe he understood his role as a president to be of the people, by the people, and for the people, for it was the *people* who voted him into the position in the first place. Just as it is written in our Constitution, "We the People of the United States...promote the general welfare, and secure the blessings of liberty to ourselves and our posterity..." Mr. Reagan did indeed promote the general welfare of the people, not only in the United States but also abroad. In his efforts to combat communism, he took it upon himself to see justice done for a people thousands of miles away just as if they were two blocks away standing in an unemployment line. I only wish that his efforts to secure the blessings of liberty and posterity for this country were not just slipping away, as it seems that we as a people today in the twenty-first century are more self-centered, envious, and greedy.

Ronald Reagan was interested in and dedicated to building a country filled with people who appreciated and remembered why we have our freedom in the first place: because there were men who were willing to die for it, write their names in blood for it, and go to their graves knowing that their sacrifices were in the name of *justice and liberty for all*. I stand strong on the issue that today we as a people are greedy and selfish and that both money and sex rule the airwaves, commercials, movies, and pretty much all the minutes of our lives. Not everyone is greedy and YES there is a lot to be thankful for in our country and with its people, but do I need to remind you of what I wrote earlier about the money-hungry kings of Enron? What about the report that headlined the first week of June 2004, claiming that the California energy crisis of 2000 was nothing more than a deliberate scam to electrocute the pocketbooks of millions of innocent investors and companies in America? Just think what it would be like if President Reagan were in office today. Believe you me, he would probably stand up to these money-hungry, selfish cowards, and throw the book at them himself just as he personally fired the air traffic control employees who went on strike during the mid-1980's.

Who is going to stand up to "bullies" and put them in their place? I don't just mean bullies in communist countries or tyrannical leaders such as Saddam Hussein. President Reagan could have just made a mental note regarding the striking airline employees and gone on about his business. Instead he made a conscious decision to accept the fact that no matter what happened in America, he as the president of these United States, accepted full responsibility. He took a stand, made a decision, and acted upon it. Even when something went wrong in his administration, he looked the public square in the eye and told them, "If there is any blame to be given then it rests in this office and with this president." Being a man of his word, he accepted the blame and continued to lead this nation. It was inspiring to have a leader who accepted wrong and continued to lead forth with a willingness to learn from life's mistakes.

I wish I could see more of that in the politicians of today; a humble character like that of Ronald Reagan! The president puts his pants on like everyone else; he just made a choice to wear pants that hold more responsibility than others. Nowadays it seems that if someone wants to run for president, the forefront of the issues fall on what and how many faults, lies, controversies, and dirty little secrets one can dig up against his opponent in order to wage a political battle against him. I am sick and tired of hearing the claim that the other party has more faults than my party so VOTE for me, and I will make things better. Obviously a man who was convicted of car theft when he was just twenty years old will not make a good candidate for president when he turns forty, but I am not speaking of the obvious misdemeanor or felony crimes. My point is that a president is like any other human being, except for the fact that he or she, for whatever reason, decided to do a noble thing and run for the chance to be the president of the United States. I mean, we are all human, capable of both love and hate, forgiveness and compassion, and what separates us from others in the world who do not wish to seek out freedom is our commitment to preserve what has already been paid for. I have said it time and again throughout the pages of this book: men paid with their very lives so that you and I and people like President Ronald Reagan could have the freedom to make the choices that we do.

On the night of Ronald Reagan's death, I was watching NBC Nightly News with Brian Williams, for Tom Brokaw was visiting Pointe du Hoc, France, commemorating the sixtieth anniversary of the D-Day invasion, June 6th, 1944. Mr. Williams had asked someone why they thought President Reagan could comfortably speak of God in various public settings and receive no flack, unlike President George Bush who also openly speaks of his personal faith in God and yet his faith in relation to his job as president has been made a side note to many political analysts. Both Brian and the person to whom his question was addressed had no real explanation other than perhaps it was in the way the very individual himself, either Ronald Reagan or George Bush, had presented their thoughts and beliefs to the public that made the difference. I disagree! God is the same as when Reagan was in charge, and He is no different today with President Bush in charge. What is the denominator then? In my observations, it has something to do with our changing world, our government policies or, for lack of better terms, a lack of moral policies. Of course there is also a big change in the very people who have the power to make amendments to certain rights, privileges, and traditions found in our blessed Constitution.

People want freedom and certain personal rights; however, it is these same people who fail to realize that the Constitution, Bill of Rights, Declaration of Independence, and countless other foundations to our very being as a government came from men who believed just as Reagan and Bush did, that God had a lot to do with our creation as a people and a nation. So there you have it straight from the horse's mouth (ME), and while some might think that what I have to say comes from the mouth of an *ass* rather than the horse himself, thank God for the freedom of speech!

In conclusion to this short passage, I want to reflect on the past generations of Americans who dedicated their lives to rid the world of an evil that kills innocent men, women, and children and offers no hope of true democracy. The "First Generation" was the Spirit of '76, and General George Washington led our nation as the first president of the United States. The "Greatest Generation" spearheaded the D-Day invasion of Normandy, France, and killed the heart of Nazi Germany while the home front sacrificed like no other generation past or present. The question now is what about the "Next Generation?" Can we honorably say that it is this generation, who was witness to 9/11 and sent its young soldiers to rain down the "rockets' red glare" in support of Operation Enduring Freedom? Or will it be the "Next Generation" who has yet to come? What I am getting at is, what truly is the heart of the people like? The values of most Americans in 1941 differed significantly from the values of people today. We have all heard it time and time again, and different corporations, organizations, the military, and even some churches have all used this excuse. And by the way, it's a feeble excuse in an attempt to cover up real issues that otherwise might infringe upon the truth, which is that the truth itself hurts. The grand excuse that is used repeatedly is this: "Times have changed and so must we."

It is true that times have changed, and it has been better in most cases. The problem is that the heart of man never changes. Even the Bible says that, "Above all else, the heart is deceitful." The heart of a man with good intentions is the same regardless of the generation in which he lives. From the heart of George Washington to the heart of Ronald Reagan, both men were *just* in their quest to lead a nation with help and direction from God. The heart of evil is also the same regardless of the generation in which a person lives. Adolph Hitler was just as much a tyrant sweeping across all of Europe as was Saddam Hussein, who marched into Kuwait with evil intentions of taking it over just because he thought he could. Even though the "times have changed," our morals do not have to change, nor our faith that God does exist have to change, nor does the very way we as a nation treat other people have to change. Maybe if more leaders took a stand on sensitive issues and made decisions based on our founding principles rather than changing because of the times or changing in favor of their peers, then our nation would be more like that of the Greatest Generation. [Note: If you have not read Tom Brokaw's book, *The Greatest Generation*, then you may have difficulty understanding what I am trying to communicate.]

All in all, I will close with the very words that President Reagan said as he faced the nation, just as he had many times in his lifetime of dedicated service. President Ronald Wilson Reagan said, "All in all not bad, not bad at all." And the question that Tim Russert asked his guests on "Face the Nation" the following morning, the morning after the president's death, was how will Ronald Reagan be remembered? As for me, he will be remembered as a "True Patriot," a man able to face his own mistakes and learn from them, a man who lived life to the fullest and truly cared deeply for the common good of others, and a man who exemplified what this great nation stands for, "That all men are created equal; that they are endowed by their Creator with certain unalienable rights; that among these rights are **life, liberty**, and the pursuit of **happiness**."

"God Bless you and God Bless America"

RONALD WILSON REAGAN

1911–2004

THE PATRIOT

In the action packed movie "The Patriot" Mel Gibson portrayed a brave-hearted American patriot during the Revolutionary War who closely resembled Francis Marion, the man known as "The Swamp Fox." Don't think that you have to swing a battle axe, shoot a musket rifle, or kill with your bare hands to be a patriot. Anyone can be dubbed a patriot. It essentially means a person who deeply loves his or her country, although not everyone can be placed in the same class of patriots as that of the patriots of 1776.

When I used to think of the word "patriot," only two things popped into my mind: the New England Patriots and the Patriot Missile that made national news during the 1991 Gulf War. Other than that I had not heard a reference to the word until the events of 9/11 when President Bush announced the signing of the Patriot Act, and then of course there were references to the patriotism of many Americans who proudly displayed flags, emblems, and banners depicting their own forms of patriotic pride. I do not believe there can be a comparison between the first patriots with their divine notations of patriotism and the love of those who poured out their lives and souls after the events of 9/11. "Give me liberty or give me death," as Patrick Henry stated to a crowd of colonials before rallying against British forces was exactly what he meant: death over the rule of tyranny at the hands of a king sapping the very life breath in the form of taxes and hideous acts was worth fighting for and even dying for if need be. That was what the "Spirit of '76" was all about, and the only comparable act of that magnitude was when Todd Beamer cried out, "Let's Roll!" and lead his little band of modern-day minutemen, and literally they only had mere minutes to act, in a daring attempt to subdue their aircraft's hijackers. The patriots of the American Revolution were a like-minded bunch of individuals with all sorts of different ideas of how to live in the New World, and yet they all agreed on one thing: in order to "Let Freedom Ring," you might have to fight for it. The following men are just a few of my favorite patriots of that 1776 era.

BENJAMIN FRANKLIN
SAMUEL ADAMS
PATRICK HENRY
ETHAN ALLEN
JOHN PAUL JONES
JOHN ADAMS
And
JAMES MADISON

The list could go on, and I sincerely hope that their legacy will live on as long as our American heritage is preserved in a way that makes future generations proud to learn of it. And just think, some people believe that a good tasting Boston lager by the way of Samuel Adam's Summer Brew is worth drinking while sitting on a piece of authentic Ethan Allen furniture enjoying a wide-screen TV as the New England Patriots kick off against the Green Bay Packers. All of that and much more was made possible by an invisible force called electricity that Mr. Benjamin Franklin, one of those "'76 Patriots," harnessed out of flying a kite on a stormy East Coast day. Now that's PATRIOTISM at its grandest!

A lot has happened in the course of our history since the Green Mountain Boys took Fort Ticonderoga and John Paul Jones declared that he had not yet begun to fight. And yet, for some Americans that fulfillment of self-pride that comes from sacrificing it all in order for others to share in the same freedoms is far and few between.

To be a **Patriot** is one thing, but a **Hero** is not easy in the making for it is not something made up or even achieved by a simple plan. There have been heroes in the past that went above and beyond the call of duty. Audie Murphy, for example, is the U.S. Army's most decorated soldier of WWII and can be confidently called a true hero. There are many other war heroes as well, and I am quite sure that to every mother who has sent a child off to battle that her child is in fact a hero. And for every little kid...well, we all had our heroes that we wanted to grow up to be like. Perhaps at such a young age we are not always able to differentiate between a true hero and a fictitious one like Superman or Batman and others, but nonetheless, the only recent living heroes in my opinion who faced a conflict and put their souls on the line for another man and died doing it are Delta Force Sergeants Randy Shugart and Gary Gordon.

The Hollywood movie version was based on the facts from Mark Bowden's book *Black Hawk Down*. It showcased the two Delta Force operators (Shugart and Gordon) who not only were willing to put their own lives in jeopardy but also requested that the Black Hawk helicopter they were riding in touch down near the crash site of Warrant Officer Mike Durant in a last-ditch effort to rescue him. The two operators knew what they wanted, made the decision to move in and secure the crash site, and did it without even thinking of the possible consequences of their not making it out alive. It is that kind of dedication to saving the life of another comrade that earns the designation of "Hero." Make no mistake about it, neither operator touched down in the midst of a raging crowd of militiamen who wanted nothing more than to kill an American soldier, for the honor of being called a hero. They did it because they couldn't live with the fact that a man lay in the rubble of metal parts, busted and bruised, with only a glimmer of hope of being rescued before being savagely killed while they hovered up above in a holding pattern watching their friend brutally murdered. Patriots? Yes! Heroes for what they did? Yes! I would dare to say that there are not many men on the face of this earth who would have done what they did.

That brings me to a touchy subject that has had a negative effect on the minds of many military personnel. Now, before I go any further on this new subject matter, let me say that the feelings I had were the same no matter where I went. From Fort Lewis, Washington, to Fort Bragg, North Carolina, the men I spoke with all agreed that Jessica Lynch was no hero—period. I believe that the American media branded her a hero in order to win the hearts and minds of the American people. Just think about it—thousands of U.S. troops headed off to Iraq while thousands were already in Afghanistan fighting, and it was almost Christmas time. What a picture perfect opportunity to display a young, vulnerable American soldier, a daughter to her father, a sister to her brother who is already serving, and a sweet, innocent little girl portrayed by the American media for all to see. She was the perfect propaganda tool to gain sentiment in the hearts of the American people by creating an emotional response for the cause of building the war effort and to support the administration's decision to spend more money. Or something like that! Why not feel sincerely for this captured American soldier who bravely fired her M16A2 rifle and killed the enemy who had all but surrounded her unit's convoy? She bravely took control of the combat situation and did what any well-trained maintenance crewman would do. She was prepared to fight to the death. Does that sound too good to be true? Was that not the initial picture painted by the media for us all to see and read about as we subsequently opened our daily newspapers or switched on the evening news?

We as a country found out later that some of the stories, including the ones about Private First Class Lynch, were either falsely written and/or abhorrently twisted. What a shame on the part of the active news agents who themselves braved combat situations to bring about the reality of war by means of pictures, interviews, and stories, and by portraying soldiers doing their duty during a time of war. Jessica Lynch herself proclaimed in her book and on national television that in fact she never fired a single round, for her weapon jammed. Instead, she hit the ground on her knees and prayed to God to make it out alive. I am sincerely happy that she made it out alive, but who is more a hero—Lynch or the Iraqi doctor who walked across an active combat zone facing death from flying bullets all around in order to see justice done? That man could have been shot as he approached U.S. Marines to tell of her whereabouts, but he did it anyway. Does that qualify as the act of a hero? I am not sure if it qualifies, but it took courage to go above and beyond his normal call to duty to help save people, and all the while facing the real possibilities of death to himself. Oh...wait a minute...I almost forgot...this man was a doctor...he was only doing what he was trained to do regardless of the situation or the person involved.

Unlike Private Jessica Lynch, in April 2004, a U.S. Ranger from the 2nd Ranger Battalion 75th Ranger Regiment died as a result of enemy fires. (The incident was investigated regarding whether or not it was enemy fire or friendly crossfire confusion.) During Operation Enduring Freedom and while directing his men to safety, Corporal Pat Tillman, former NFL football player for the Arizona Cardinals, paid the ultimate sacrifice in the face of danger. At what price does someone leave the comforts of home and all that is important to him to go and die in the harsh sands of another country? You cannot put a price tag on freedom; however, in relative terms it cost the sum of about three million plus dollars, for that is what Pat Tillman gave up in order to serve his country.

-SERVE HIS COUNTRY-

Pat Tillman didn't do it for the glory or the fame. There were no trophies, no NFL draft, no big contract, and no stats or bragging rights. There was only discipline and the creed that says, "Leave no Ranger behind." Pat Tillman, simply put, wanted nothing more than to serve his country in a time of war, and he did it in a way that was unknown to many. Leaving the NFL and all its glory for a position that paid around $30,000 when he was used to earning in the six-figure range is patriotism. I wonder how many critics chastised him under their breaths because taking that kind of a pay cut, let alone giving up some of your rights as a civilian, is too much for the average person to understand. I mean, not everyone can sleep on the ground in places that harbor little creatures that like to bite you. I have slept in the jungle, the desert, the woods, on rocks, and in other places that are either too hot or too cold and would not be suitable for average Americans.

Not everyone can handle the physical challenges of being a soldier, and Pat Tillman wanted to be a RANGER, the Army's toughest infantry soldier. I have profound respect for Corporal Tillman, and I work with Rangers who have either been let go, so to speak, or are waiting to return to "Batt" to fill positions already taken. The Ranger mentality is like none other in the Army and I dare not even compare myself to them. The Rangers I have worked with are dedicated to their profession. Just as Pat Tillman took it to them on the fifty-yard line, he took it to them as a Ranger as well. Who are "them" you might ask? Tillman the defensive line backer went the distance and took the hit. He made other athletes pay for being on offense, and set up the play that ran for the end zone. Then there is Tillman the soldier, who raised his right hand and swore an oath to God and country just like I did. He turned "blue" in Fort Benning, Georgia, went to RIP along with Airborne School, and then was assigned to a Ranger battalion. He took it to them—whoever challenged him as a Ranger, either his buddies during combatives or the enemy on the battlefield. He never quit and because of that men are still alive. *Hero* or *Patriot*?

Pat Tillman is a symbol of what America is all about: enjoying all that America has to offer from sea to shining sea and yet being willing to die for it. Die for what? It! He was willing to die for the seven-letter word that our Founding Fathers died for—FREEDOM. Remember that freedom is not free and someone must go and stand in the boots of the men and women who didn't make it. Will it be you? There is an old saying that goes, "Old soldiers never die, they just fade away..." I hope that our memories of why we are doing what we are doing will not just fade away. I hope our lives will not just be consumed with the new technologies of all that is to come as a way to make life easier. Life is already too easy when you live in one of the greatest countries in the world. As the song says, "America, America, God shed His grace on thee...." Let us not forget those who are willing to fight for FREEDOM because that would be a shame and already we have enough to be shamed about. We as a nation are not perfect, for the Bible says that "No one is perfect not even one," (Romans 3:10) and yet our Founding Fathers, patriots, and heroes paved the way for you and me to live and breathe and have our own being. Please, let us not forget what our independence is all about: "And the rockets' red glare, the bombs bursting in air, gave proof through the night that our flag was still there...o'er the land of the FREE and the home of the BRAVE." God Bless America!

THE FARM
GOOD OLD HARD WORK

Wat is the value of hard work and how can one define oneself through it? Hard work could be described as "a job well done," no matter how big or small the task. Perhaps if you were to ask a farmer to describe hard work he might reply with something like this: "Everything from sunup to sundown, six days a week." Compare that to a Microsoft employee, and his/her version of hard work might be meeting software deadlines or standing in line for a hot cup of java from Starbucks to stimulate the brain cells. Either way you put it, no matter what the job or career consists of, if a person can honestly say he or she put forth 100% effort during the day, that person had a hard day's work. Work is not easy. Since our fluctuating economy has been up and down in the past several years, just finding good work has become in itself "hard work."

The process of defining oneself through hard work comes from the gratification of doing the job right. After you leave the job, it will speak volumes regarding who you are. If the job is sloppy, that might be a good indicator of who you are as a person. If you are stricken with laziness, then laziness certainly will not get you very far. Just where or how do we learn the value of hard work? Some learn it from their parents, who in turn learned it from their parents, who probably learned it from theirs as well. Whole generations learned how to work, as that was the way things were before the information super-highway came about. Today it seems that more and more children are graduating from high school without knowing the basics of house cleaning, yard work, cooking, and simple car care. Ask me, for I should know; I am in charge of young soldiers who come to the Army and have no idea how and why it is important to keep a clean room. Not all children fit this description, however, and it could very well be that for various reasons the ones who don't have a good grasp of what work is also have a lack of strong family values. More and more children are raised without a father figure in their lives, a mentor to help mold and develop them into confident, competent young adults. But that story is for someone else's book...Back to the values of hard work.

Why did I decide to include a chapter about "good old hard work" in this book? For several reasons. First, because I learned the value of hard work on the farm, and I learned about it the hard way. Second, the U.S. Army taught me the value of hard work through the basic fundamentals of becoming a soldier. Third, as stated previously, anyone who reads Tom Brokaw's book, *The Greatest Generation*, will be transformed in their minds about what true hard work is all about.

THE FARM
ABBYVILLE, KANSAS

I was not born on a farm like so many of America's farm generations are and neither were my parents. Instead I became a "foster" child to a farmer by way of Abbyville, Kansas. Up until my freshman year in high school, I had never really held a position of great responsibility, except for my local city paper route. After leaving the city and moving halfway across the state, my world was no longer paved streets and flashing lights but rather dusty dirt roads and an occasional stop sign alongside the county black top highway. As a freshman at Fairfield High School, in Langdon, Kansas, I made friends with Daniel Foster, who asked me if I would consider helping out during the summer harvest on his father's farm. I accepted the offer because I could always use some gainful employment. Now, just how gainful that employment would come to be, I did not know at the time.

In looking at my life now, however, I realize I learned more than just driving a truck or scooping out grain bins in the middle of July. At the end of the first summer I was not sure how I had fared as a young, inexperienced farm hand, but I found out with a good ole firm hand shake and this question, "So do you think you might want to join us again next summer?" A lot of emphasis should be placed on the word "might," for I think the *boss* was afraid he'd mistakenly worked me too hard and that I, as a city boy, was not cut out for the farm life. I blissfully agreed to return, because I liked the work, and the pay at the time was decent for a boy like me. So what impelled me to want to come back to an early morning "roll call" from Daniel's mother? Like precise clock work, she would stroll downstairs each morning at the crack of dawn and sound off with a gentle voice saying, "Rise and shine, boys, time to get up." Well, to tell the truth, on my city paper route I didn't have fresh-baked wheat bread served with steak and eggs waiting for me each morning, and don't forget that those farm fresh eggs were cooked to order! And, boy, did I love eating, so food was a big reason that I decided to return the following year. Another reason was that I was having fun! Yes, you can call farming "hard fun" as the Fosters called it. For anyone who wishes to understand what and how farming can be described as *hard fun*, then I can only say that you have to experience it for yourself.

"HARD FUN"
FARMING

I know that "hard fun" farming sounds kind of weird, but its one of those occasions when you just had to be there. Gary and Lana Foster are the folks who run the hard-fun farming operation, and they are the folks that took a green kid from the city and made him into a certified hired hand. Earlier I described that working for Gary Foster was gainful employment in more ways than one, and consequently, I learned not only the value of hard work but also the meaning of life. You see, I believe that God makes or allows things to happen for a reason. Why did Dan pick me? I have a twin brother who is equally talented and also has a good work ethic. What about the other boys from our class? They too might have been a good pick. For some reason, however, Dan picked me, and I was glad for it.

I was raised with my twin brother Matt and with my other siblings, three sisters and an older brother. I never knew what a real family was for my parents divorced when I was still learning to walk and talk. How ironic that after years of moving from one town to another and never having any stability in my life that I would come into the company of a family with the last name of "Foster." Gary and Lana Foster took me in— red-headed, fair skinned, and green as a carrot top—and taught me the ropes of farm life. Soon enough I was ceremonially added to their family as the "foster son." Besides, my red hair was a perfect match to Gary's red beard, and for some reason they all took a liking to me. So there you have it, the making of a story that has more meaning than a summer paycheck. It meant being introduced to a real family who sat down to supper each night—I mean dinner, as there is no such thing as supper on the farm—gave thanks to God, and talked to each other about life. Wow! I was loving the farm and the true essence of learning about the Fosters' history. It made me wonder about my own family history and how people's lives are different. Yes, I was loving it, a family that talked to each other, laughed, and hardly escaped a lecture or two from the old man himself. What father can tell his children lessons on life without a long lecture dabbled with one line openers such as, "Back in my day," or "When your grandfather was a boy...?" Such precious and timeless stories bring generations together, but only if the bond of family is strong enough to carry on those stories, like that of the Fosters. I am truly grateful. I remember thinking to myself after that summer that I felt a part of something—a family that had opened their home and hearts to me. Thank you, Gary and Lana!

Before I knew it, it was summer again and I was back on the farm having fun. Having fun? You could call it fun—trying to change the front tire of a combine in a hot metal shed in the middle of summer without a breeze to cool the drops of dirty sweat collecting on your forehead. I also remember the satisfaction of getting done with one job only to start another. The first job was to gather up round bales with the old 1086 (International Tractor) followed by earning a Ph.D. (Post Hole Digger), which consists of digging new post holes the old-fashioned way in order to replace old ones that are not adequate any longer in keeping cattle in their rightful pastures. Something else I learned on the farm was that men, mainly the farming kind, like to keep account of their cattle. They know each by name, and if just one gets out of its pasture, then all work ceases and all hands pitch in to help round up the lone escapee. It was amazing to me that Gary knew all of his cattle by name, and in turn they knew his voice and the distinct sound of his old Ford pickup truck.

Last but not least, I believe it was the dirty jobs that forged inside of me the value that hard work does pay off in the long run. Those dirty jobs included, but were not limited to, the following: bucking alfalfa hay bales all day long inside a dusty, hot barn in August, scooping out the bottom of a grain bin with a broken shovel until your back screams with pain, digging post holes in ground hard enough to serve as a county runway, and the most painful farm experience of all: finding out that after you have spent all day dismantling various engine parts to get at a worn fan belt, the belt you purchased in town at the local co-op is one size too small. All in the name of fun, now, isn't it? I can hear Gary saying that right now!

We as farmers tried real hard not to allow incidents like the worn fan belt to disrupt a precious day's work by having to run into town and possibly be sold the wrong-size part. We accomplished this by doing a good job of keeping a stockpile of various parts at the farm, and no feeling is better than when a part breaks and you have to get the machine up and running again to be able to simply say, "I have the part we need around here somewhere. I just need to find it first." [NOTE: Most farmers, to my amazement, practically have an entire parts store located somewhere on their farm. You can start by looking in the most obvious of places, the machine shed. Now the machine shed holds an array of "extra parts," scattered tools, grease guns of three different sizes, buckets with holes in them and buckets without holes, nails, screws, bolts, batteries galore, an axe and hatchets, hammers of all sizes, a wedge and an anvil or two, a homemade work bench spot welded from two 55-gallon steel drums, and of course the wall of glory. The "wall of glory" consists of little boxes of washers, wing nuts, and spark plugs, cotter pins of different sizes, hose clamps, fan belts, universal joints, 10w30 motor oil—enough to change the oil in your whole family's cars and all of your neighbors' as well—tubes of grease, welding rods, keys with locks and keys without locks, and the most important number one item found hanging on the wall of glory: bailing wire used to help hold "stuff" together. Also there are other places you can find extra parts. To name a few: always look under the truck seats, between the truck seats, and behind the truck seats. You would be amazed at what one can find in the confines of an old pickup truck! And last but not necessarily least, if you have misplaced your 9/16 open-end wrench and your must have needle-nose pliers, your best bet is that they can be found on your secondary work bench. It is next to the drying rack on the kitchen counter top.]

Thanks to the Fosters, my life is well rounded. I hold many fond memories of the four summers that I worked on their farm. Nothing could have prepared me more for joining the Army than learning the values of hard work during those long, dusty, hot, Kansas summers. I will always consider the farm in the realms of "there is no place like home," and Kansas is home to me. Thanks to Daniel for seeing something in me. I am sure we will never forget the many times we drove too fast in the "Blues Mobile" or the times we spent down on the river, hand fishing for catfish. I have shared with you but a taste of farm life and how it impacted me—"Really Living, Ain't It!"

365 DAYS IN IRAQ
WAR! IT'S NOT WHAT I THOUGHT IT WOULD BE!

I n the pages of the book *Band of Brothers* by Stephen E. Ambrose, an accurate account of what war really is like is described by the men who faced the Germans during the numerous battles of WWII. The way in which these men describe coming face to face with their evil enemy and at times having to plunge a cold, steel bayonet deep into the chest of some cold-hearted Nazi only to remove it and carry on as if nothing out of the ordinary had just happened stimulates the imagination. That is what I pictured war to be more like: coming face to face with my enemy and shooting it out in the streets of Mosul, Iraq until the last bullet had been fired.

I have taken into account that I did not participate in the active ground assault that started the war in March 2003. Nevertheless, as part of Operation Iraqi Freedom III, I have battled with the AIF (Anti-Iraqi Forces). Long before I recognized the acronym "AIF," my only account of the war was through the broadcasting of Tom Brokaw and the NBC Nightly News. It became a daily routine for me, fighting traffic on I-5 trying frantically to make it to my driveway in time to hear Tom begin the opening headlines.

As far as seeing any AIF on the news, it was the usual plain-clothed street fighter with a yash'mer (usually black and white checkered head piece) wrapped around his head and shooting his rusty AK-47 assault rifle horizontally from left to right in a spraying pattern while praying that a bullet hit its intended target. To me, that was the enemy I was looking to go after once my boots hit the streets of Mosul. To my surprise, things turned out somewhat differently.

As the days grew closer to deploying to Iraq, I would often wonder what WAR really was going to be like, and I started telling myself and my men, "I know one thing for sure; it's either me or them, and you can bet that I'll be the one coming home." I guess that was my way of making myself feel better. Little did I know that six months into the operation I still would not have seen my enemy face to face, other than a picture of a dead AIF cell member or the suspected ones we rounded up during cordon and search operations.

Unlike Lieutenant Winters from Easy Company 506th Parachute Infantry Regiment, who successfully held the German line on D-Day after parachuting in from the night sky, allowing for follow-on forces to secure the French town of Carentan (*Band of Brothers*, Stephen E. Ambrose), I did not meet the enemy face to face. Not only was Winters wounded during that engagement, but inevitably he met his enemy face to face. I do not envy the men of WWII, or any other conflict for that matter. Not seeing your enemy during a war that has many conflicts in and of itself can be both frustrating and downright mind boggling. The first night they landed on foreign soil, the men of Easy Company knew what they were made of. Like the "Duke" (John Wayne), they didn't take crap from anyone, let alone a German trooper waiting in the mist of the night ready to kill any G.I. who came into the open. It has been said before that the AIF are like ghosts. They stay in the shadows and shoot at you when your back is turned, or they fill a car with explosives and drive themselves head first into your combat vehicle. They are not quite the enemy force from the 1940s, but who am I to compare the AIF of Iraq to the Germans?

WAR! When I think about it now that I have seen the effects of it, I agree with Thomas Jefferson when he said, "I have seen enough of one war never to wish to see another." At the same time the people of Iraq, like so many other nations worldwide, have lived with the effects of war for many, many years. On one particular mission my men and I occupied a sniper position from inside a doctor's house. The house was not only isolated but in direct alignment with a suspected enemy mortar-firing position. It was a perfect specimen of an OP (Observation Point) that would allow us to engage and destroy the enemy if he were to enter our designated kill zone. Although we never engaged the enemy, we occupied the young doctor's house for eighteen hours. His name was Omar and he was only twenty-eight years old. He told me that his entire life has been war and nothing but war. "Since I was a little boy, I have seen war. My entire life has been war. War with Iran when I was boy, war with Kuwait when I was teenager, and now as a young man, this war (Operation Iraqi Freedom). I never had a childhood, just war." I cannot fathom what that kind of life must be like, to see your country suffer under the hands of fighting men and to never experience the freedom we have in America, a freedom that is undeniably the richest gift God himself could ever give to a nation. It is, however, because of men like Lieutenant Winters and the thousands of other fighting men and women who have braved the many battlefields of our time that we have been able to preserve what we so desperately sought during our American Revolution—the spirit of freedom and democracy that is solely for the People, by the People and of the People.

Getting hit with an IED (Improvised Explosives Device) for the first time is an experience that I will never forget. Like I mentioned above, war is not what I thought it would be, and getting hit from an explosive device is not what I thought it would be either. In my mind I could only picture the Hollywood version of war, which was walking down a two-lane dirt road in central Vietnam when, at the precise moment the point man thinks he sees something strange and gives the hand and arm signal to halt, an ambush kicks off with anti-personnel mines, the crackle of automatic machine gun fire, and the screams of men getting hit and falling to their potential deaths. NO, it was not like that. Instead it comes when you least expect it, when at the last moment you never saw it coming. It comes at moments of laughter, when joking with a fellow comrade or perhaps when your mind has momentarily slipped back to reality instead of being forced to stay alert in order to stay alive. But then again, what man can find a moment of reality inside a combat zone, knowing that at any second his life breath could be stolen from him?

I remember the events well: the assassin platoon getting hit for the first time in Mosul, Iraq. It was our second month in country when the battalion had us conducting daily patrols for what they liked to call "counter-mortar patrols." We all knew that the counter-mortar patrol was more like looking for a needle in a haystack, and we were really conducting a movement to make contact with the enemy.

This is the account of how the patrol went:

1400/1500 hrs. NAI (Named Area of Interest) 856 Counter-Mortar Patrol to deny enemy use of mortars in and around Al Palestine Neighborhood

It was the night before this particular patrol when Assassin 7 (who was also our platoon sergeant) said, "Well, boys, our day is coming. We've been patrolling this neighborhood for over a week now and our day is coming." And come it did. It was a rather warm November day. The day before the neighborhood kids were out in droves following our Strykers, hoping to get a free handout. In the middle section of Al Palestine there was an open lot the size of a suburban American grocery store parking lot. Instead of neatly painted lines marked for cars to park in and baskets of flowers attracting butterflies, the semi-empty lot contained some old, rusty, broken, playground equipment and piles of scattered trash. At the southwestern edge was a cesspool filled with garbage and sewer water. That did not discourage the geese, however, that congregated at its edge and drank down the liquid death. There were also goats that called the lot home. They, like the geese, found bits and pieces of trash and garbage to nibble on, and all the while the surrounding neighborhood children played soccer as if it were the greatest soccer field on earth.

On that particular fall day, not as many kids came out, and the ones who did persisted in throwing rocks at us as we passed by on patrol. We had headed due west when our lead victor (stryker) headed into the black hole, as Assassin 7 referred to it. The black hole was the western-most edge of Palestine that led to a dead end. It was paralleled on the north by residential homes and on the south by an all girls elementary school. Inevitably we were channeled into a potential kill zone with only one way in and one way out. Over the radio Assassin 7 called Assassin 6, our lieutenant, "Hey, Six, I don't like being here; it's a black hole like I said yesterday. Let's make it our last time we head down this road. Seven out." We turned around, heading back northeast, and turned left adjacent to the open lot. The order of movement was 2 Victor, 3 Victor, and 1 Victor with Assassin 7 in the rear. It was a strange feeling to have had the streets filled with onlookers and kids the day prior but on this day the neighborhood was almost empty, like a ghost town. That's when it happened. At that moment the strangeness crept in and the unexpected occurred. As 1 Victor approached the corner to make its left turn, a young male came running at full speed from across the field in the direction of 1 Victor's seven o'clock and was carrying some strange apparatus in his hand. Now picture if you will a column of Stryker combat vehicles conducting a patrol in an urban setting, the men rich with anticipation to let loose some God-forgiving firepower upon the souls of an unforgiving enemy, and from across a dirty, trash-ridden field, a teenage male with the likes of an Olympic javelin in his hands comes running full speed toward you. We were kind of awestricken and it made for the brunt of jokes afterward, but at that moment of sudden bewilderment, the enemy closed in on the trail victor and hurled the sticky bomb at us.

In an attempt to throw a sticky bomb affixed to a pole, hoping that it would become a deadly projectile and land on top of and inside the vehicle, the young man missed his mark. At the instance that Assassin 7 knew what was happening, he yelled out, "Get down, get down!" The bomb landed on the side of 1 Victor and only mere heat and some gassy residue fell upon the men inside. Assassin 2 and I were pulling air guard in the lead vehicle when I heard the explosion. I turned my head in time to see a puffy white and black cloud surround 1 Victor.

Immediately I thought to myself, "My God, it happened, they just got hit!" Our procedure, or SOP (Standard Operating Procedure), was to enclose the enemy contact, return fire, fix the enemy, and gain fire superiority with little or no friendly losses. All this concentrated on a young man brave enough to run unarmed at a 30,000-pound steel cage with nothing except that sticky bomb in one hand and two swift feet like that of Carl Lewis. If ever in his day did he run for his life, it was then and there because as soon as the explosion was over, the radio squelched out with a fierce voice, "Make 'em pay!"

In a time like that when you have no idea if the initial contact is a signal to trigger a larger ambush of some sort, you react the way you have been trained. As the butterfly trigger was depressed and .50-caliber bullets screamed down the street, the young heathen "dealt aces with the devil himself" and hurtled a wall, missing being hit by only fractions of a second. We encompassed the neighborhood and did our best to find the man who had thrown the sticky bomb, but unfortunately he got away.

At the same time we had radioed to our headquarters about our contact. They asked if we needed immediate assistance. Assassin 6 responded with "No," and we continued to search the area, asking the local populace for information. Battalion had rallied the Kiowa OH-58 and the Apache AH-64 helicopters to provide overhead, close-air support. We stayed on the ground for what seemed like an eternity, and yet only an hour had passed. But in that hour the AIF had fixed our position, calculated our likely ex-fill route and planted a powerful car bomb in the northbound lane of route Lexus.

Prior to deploying to Iraq, we received instructions on likely enemy courses of action. That meant becoming familiar with the actions that our enemy could possibly do or not do in any given situation while on the battlefield. On many occasions the enemy would set up an IED, wait for a U.S. convoy, particularly of light-skinned vehicles, detonate the bomb, and then commence observing our own actions on contact. They found that at first contact we would pull back some 300 meters, so bingo, at about

300 meters from the emplacement of the first IED, several more were strategically placed in hopes of causing the most devastation to American troops as possible. You can imagine that it is an ever-changing bout of tactics from friend to foe. And with that aspect in mind, President Eisenhower once said, "In war, before the battle is joined, plans are everything, but once the shooting begins, plans are worthless..." (Stephen E. Ambrose, *Undaunted Courage,* p. 81). And that could not be truer in combating terrorism.

After a time the AIF found that against the "Ghost Riders" (a nickname given to the First Stryker Combat Team, 3rd Brigade, 2 ID, due to the fact that the Stryker vehicle is a quiet combat vehicle that often surprised Iraqis), most IED's, including RPG's, had very diminutive catastrophic effect. More and more, though, the enemy was rigging up two types of car bombs known as vehicle carried and vehicle borne IED's. The former was a vehicle with a lucky gentleman who wanted to reach the Promised Land prior to retirement, and the latter was an abandoned car left stranded on the side of the road. Sometimes both had enough explosives that it caused significant, if not catastrophic, damage to the Stryker and its crew, not to mention unlucky bystanders. For the most part, however, the vehicle was designed in a way that its eight wheels and slender body with the addition of the outer cage know as the "bird cage" detracted from most car bomb detonations and RPG attacks and allowed the vehicle to maneuver itself back to a secure area. [Note: At times all eight wheels of a Stryker Combat Vehicle have been blown out and the vehicle is able to maneuver back to a secure location.]

Assassin 6 called battalion, "Gimlet 3A, Assassin 6. We are finished conducting a patrol and could not find the individual at this time. We are green and headed back to the FOB (Forward Operating Base) at this time, over." "Roger Assassin 6, Gimlet 3A out." We picked up in the same order of movement and made our way north out of Al Palestine back to Lexus for the return trip home. Just as we turned left onto Lexus, Assassin 3's vehicle commander called out over the radio, "Low left, low left," which was our signal that there was possible danger and for everyone to take precautions. Just as the call was made an additional call was transmitted over the radio, "Hey, man, that car looks shady, like it's real low." 3 Victor rolled past the car cautiously as did 1 Victor, and then the loudest explosion I have ever heard ripped through the heat of the setting sun, and a fireball that engulfed the space between our victor and 1 Victor came rolling with it. The blast was so intense that it jarred both my knees and elbows. Bits and pieces of the car were shredded into fragments the size of a Matchbox car, the kind I collected as a seven-year-old boy. Luckily for us the timing was off and that 3 Victor had called out "low left," giving us all ample time to get down.

On that day we all made it back to the FOB in one piece, thankful to God to still be alive. We got hit not once but twice in the same day, our baptism with fire, if you will. Our enemy did not show their faces, did not come out and decisively engage us with their rifleman, nor did the enemy run in a fearful retreat when we reacted with a vengeance from the sticky bomb. But what they did do is show that at any time and any place, with comfortable ease, they could plant several bombs and have a hide-site position somewhere within 100 to 300 meters away to watch our every step. To me, that is the kind of intimidation tactic reserved for a sophisticated military, but then again the war on terror is an intimidation tactic aimed at destroying its target at whatever cost and with little or no real sophisticated technologically advanced group of individuals. Instead they have a band of renegade men with one sole purpose: to kill whomever shall infringe upon their so-called religious war.

It was not too long after we got hit for the first time that the Mosul massacre happened—Tuesday, December 20, 2004, at approximately 1200hrs (0400 in morning East Coast time). We were scheduled to receive our CIB's, Combat Infantrymen Badges, for having served over 180 consecutive days in a designated combat zone. Lancer 6, Colonel Robert Brown, and Task Force Olympia Commander General Carter Ham were present along with our chain of command to both present the awards and to pin them on.

Shortly after leaving FOB Patriot, Lancer 6 headed to FOB Marez to present more CIB's. We, the Assassins, were scheduled to conduct more so-called counter-mortar patrols later in the day, so most of us either headed back to our rooms, lifted weights, or moseyed on down to the chow hall for lunch. The food at Patriot was not what you would call anything spectacular, unless you were being sarcastic and spectacular was your way of saying the food royally sucked. For starters the food was brought in by way of convoys and that alone made you feel a little less fortunate when you knew the other FOB's were eating meals prepared in kitchens and sitting down inside nice dining facilities. Breakfast consisted of cold cereal, canned fruit, and pastries. Lunch was good old-fashioned bologna sandwiches with more canned fruit, and for dinner we at least had something hot. In no way am I making light of the subject of a massacre that took the lives of over twenty U.S. soldiers. However, the mood set forth from the chow that winter afternoon added to the breaking headline news as FOX NEWS LIVE reported that an attack on a U.S. base north of Baghdad had killed and/or injured some seventy soldiers and civilians.

We had heard a loud explosion during the CIB ceremony, but it was rather far away. After spending over 180 days in Mosul, hearing random gunfire and loud explosions was very common place. We sort of thought nothing of it and went about our day. The week prior to the massacre was filled with AIF activity, for it was the end of the holy Muslim holiday of Ramadan. There were also daily attacks against both U.S. forces as well as the ING (Iraqi National Guard). On one particular day, heavy fighting occurred just outside and to the east of our FOB, Forward Operating Base Patriot. AIF forces attacked Bridge One killing several ING soldiers and destroying five ING light-skinned trucks. Bullets and 60mm mortar rounds impacted our FOB daily, so it was no surprise to witness such activity.

One thing that does go through your mind when you hear an explosion, though, is, "I hope no one got hurt." I was in my room when I overheard someone saying that the explosion impacted on Marez. That's when you begin to take things seriously. We knew men on Marez. Immediately reports came down the pipeline that an 82mm or perhaps a 102mm mortar round impacted a direct hit on the Marez dining facility. "Damn," is what you want to say, and your gut starts to tighten up. You wish you could be there to help your comrades, and you get a weary feeling inside because you know that someone you know might be a casualty. I headed to the infamous chow hall, not for the food as you would expect, but because FOX News showed live coverage.

"LIVE coverage" meant an attack had happened just moments earlier, across the Tigris River and just west of our location. I could drive a Stryker and be there in approximately ten minutes. Nevertheless, as I sat there on the wooden bench along with about fifty other soldiers watching the reports and seeing the news correspondents do their best to positively identify the what, when, who, where, and why of this most tragic event, I was perplexed at the media's feeble attempts to be so sure of the mode the enemy used to launch such an attack. Earlier the reports came down on our side of the river, not to mention our side of the world where the war was taking place (and not back in New York City), that the attack might be from a large mortar round. That was one likely avenue since mortar rounds had in fact impacted both FOB Marez and Patriot along with other camps in the city that same week, but it was just way too early to tell. Another suggestion from the media was that a 107mm rocket used to fire at aircraft was what actually impacted the chow hall, due to the fact that whatever had caused the explosion left a monster sized hole in the canvas ceiling large enough to drive two Chevy trucks through. It was only a matter of minutes before a military analyst gave his expertise to FOX News as to the specifications of a 107mm rocket. When asked by FOX if in fact the rocket could have done the massive damage shown, the answer was inevitably yes.

It could have been the 107. As part of our counter-mortar patrols, we were to be on the lookout for anyone trying to shoot down incoming aircraft using such a rocket, but we all had our doubts. As we sat and watched the news, the time had expired to about one hour since the explosion, and we had suspected that a suicide bomber somehow got himself and a bomb inside the chow hall. Remember, one thing that FOX News and/or any other news organization did not know was that, on a daily basis, military intelligence gives out its likely course of enemy action. We already knew from the heavy fighting the prior week that the AIF were launching attacks to coordinate with the ending of the holy month of Ramadan. We also knew that the AIF wanted to demonstrate their so-called power to inflict a devastating event to kill as many American soldiers as possible—all at the same time. Unfortunately it did happen, but then again this was WAR.

I like FOX News, but I don't always like how they choose to report on the war. I just don't like the fact that after it was all said and done twenty-two AMERICAN SOLDIERS lost their lives and some seventy others, including civilian contractors and several coalition force members, were injured. Men that I knew and had worked with were hurt. Men that I knew and served with helped pick up the body parts and assisted the medics in treating the wounded. And all this while someone back in the United States reported on the possibilities of what had happened that day, why it happened that day, and how it could have happened that day. The very man who addressed my men during the CIB ceremony earlier that morning, General Ham, gave his respects and condolences to the families of the men and woman who had died in the explosion. Nevertheless, someone back in the newsroom was gathering his own ideas, his own conclusions and his own hypotheses as to what might have happened that day. That is what bothers me so.

Immediately the experts were pulled out of the closet, and they sounded as if they knew what was going on. Questions were asked as to how this could have happened, and if it were a suicide bomber, how did he or she get access to a gathering of perhaps one hundred or so soldiers in one setting? And then there were more reports about the 107mm rocket and how it is aimed, how the enemy gets their hands on such weapons, and so forth, and on and on and on.

Enough questions! The reality of the matter was that the most devastating attack on U.S. Armed Forces since the start of the war in March 2003 had just occurred. Good men and woman lost their lives that day. Regardless of the media's Mickey Mouse questions and hypothetical reporting, *WE* the men and women serving in Iraq, fighting for the freedoms of another country, were going to wake up the next morning and continue to do our jobs. The media reporting the situation, however, were going to wake up the next morning without fear from another attack and instead go about their so-called normal, daily routines, looking for yet another breaking news flash and start the process all over again.

Another fact that came from the military's initial investigation was that an individual working with the security force on FOB Marez had infiltrated and been recruited by AIF members to carry out a suicide attack on the chow hall. Unfortunately, he was successful in his cowardly attempts. How does that make one feel, knowing that a suicide bomber could infiltrate your "ranks" and take your precious life? I was mad and upset, and I felt great sorrow for the losses that afternoon as I sat there watching the reports. Later video of the attack surfaced on extremists' websites. It was disheartening to see that they had waited for the precise moment of the attack, with camera in hand to capture their work, and all the while they were watching us from afar. Little did they know, however, that the Assassins, with the help of the 160th SOAR (Special Operations Aviation Regiment), were on our way and we were ready to bring HELL with us.

Intel reports indicated that the persons responsible for the Marez attack lived in a small village approximately forty kilometers south of the city of Mosul. Along with the Annihilators (Alpha Company, 3-21 IN), the 160th SOAR who flew the Assassins, and members of the battalion TAC, a coordinated effort was pieced together to go and intercept these individuals. The Assassins would conduct a tactical air assault into their blocking positions on the southwest side of the village, closest to the target house, and prevent any persons on foot or via vehicle from entering or leaving the area. At the same time, the Annihilators would drop down from the north with the Strykers and conduct the same cordon in the north, again preventing any persons from entering or leaving. Simultaneously they maneuvered a team to seal off the target house and go in for the "nab and grab." The 160th SOAR consisted of the following aircraft: two MH-60 Black Hawks, one DAP (Direct Action Penetrator, a specially modified Black Hawk designed and used exclusively by the 160th SOAR), and one MH-60 designated for MEDIVAC purposes. The DAP would be conducting a holding pattern west over the Tigris River, ready for immediate CAS (Close Air Support), which, when needed, could provide a hell storm of firepower from its 40mm automatic grenade launchers and two 7.62mm mini cannons that spit out thousands of rounds of ammunition per second. One of the MH-60's, with a sniper carrying a match grade M4 carbine capable of putting a 5.56mm bullet center mass of a human target, picked up a rotation pattern over the objective. The other two aircraft were approximately two minutes away and on the far west side of the river. The conclusion of the operation came down to this: the main individual was not at home. His brother, who was a person of interest, was home and said his brother was at work. All in all, the operation was successful and lead to several persons taken into custody.

Whether or not any "justice" was found for the lives lost at Marez I leave up to the individual soldier to decide. Unfortunately, I was unable to fly with the 160th that night. Due to the need for sufficient space in the event of an air MEDIVAC, the 160th flight commander tailored the ACL, the aircraft load, at the last minute. I put my second in command, Sergeant Ryan Wells, in charge of the sniper section and I stayed back. My decision to do this was sacrificial on my part, confident to put my second in command, and an opportunity to allow my men to conduct a tactical air assault mission with the best combat pilots the world has to offer. During the planning phase of the operation, inside the SOAR's planning bay, I felt somewhat out of place at first. This was due to the fact that I was surrounded by men who had gone through some of the toughest training the military has to offer. The level of professionalism inside that planning bay astonished me, and my mind drifted back to the book *In The Company of Heroes* by Michael Durant, where Durant said that every member of the 160th knew that he wanted to be there. It's a special community, and I would have to say I am fortunate, along with my men, to have conducted several combat missions with these men. My hat goes off to the members of the 160th!

In January 2005, the Assassins encountered a situation that had been predicted might happen but never embraced fully and for the most obvious of reasons. It is talked about and rehearsed during field training exercises, but to lose your platoon sergeant firsthand is like stabbing yourself in the heart. You can feel the pain and see the pain, but you can do absolutely nothing about it. On January 13, 2005, Assassin 7 was killed in action while conducting a combat patrol on Lexus, northeast of the Al Palestine neighborhood. The mission seemed easy enough to conduct: escort several members of a Navy Seal team around the Gimlet AO (Area of Operations) and give them specific information as to the enemy activity that would allow them, the Seals, to become familiar with the area for future operations.

Just a few days prior to the incident, I left Iraq for my R&R back in the States. Assassin 7 had walked up to the battalion TOC with me to wait for the midnight LOG PAC. I remember clearly he was happy for me to go home to see my family. He shook my hand and told me to have a good time. That was the last time I ever saw him, and I will hold onto the memories and lessons that he provided to me in order to help make me a better leader of men. When I arrived home that first night, I was glad to be home and yet I felt like I was missing something. Perhaps it was being away from my men, knowing that their lives were still in danger in Iraq and that I was at home enjoying myself.

The call came that next morning as I lay in bed with my wife, talking about how much we loved being married. Immediately I knew something had gone wrong when on the other end of the phone I could hear solemn sadness and crying in a soft, gentle southern voice. The voice came across from the other side with these words: "I am so sorry, but Mack was killed today." That message will live forever in my heart. I could not believe what my ears had just heard. Mack had been killed. How on earth could this have happened since I had just seen him and spoken with him not more than forty-eight hours earlier?

The death of SFC Brian A. Mack was a shock to the entire 25th Infantry, and not just the "GIMLETS" but also the brotherhood of Duce-4 (1-24 IN) as well. His career involved not only special operations, but also Ranger training, and the regular infantry also. He was the scout platoon sergeant in 1-24 IN before starting the Stryker Brigade Advanced Skills Center located at Fort Lewis, Washington. The skills center focused on advanced marksmanship, sniper, and pre-ranger training for the entire brigade. He was assigned to the 3rd Battalion 21st Infantry just prior to deploying to Iraq and again took charge of the scout platoon. After his death he was promoted posthumously to master sergeant and awarded the Bronze Star and Purple Heart. For the rest of my life, whenever I see "Old Glory" waving proudly in the wind, I will think of MSG Mack and the sacrifice he made so that I, we, the Assassins could all come home safe and sound and in one piece.

I was not there that afternoon when the Assassins escorted the Seals, yet in my mind I could see the exact location of where 7 went down. It was south on Lexus near the Buick and Ford intersection just north of Al Palestine where the AIF had concealed a 107mm rocket in a row of bushes and then waited for an American convoy, presumably Strykers, before initiating the rocket. They say it happened so fast that it was surreal and the explosion was not loud enough to cause any pulsating alarm, unlike a car bomb that can be heard miles away. The rocket slammed into the mounted M240B machine gun, tearing it in half, and then it went up and over the Stryker and kept going in the two o'clock direction of travel. Fragments of metal dispersed in a 360-degree radius spraying both Mack and the Seal. A fragment of metal several inches in diameter penetrated Mack in the back of the neck, close to the base of the skull. As the Seal fell down into the Stryker, semi-conscious, Mack was still standing in his hatch.

The men did not know the extent of Mack's injuries and started treating the fallen Seal. Thinking he was okay and looking to return fire, everyone at first thought Mack to be good. When blood started to drain down into the back hatch and Mack did not respond to any verbal communication, that was the moment the men knew he was not good. Someone went to physically grab Mack and his legs went numb, for Mack was still standing because his web gear was in fact caught on the rear hatch locking lever. From that point on and until the crew rushed to the combat hospital, located approximately five miles northwest, every effort to sustain Mack's life was exhausted.

Immediately Assassin 3 took charge, radioed to higher that they had an urgent surgical and were in route to the CSH at LSA Diamondback. Subsequently both commanders, GIMLET 6 and LANCER 6, were aware of the critical situation, rallied their TACs and proceeded to Diamondback as well. For a commander in combat, knowing that the loss of soldiers is and will forever be inevitable, it is still hard to deal with, especially when it is a senior in command who has served his country well and for many years at that. I cannot imagine what was going through everyone's minds, but I was in shock. I know that as for LANCER 6, Colonel Brown, Mack was not just another sergeant first class in the brigade, but also a true leader, warrior, and man who could be trusted to lead fine men into combat and win the fight.

When the news of Mack's death came to the men, it was hard to swallow. Everyone that day shed tears and felt pain in their hearts for the man who had just lost his very life, for the man who made the Assassins who they were, the man who was the "backbone" to each and every one of us, and the man who smiled at you after he chewed your butt and then cracked a dumb joke to make you feel better. A fellow Assassin from Alaska told me, "I rested my hand on his cold body, closed my eyes, and said in my heart…goodbye Mack." After I received the news, I knew I had to go visit his wife and daughter in Dupont, Washington. Lt. Rob Decker and I were on leave from Iraq, and we would be the closest thing to the real Mack that his family would be able to experience.

After all, I was MSG Mack's roommate and I held certain bits of personal information that I knew his family would want to know. In short, I told his wife that I was deeply sorry for her loss, and I held her delicate body in my arms for what seemed like hours. Before I left I told his daughter that every day Brian looked at a picture of her, with her big smile and bright eyes, and said out loud, "That's my girl." Then he would chuckle like he always did, an undeniable little laugh that only Mack himself could produce.

Left with feelings of immense guilt for not being there the day Mack died, I spent hours each morning of my R&R reflecting on the matter. On one particular morning as I habitually sipped my cup of coffee, I watched the water roll in from Puget Sound hitting Owens Beach, and I broke down into uncontrollable tears. I was in shock. I guess I thought that the first to die in combat would have been someone other than the veteran Mack. Mack was always out front, leading "us." He was the last person any one of us thought would have died first, and at the beginning of our combat tour at that. The song "When I'm Gone" by Three Doors Down helped me to deal with my emotions. My wife, Sarah, held me one night when I suddenly woke to a dream of being in combat, and I then realized that Mack was really dead.

After returning to Iraq, it was back in the saddle again. On my first patrol back out into the city, we left the FOB just before sundown to conduct a route recon for a mission the following day. Assassin 1 and I took the air guard hatch and our victor (vehicle) was the trail of three Strykers when we approached the Chevy and Buick overpass. Just as we descended the downhill approach to the overpass, "low left" came over the radio. "Low left" was the code word for any vehicle left on the side of the road, and all persons took evasive actions until each vehicle passed the vehicle in question. A suspicious looking abandoned car sat in the eastbound lane and sure enough, as we came to find out, it was a vehicle-borne improvised explosive device (IED), better known as a car bomb. The initial detonation, although not as impressive as others in the past, still rocked our world. As we all gave the thumbs up and called each other on the radio to follow up on each other's status, we turned around and immediately started to scan the area for any would-be AIF waiting to shoot at us. Our Strykers picked up a 360-degree security formation and prepared to counterattack. Several minutes had expired and then came an even louder explosion, and this time car parts fell from the sky on top of my Stryker. A third explosion occurred and then a fourth. To our best knowledge, which is a good calculated guess, the first explosion only detonated a section of the entire explosive body and the heat from the car fire ignited the remainder. Lucky for us, perhaps, since if in fact the entire bomb would have exploded as we passed by the first time, the results could have been fatal.

Later that same month, we were conducting dismounted patrols southeast of the Isuzu and Buick intersection when we had been on the ground for approximately two hours. Our mission was two-fold: one, to look for possible sniper positions overlooking two suspected mortar POOs (Points of Origin) and, second, to look for an over-watch position that gave good fields of view on route Isuzu (a main road notorious with car bombs, shootings, and drive-bys). With only one last position to search, we made our way across a rather large open field with a Stryker in trail to cover our movement with its .50-caliber machine gun. The house sat back from Isuzu a good four hundred meters and its front gate faced due north. As we finished searching the house and found that it was in fact the best location that we had visited all day, giving a great field of view, both left and right of the western-most POO and a good birds-eye view of a fair section of road east on route Isuzu. We funneled out of the front gate, picked up our dismounted order of movement and headed northwest.

I remember it clearly as if it happened yesterday. I know who was next to me and I know the precise location of the Stryker in over-watch. I know which team was on point and who was picking up the rear. I can see clearly the shape of the field which we were entering and the precise color of the dirt; it was a rust-colored red, mixed with shades of dark brown, with debris strewn about.

Not more than fifty meters after we shoved off from the house, bullets riddled the rust-colored dirt throwing pieces into the air. The sound was so distinctive—automatic machine gun fire and the snap of bullets whizzing by at thousands of feet per second. Our actions were automatic as well—get down, seek cover if any, and return fire. I dropped like a sack of potatoes, looked around me, realized that I was not being decisively engaged, and then Sgt. Ryan Wells, North Dakota, and I ran back twenty feet to the front gate. Along with the other men, we started to return cover fire in the direction of the enemy contact.

We still had men out to our front who were being decisively engaged and pinned down behind a shallow mound of dirt. After a few seconds, though, Wells and I glanced at each other and gave a distinctive nod. We had heard a sound that we both knew very well. It was none other than the pop, pop, pop, of automatic 5.56 from a SAW (Squad Automatic Weapon). It was Sgt. Andrew Spiess, Vermont, returning fire with his squad automatic weapon. Later that day Spiess recalled to me that they (AIF) must have had me fixed in their sights. For one thing, he was part of the point element, hence the SAW up front and, two, he became very intimate with that shallow mound of dirt because the bullets were impacting to his left, front, and right sides. "All I could do was curl up into the smallest ball possible and say to myself, "Oh God, oh God, oh God." When a momentary pause came to the enemy fire, Spiess said, "I raised the six-inch barrel over the top of the mound and let off the entire two hundred-round drum."

The reason for the head nod from me to Wells earlier was because we knew that Spiess must have been okay and that his firing that SAW meant that our cover fire was working. All in all, no one was hit from any enemy bullets, a far cry from what our returning fire accomplished on the opposite end. There were three dead suspected AIF members and several others wounded. Everyone learned a lesson that day. You can never underestimate your enemy, and your guard always has to be up and ready to return fire. Sergeant Wells recalled saying to someone that when we headed southeast for that last position, and as our platoon was spread out in its wedge formation, "I looked out over that field and said, Yep...if there is any place to get hit, it's gonna be right here." Indeed he called it that day. Sergeant Spiess, after safely being able to retreat to the confines of the house, sat there and counted his blessings. He looked me straight in the eyes and said, "Just one bullet, and I could have been shot out there—just one bullet."

Nine days, just nine days later, it happened again. Assassins made contact. Again I remember the day quite distinctly. It had been rainy out that night and most of the early morning as if it were just another winter day in March. But then again, when is a day just another day in Iraq? It will never be just another day in Iraq for as long as I live and for the families back in America who have lost loved ones in combat. Another day is never closer to bringing the ones they love home again. Our mission was to conduct a dismounted sweep of the entire Santa Fe loop, starting from the west side of Buick and heading east to the Santa Fe bypass. Most of the area was industrial and fairly empty, for it was a day of rest in the Muslim faith. The process was slow and cumbersome due to the fact that the dismounts had a large area to cover, and the occasional stop to converse with the local populace takes some time. All in all, the mission was completed in about three hours.

The details that encompass the next several pages are the truest account from my perspective of what took place next.

Depending on whom you asked about that day, the events could be related differently. This is my own true and professional account of what happened. Some of the details will be graphic. But then again this is WAR.

We left Santa Fe in the following order of movement: 3 Victor, 4 Victor, 1 Victor, and then we turned north onto Buick. It was a fairly straight shot back to the FOB; however, we all knew that the Buick/Chevy overpass was always a potential hotspot for AIF activity. We just got hit there last month, and then the very next day the Annihilators rolled up on some AIF trying to plant yet another IED. Already our emotions were running high! No one had to say anything. Nothing had happened during our three hours spent dismounted and now, just because we were inside our Strykers as if "scot-free" and heading home with time left for some hot chow, the sense of security was elevated. We all knew that it took just a few seconds for all hell to break loose. Like I said, no one had to say a single word. The air guards all knew it, even if they joked on their headsets calling out to someone else, "Yeah, I saw your mom last night." Ha, ha. All jokes aside, the very real possibility of getting hit was imbedded in the backs of our minds. We knew that it could happen, and it was just a matter of when and where.

"All elements be advised that a suspected IED is located at grid LF 1234 5678, (for security reasons the real grid coordinate cannot be used) just west of the Buick and Chevy overpass. Gimlet 3A OUT." Assassin 6 (Lt. Decker by this time had been assigned as the executive officer of Charlie Company 3-21 IN) called all victors passing on the information. All victors responded in sequence, "Roger, OUT." As the lead victor responsible for the route reconnaissance, Assassin 3 made recommendations as to the routes we should take or the routes we should not take. With the information that had just come across the radio, a decision had to be made. I do not know the entire conversation that took place inside of 3 Victor, but over the NET came this transmission: "All Assassin elements, we have two choices. One is to turn west on Ford and bypass Buick and head north on Lexus, or go straight on Buick in the direction of travel. Stand by." Several seconds passed and the final decision was made by Assassin 3 himself, 3 Victor, and the rest of the crew. "Okay, this is what we're gonna do, BREAK." Another few seconds passed and then the final decision came across the speaker box, and this was all it said: "Let's take it (the fight) to 'em."

On that day I was in command of 4 Victor and manned the vehicle commander's hatch. Assassin 1 called me on the headset. "Mike, we're about seven hundred meters out," he said. I responded with, "Okay, let me know when we get closer so I can get down. Roger." Five hundred meters later, "Hey, Mike, were coming up on it now. Get ready." As I told my men in the rear to get down—BOOM!—it was already there. A moment paused in time, as if time was motionless, and I saw the explosion engulf 3 Victor's rear half of the Stryker, and then again, the sound of automatic gun fire! It was a near ambush, if you want to get technical. The fact was that 3 Victor had run over a pothole with an IED sandbag inside of it. At the last moment 3 Victor called to his driver, "Shift left...left...left!" In an attempt to avoid driving directly over the bomb, the driver shifted as far left as possible. I saw thick black smoke and could taste a sulfuric acid type residue in the air. For several seconds thereafter, I was paralyzed from the loud explosion, for it had happened less than one hundred meters to my front. The explosion pushed the air guards down inside of 3 Victor straight to the floor. I charged the .50 caliber, swung the turret to the three o'clock, and let loose some rounds. My two air guards immediately returned fire with their M4's and then one got his hands on the M240B machine gun—his first mission out with us, by the way—and he gunned down three men standing at the site of the near ambush. We believed them to be suspected AIF. As I fired the fifty, I kept wondering to myself, "I don't see any enemy. Where is the enemy?"

"Three's down, three's down, three's been hit." That was the next radio transmission to fly over the airwaves. Assassin 1 called 3 Victor, "Hey, I need his vitals, OVER." Then the return transmission was the worst for any man to hear after a friend or comrade just got hit. "NO VITALS—THREE's DEAD." Not quite the proper radio transmission, but in the heat of the moment it was justified. At that precise moment every man takes into account that he just lost a friend, a confidant, and a comrade. As we raced the Strykers back to FOB FREEDOM, no more than a few minutes away, everyone in the platoon kept thinking, "How bad, how bad?" As for the men who were there the day Mack got hit, their hearts felt the coldness all over again. The words "Seven's been hit" or "Three's been hit," creates a distinctive cold, dark, and empty feeling inside of you. It is an emptiness that cannot be explained by words alone, and it is nothing like what is splattered upon a Hollywood movie screen when a "buddy" bites the big one. I can only tell you that when a fellow soldier dies in your arms or right in front of you, a part of your eternal soul dies along with him. After it happens, all you can do is wait and wonder and hope and pray for the best.

Assassin 1 called an immediate Air-MEDIVAC request to "Gimlet 3A." By the time we reached the CSH (Combat Support Hospital) on FREEDOM, our battalion commander, Lieutenant Colonel Michael Gibler, and several other members of the TOC were there waiting for us. Three Victor stopped adjacent to the front entrance of the CSH with 4 Victor right behind him. One Victor went on to the PAD to park the vehicle and then walked up the hill to meet the rest of us already at the CSH. We all congregated outside in somber silence waiting for the news.

Three's vehicle commander, known as just 3V, had built a strong bond with Assassin 3, as if the two of them were thinking the same thing at the same time. Three V was our most experienced vehicle commander, and if you needed help and help in a hurry, you could count on 3V. You knew it was him coming, too, for you heard the sound of the .50 caliber blazing a trail fast and furious. That's just how he ran things. As 3V raced to drop all his combat gear, the ramp had hit the ground and the men inside carried Assassin 3's lifeless body inside the CSH. I will never forget that sight. It is engraved on my mind with surgical precision: full-grown men carrying the body of another soldier wounded in combat, trying desperately to save his life. By the time I had dropped my gear and gotten down off the Stryker, 3V was visibly shaken. He was upset and angry at his driver. "If only the driver had swerved more to the left, if only...," was what he perhaps thought. But it was not the driver's fault, and we all knew that. Even 3V knew that, and it wasn't even the IED that killed Assassin 3. But in the heat of the moment, when your blood is boiling, you might say or do things that are neither normal nor rational but are later forgiven.

Now even LANCER 6, who knew both Assassins 7 and 3, was standing by with several more soldiers who knew "us." Up to that moment everyone had been asked by medical personnel to leave the CSH and to wait outside. I cannot speak for the others, but I was in shock. Just minutes ago I had spoken with Assassin 3 on the radio. I saw him laugh out loud in response to some stupid thing that meant nothing, but it gave us something to laugh about. I had just given him a report as to our next movement. How could this be happening? "Was it real?" is what I thought, and "Is he going to make it?" is what I wanted to hear. Will he be alive in the morning is what I wanted to know!

The Assassins had gathered outside at the edge of Bushmasters' (Bravo Company, 3-21 IN) gravel parking lot. We knew that Assassin 3 had suffered a traumatic head injury, but to what extent we did not know. Silence and a solemn demeanor had overtaken all of us. GIMLET 6, Lieutenant Colonel Gibler, walked out of the CSH, turned left and headed in our direction. Nothing was conveyed on his pale face, nothing but a square jaw ready to address his men. At that time, when a commander is about to address his men on the state of a fellow comrade, all rank goes out the window. GIMLET 6 held out his arms, motioned to us to gather closer, and solemnly said with a soft yet commanding voice, "Men, I am sorry...he didn't make it."

Like a brick wall crashing down upon us the news hit hard. Most of us cried, others walked away to find comfort in solitude, and others embraced each other. I hit the ground on my knees, crying out loud. A strong hand rested upon my shoulder and then pulled me to my feet. Our S-3 Plans Captain took me into his arms and embraced me and said, "It's okay, brother…let it out…now be strong." After a few moments we all gathered inside to see Assassin 3. When we saw him laying there, a lifeless body, we did not want to believe that he was dead. Just forty-five minutes before he had been walking, talking, and laughing with his men, and he had that "I'm a guilty bastard" look on his face. Now his body was cold and pale and covered with an O.D. green Army blanket with only his face showing. We all stood there looking, waiting, and looking some more, as if any moment he would spring up and yell in his obnoxious voice, "Hey, what's going on over here?" but it never happened. At that time some men prayed out loud, and some said their final goodbyes, but I walked out of the CSH and wanted nothing more than to be left alone.

On that day, March 4, 2005, Staff Sergeant Juan Solorio, Assassin 3, a.k.a. "Solo," died in combat in Mosul, Iraq. He had survived eight enemy engagements, a dozen close mortar attacks, and one rocket attack. He was shot in the head with a 7.62mm rifle round. The round impacted the side of his "Mitch" helmet and killed him instantly. At the time of the contact, every effort was made to render first aid to him, and yet he passed with no pain and no suffering. The only suffering will be from the ones who loved him, his friends and family, the ones who fought beside him, and the ones who will never forget him.

After his body had been taken inside the CSH, it was reported that medics were able to bring about a momentary pulse, but he had lost almost all of his life breath. I will never forget that day, although at the present time, I am trying to forget a lot about my experiences in Iraq. Everyone deals with situations in different ways. Lieutenant Winters and his men had to deal with the Germans, the long cold winter nights stuck inside open foxholes, and the reality that their enemy at times would come face to face with them, ready to engage in battle. I am quite sure that every man or woman who has faced combat—no matter what the conditions—who has been shot at no matter how many times or how close or far away, and who has heard the sound of shrapnel whiz by his or her head, deals with the emotions in a completely different way.

The war against terrorism is nothing like the wars of the past, and I dare anyone to compare today's infantrymen with the likes of the men who first jumped on D-Day, or the men who became the first Rangers, or still more the men who paved the way for the Special Forces. One thing that remains the same today as it was back then, however, is the passing of a comrade on the battlefield. That in my mind is an experience that only a few men will encounter, and after the fact, it changes you. It...changes...YOU. I can only hope that like the "Greatest Generation," I too can return to my beloved America, "Land of the free and home of the brave" and do what John F. Kennedy said, "Ask not what your country can do for you, but ask what you can do for your country."

The Assassins moved on from that day. The command gave us a few days to refit and then it was back out on the streets of Mosul. As far as the rest of the battalion, the Assassins were not the only ones to suffer losses. The Annihilators, the Tigers, and Bushmasters had either lost or had wounded men also. But the fact remains that NO single platoon of men had suffered more than we did. We lost Assassin 7. Just five days after his replacement took the reins and went on his first mission, he was hit with a huge vehicle-borne IED. Can you guess the location? That's right! The Buick and Chevy overpass has been a magnet for AIF activity. The replacement Assassin 7 was wounded and lost his left eye and partial hearing as well. Then Assassin 3 was hit and died. All this happened in the span of just fifty-some days. After a while it starts taking a toll on you.

When I witnessed the fact that able and young Iraqi men, who are too afraid to pick up arms and fight for their country but will idly sit by and let you, an American soldier, die for their (Iraqi) country so that they can shout out in the streets, "American, we love you," that burned a deep hole into the bottom of my blood-stained heart. I washed American blood out of the back of a Stryker for the cause of Iraqi freedom when there were at least one hundred, if not more, young Iraqi men who could have taken that bullet just as well. I will never understand the politics of this war and don't care to have it explained to me. One thing I do know: If ever in my lifetime I bear witness to the day that a terrorist invades my neighborhood, I, like my patriotic next door neighbors, will take up arms, stand up and fight to the death if necessary, and root out any and all evil from where it stands, so help me God. I will pursue that evil to the ends of the earth and be like my brethren before me who, with musket in one hand and ball and powder in the other, fought the glorious battle, waved the glorious flag, and died the glorious death. Now that I can understand. For that I can appreciate the sacrifice of death for the cause of a greater good to mankind for the peace and freedoms of a people, and a nation, who wants it and is not afraid to go and fight for it. Only God Himself can save me from this place. I can only hope that if in fact you are reading the pages of this book, perhaps at a local Starbucks or in your home next to a warm fireplace, then bravo, I am alive and well and was able to finish writing this book. To God, then, be thy glory, until I shall return home. [NOTE: In order for you the reader to fully understand the emotions from the events just described by the author of this book, rather than alter it to reflect the year of publication, I have chosen to leave it all as it was originally written.]

If I took the time to write every detail of my 365 days in Iraq, like I had initially intended to do, then I could literally compile an entire book aside from this one. I decided, however, to combine my tour in Iraq within the pages of *Let Freedom Ring*, since I do speak of war and battles, both the spiritual and physical kind. I guess you could say that this book is a compilation of several topics. But then again, I stand firm on my conviction to write from the heart as I have from the very beginning!

For twelve months I was rated in the position of the battalion sniper section leader and carried that over for another four-and-one-half months. Although I will not discuss the situation in this book, or at a later time afterwards, a situation developed within the reconnaissance platoon that ended on a rather bad note. Many of my peers as well as subordinate soldiers and fellow team members feel that the situation could have been avoided altogether, and I am quite certain that a few feel as though NO situation existed in the first place. Nevertheless, a situation did arise and I believe it had its beginnings long before this unit ever deployed to Iraq. Back in garrison at Fort Lewis, Washington, when soldiers could not and would not adhere to certain standards, a pattern developed and was carried into the realms of combat. Don't get me wrong—soldiers will be soldiers and "Joe will be Joe." But the bottom line still stands that in the military a certain level of compliance is expected from each and every individual regardless of his or her rank. When that level of compliance is not adhered to, and the sergeant in charge does not enforce that standard of compliance, then you get what we had over here in Iraq: a platoon that was undisciplined, filled with bad attitudes, and had a general distaste for the common disciplinary standards set forth by the United States Army. [Note: Even though I describe the above situation as if "we" were an undisciplined unit, good things were still accomplished by the men of this platoon.]

Now I get tired of rules just like everyone else. When it gets to a point that is deemed "out of control," however, then a decision has to be made. I made my decision. I requested to leave the platoon and to seek a staff position. It was a difficult choice, leaving my men in the middle of a combat zone for the comfort, if you will, of a desk job. As I looked at it, and as I was counseled about it, however, I realized that the time had come to allow for a new leader to step up to the challenge. After thirty-six months in the same platoon and after serving in two different leadership positions, the time came to let someone else take over. Do I have regrets about it? Some regrets, YES, but life goes on and my career path will take me to a new location, a new group of faces, and a new set of challenges.

For the last account of my combat time in Iraq, I want to share with you the details of one of our sniper missions. One of the most effective tools the enemy had employed on their end of the spectrum was the use of mortars. When we first set boots on the ground in Iraq and lived at FOB PATRIOT, we were hit with mortar fire almost daily. It usually started early in the morning, so it became a sort of wake-up call to us. Farther up the river, at FOB FREEDOM, the mortar attacks were just as common but with more deadly accuracy. The reason for the difference was that PATRIOT was shaped like a perfect rectangle and set up parallel to the Tigris River. It almost took a miracle to hit our base and the rounds usually impacted long or short of the box.

FREEDOM, on the other hand, was like a dream come true. Set on a slightly higher level of ground and laid out in almost a perfect circular shape, FREEDOM was almost a guaranteed hit. We had been living at camp FREEDOM, renamed COURAGE thanks to the 11th ACR from the infamous desert training camp of Fort Irwin, California, since early January 2005. (I hold a personal grudge against the 11th ACR, but for professional reasons, I will keep those thoughts to myself). We had been hit with mortars numerous times. On one occasion, twelve or so 82mm rounds impacted the FOB. Both U.S. military and civilian contracted personnel died as a result of these enemy mortar attacks, which sparked numerous counter-mortar patrols throughout the city of Mosul and the emplacement of sniper observation posts. The results were fantastic! Mortar attacks went from over 300 a month down to 10 per month, 142 various mortar systems were captured and/or destroyed, and 233 enemy caches found (Lancer Brigade, 25th ID, in IRAQ, OIF III, Sept. 04-Sept. 05).

OPERATION ANNIHILATOR
MOSUL, IRAQ 2005
Within the scope of the U.S. Army's most technologically advanced weapons systems of the modern battle field, there remains an old-fashioned form of warfare that dates back to the late seventeen and early eighteen hundreds. Nevertheless, throughout the last handful of the world's most intense conflicts, this form of fighting has changed very little from its true warrior

form—waiting ever so patiently for your enemy to appear between the intended kill zone and a sniper's crosshairs.

The following is an accurate account of a sniper team's mission to destroy an anti-Iraqi mortar cell operating in and around the city of Mosul, Iraq. The facts are true, but soldiers' names have been changed. This is how the mission began:

OPERATIONS ORDER

2030 hrs.

I attended the op-order given by Annihilator 6 of the 3d Battalion 21st Infantry Regiment of the 25th Infantry Stryker Brigade Combat Team. An active AIF mortar cell was working inside the company commander's area of operations, and he was hell bent on killing every last one of them. His own company sniper team had logged some eighty hours of observation time with some big payoffs. The order was cut and dry: establish three separate sniper OP's over-watching three different mortar POO's that had been identified as being used recently, and be ready to shoot to kill.

SITUATION: AIF are working in and around Alpha Company's AO firing mortars in an attempt to disrupt coalition forces and present a show of force amongst the local populace.

MISSION: Infiltrate during the cover of darkness and occupy these pre-established OP's—COWBOYS, REDSKINS, AND BROWNS. Establish observation and annihilate the mortar team.

The rest of the order was standard operating procedures that were both well known and an infantryman's forte. The communications plan called for hourly radio checks followed by the no-commo plan, a primary and alternate infill and ex-fill site, and a standard ten-digit grid for an NFA (no fire area) with a VS-17 panel on the rooftop for a means of identification. The OH-58 pilots conducting combat flight operations could visibly see the bright orange panels and know that U.S. forces were inside.

THE MISSION

With the op-order complete and a day for mission planning and rest, my sniper team was ready. Our basic combat load was tailored to each individual's personal preference; however, each man carried certain team equipment that was evenly distributed among them all. "Emmett" carried the least since he was both the point man and primary shooter: a map, wrist Garmin GPS, and his M24 sniper rifle. "J" carried the extra batteries and his M203 grenade launcher. "Joey" carried the ASIP radio and another M203 with extra rounds. I carried the VS-17 panel, strobe light, star clusters, and M18 smoke grenade. Last but not least, our extra man carried the M240B machine gun plus four hundred rounds. Our ammunition count amounted to the following breakdown:

1200 rounds/5.56mm
400 rounds/7.62mm link
60 rounds/7.62mm long range sniper ammo
30 rounds/M203 grenade
2 M18/smoke
2 star cluster

With that firepower and our ability to overwhelm the enemy with both substantial rates of fire superiority and expert marksmanship, the likelihood of maintaining a short but effective firefight until the QRF force could arrive driving 30,000 tons of Stryker steel and spitting out .50 caliber armor piercing rounds from its RWS (Remote Weapons System) was pretty good in my book.

OBSERVATION POST
"COWBOYS"

The grid to OBJ Cowboys was LF 123 456 and it placed the point of origin at the edge of a creek in some low ground looking north in a basic direct flight path to FOB COURAGE. We were inserted northwest of Cowboys, approximately eight hundred meters away and at 0400 hundred hours on 17 April 05. Morning prayers started at 0500 so I knew I only had roughly fifty minutes to walk the eight hundred meters, staying in the shadows and trying to avoid house lights that were still on. We all knew there was one four-legged creature that would inevitably sound the alarm of our alien-like presence. Dogs! And a whole darn pack of them, too. We scaled a small concrete wall that led us into an orchard and allowed us to elude the four-legged barking patrol. We stopped to set up an ORP (Objective Rally Point) and kick out a leaders' recon to pinpoint what house we wanted to occupy. (A map recon is essential but with boots on the ground and darkness all around, things can be somewhat deceptive.) Emmett and I conducted the leaders' recon while the others stayed at the ORP and provided over-watch for our movement. We moved out due south for three hundred meters and came to a small ditch. As we crouched down to discuss what looked like the best possible position to set up in, we both agreed that the house directly to our front would suffice. It was a solitary structure that gave good observation south, straight to the objective.

THE "OP"

I radioed Joey and told him to pick up the rest of the team, head due south, and look for my IR flash—One Two, One Two. With a quick "Roger OUT," he picked up and moved out. My IR flashes were matched with his—One Two, One Two—and soon we all were crouched down inside that ditch. The plan was simple, somewhat hastily made, and very unpredictable. What waited for us inside the house was unknown. We moved out in the order of march: Emmett, "J", me, the 240 gunner, and Joey as rear security. Almost all Iraqi homes have a nearly five-foot wall surrounding the home and a locked metal gate to the front. "J" and I jumped the wall and unlatched the front gate. We all moved inside and took up defensive positions near the front door. This kind of operation called for patience and cool-headedness, so a violent kicking of the door followed by an explosive front-entry room clearing team was out of the question. A firm knock followed by "Amerikey, Amerikey," was sufficient enough to wake up the resident, who turned on the kitchen light and opened the door. Cautiously we moved inside, clearing the downstairs and gathering all occupants. Placing security on the stairs, we proceeded to move upstairs with the man of the house in the lead. With everyone awake and the family's AK-47 secured, I took the remaining family members back downstairs to explain in broken Arabic and slow English what our intentions were. The rest of the team automatically started preparing the south room for sustained sniper ops.

0600 OBSERVATION BEGINS

Three days prior to our occupation, the man of the house, Ah'kmed, told me with both hand gestures and broken English that he had heard a boom coming from the south and simultaneously said the word "mortar." This was perhaps true since a mortar round had in fact impacted our FOB a few days prior. One thing was for sure: we had plenty of time on our hands and if the enemy came to fire mortars at OBJ Cowboys, it was going to be the 4th of July in April. We instituted our security/observation/rest plan since the next fifteen hours were going to be long and tedious. One man stayed downstairs to monitor the family's activity and to ensure no one entered the home, two other men observed the objective area, and two men rested. The cycle rotated like this every hour so that we stayed fresh and attentive during the entire occupation. You may think sitting in a house for hours upon hours looking at the same piece of ground is somewhat easy, yet it drains all the energy out of you.

1800 OBSERVATION ABOUT TO END

Three hours until we departed the OP and walked back north to the extraction point. Nothing relevant to report at this time. However, we all knew that the AIF, although unpredictable and tactically stupid sometimes, fired most of their mortars at or just after dusk. The chances of one of us having the opportunity to engage this mortar cell was high and yet uncertain at the same time. Our enemy was not set on any objective timetable. At approximately 2030 (8:30 p.m.), I decided to pack up and move out to our extraction point. I did this for two reasons. One, Objective Cowboys lay on the outskirts of the neighborhood and the closest road was the actual pinpointed objective site itself and I didn't want to bring the fleet of Strykers roaring down south to pick us up. And two, I wanted to be in pick-up posture prior to the Strykers arrival so that our extraction was on the go, smooth and fast. The longer a Stryker sits in a fixed location, the longer it becomes a target of opportunity. Therefore, my reasons were both sound and consistent with the principle of "common sense." Both OBJ Redskins and Browns would stay in their perspective OP's until 2115 (9:15 p.m.) and then be extracted just prior to 2130 hours. Our position was the first to infill and the last to ex-fill.

2040 HOURS:

SHOT OVER, SHOT OUT

Every infantryman, whether he is from the Rangers, an SFODA team, or the SBCT (Stryker Brigade Combat Team), knows what it sounds like when a mortar round is hung from a mortar tube. "Shot, Over" is when a round is hung. "Shot, Out" is when the round is released from the tube and is headed in its direction of travel. "Splash, Over" is when the observer witnesses the round as it impacts its intended target. When the round is hung, or makes contact with the firing pin, it makes a distinct *thud*...a very distinct *thud*!

We had just stepped foot outside and into an open field near the point of entry from earlier that morning. We turned north and headed out in the same order of movement. At 2040 hours we heard that distinct thud. The succession of several thuds was followed by the sound of impacting rounds hitting somewhere north of us—boom, boom, boom. Instinctively we hit the ground and turned back in the direction of the objective site scanning with our NVG's. We knew the rounds were being fired from somewhere southwest of our current location and our estimation was about half a click, or five hundred meters. The thought of spotting the enemy at or near our position crossed all of our minds. We had waited fifteen hours to shoot our weapons and perhaps our trigger fingers would be satisfied with the sting of 7.62 hitting its target at over 3000 feet per second. When you are in the business of killing, and you have trained your entire career for it, the chance to exercise it gets the blood pumping, especially when you know you have the upper hand. I motioned with a hand signal for Emmett to move out and for Joey to listen for any radio traffic that might indicate if in fact the other two teams were about to make contact. The time was now 2050 hours.

ROTARY-WING AIRCRAFT
INBOUND AND CLEARED TO FIRE

We were now less than one hundred meters away from the point of extraction and holed up near a mound of dirt pulling 360-degree security. We were attentively listening for any radio traffic regarding the enemy mortar cell and to hear if the other teams were making contact. We intercepted the QRF talking to the other two teams, telling them to remain in their current positions and wait until the inbound air craft, an OH-58 Kiowa and an AH-64 Apache Attack helicopter, could ID the target, fix and destroy it, and then clear the air space. Both helicopters were equipped with state-of-the-art night vision and camera equipment that allowed them to visually see at night as if they were a lion hunting an antelope in the middle of the Sahara Desert on a cool summer night. Unfortunately, we did not receive the transmission to stay in our current hard structure. Fortunately for us, however, we were well outside the impact area that the "birds" were trying to acquire. With all these facts present, keep in mind, though, that as soldiers on the ground at night, with known enemy in the area, and knowing that the pilots up above could spot our heat signatures, we still felt very uncomfortable sitting there on the ground, in the open, in a rather large grassy field waiting for two Army helicopters to do their "thing"! Our enemy, for Pete's sake, was in or near an open field and produced the same heat signatures as us, so we knew that mistakes could and did happen. Nevertheless, please God, no mistakes tonight!

STALKER 6, OVER

FM radio has a mind of its own from time to time and some have come to call it "Freaking-Magic." At that most critical moment we were experiencing some kind of atmospheric interference that would not allow us to effectively communicate with the QRF or any of the other two sniper teams. We could hear transmissions over the radio, but we could not transmit. Believe me, that tends to happen from time to time. Our QRF kept calling for our current location in order to know if we were clear for the aircraft to fire in the direction of the mortar cell. Now picture the five of us in an open field, enemy on the ground, and inbound helicopters with clearance to fire. We could visibly see the birds headed in our direction. I yelled at Joey to keep calling the QRF and give our location. The birds got closer and closer. The QRF kept calling us to seek cover and we kept responding with "Roger, we are at the extraction point. Over."

Even though we knew in the backs of our minds that the POO was southwest of us a good six or seven hundred meters, the sound of helicopters, the frantic calling on the radio for us to seek cover, and the possibility of friendly fire, tends to make the pucker factor rise from a three to a ten plus really quick. I had an IR chem-light fixed to my Mitch helmet but I was digging into my assault pack for the IR strobe. (I knew better than not to leave the OP without it on my person in the first place.) Now both aircraft were headed straight for our position and fast. At that time both Joey and Emmett were roping the birds using their PEQ-2's (a combat laser designator) letting them know, "Hey, this is us and we are friendly forces!" We all hoped that the pilots could see our IR signatures, for at that very moment we were all thinking in our minds, "Oh God, here they come."

We knew running was NOT an option and we were sure the pilots could distinguish between friendly forces set up in a perfect 360-degree security formation and a group of lanky terrorists scattered about in an open field. At that point the birds were fast upon us, and I looked up and thought two things, "Wow this is gonna hurt," and "I miss my wife." Then I continued to do the only thing I knew to do, pull security. In the end the helicopters had come inbound from the southwest over our position on a heading of north, northwest. They then conducted a dog-leg left turn heading back south and fired a small barrage of bomblets into an open field that had been designated as the point of origin of the mortar fire. By this time, unfortunately, the enemy had packed up and moved out of the area, but the gunmen on the helicopters still fired the shots as a show of force telling everyone around that they, the helicopters, were not afraid to fire regardless. We all took a deep breath, exchanged some true feelings on the matter, joked about it for a minute, and then waited for the ride back to the FOB.

FOB COURAGE

Although it was unknown to us at the time, the rounds had impacted a direct hit on the FOB. There were deaths, both U.S. soldiers and civilian contractors. My emotions over the ordeal ranged from anger to a relentless thirst for revenge. I sat watching and waiting in position for fourteen hours to kill these "guys," yet as a matter of luck (lucky for them, that is), they happened to fire some three hundred meters away from where we had been observing. As described earlier, the patient waiting of a sniper for his enemy to appear between the kill zone and his crosshairs is in fact the name of the game. The urban setting prevented us and the other two sniper teams from getting off a shot, but for the next two weeks we flooded the area with different positions, waiting with diligent patience for the chance to kill those lucky bastards. On April 23, 2005, after infiltrating our sniper teams, the QRF spotted a lone AIF insurgent with a fake taxicab used to transport mortar systems. They engaged the man with small arms fire, captured the taxi, and found one 60mm mortar tube and several rounds. As a combined effort, the mission was a success, for that amounted to one less mortar tube on the battlefield. My only regret is that our sniper teams never fired a single round during this mission. Nevertheless, we all came away alive, in one piece, and with a whole lot of combat experience to boot!

END OF MISSION

[NOTE: From the time this account was penned, the Annihilators, A Co 3-21 IN, have killed and/or captured several mortar cells. During one combat patrol, they discovered a complete terrain model of FOB COURAGE outlining the various buildings and such. The efforts of the entire GIMLET Battalion to rid Mosul of AIF have been both sacrificial and downright hard, dirty work.]

Three hundred sixty-five days in Iraq. Three hundred sixty-five days away from my wife and newborn son. Three hundred sixty-five days away from the greatest country in the free world, and three hundred sixty-five days away from the closest thing to sanity—a nice hot Grande Sumatra with room for extra cream from my favorite Starbucks coffeehouse! There are other stories out there that are far more in depth or perhaps show a different perspective than mine. By reading these stories I have related, however, I hope they have painted a picture for you of but a taste of what Iraq was like for me. I could write more about my ordeals but I choose not to do so. My goal was to allow you to feel what we went through on a daily basis, the emotion of losing a comrade, and the feeling of what it is like to conduct a combat operation. This last segment is reserved for the honor of the two friends I lost in combat. They were not just my friends; they were also sons, fathers, husbands, leaders, and brave men.

IN HONOR OF ALL WHO SERVE
OPERATION ENDURING FREEDOM
OPERATION IRAQI FREEDOM
MSG BRIAN A. MACK
"ASSASSIN 7"
HHC 3rd Battalion 21st Infantry
23 February 1969 - 13 January 2005
Mosul, Iraq

SSG JUAN SOLORIO
"ASSASSIN 3"
HHC 3RD Battalion 21st Infantry
23 November 1972 – 04 March 2005
Mosul, Iraq

SSG Juan Solorio was born in Dallas, Texas. He joined the U.S. Army in August 1993 and served in the following units: 1-67 Armor Battalion, 1-27 "Wolf Hounds" Schofield, Hawaii, 2-505 Parachute Infantry Regiment, Ft Bragg, and 3-21 "Gimlets," Fort Lewis, Washington.

SOLDIER'S TRIBUTE
FOB COURAGE, IRAQ

Over two hundred years ago a Founding Father said that liberty must be refreshed from time to time with the blood of tyrants and patriots. On Friday, March 4th of the year 2005, a patriot lost his life. SSG Juan Solorio, Assassin 3, died. He died fighting for everything that his country stands for, which is Freedom, Liberty, and Justice for all. But more than that he died doing his job—that is all—just his job. If you ask his men, they will tell you that he died fighting the enemy. Today before you, an empty pair of boots is displayed as a reminder that at one time those boots carried the living body of a combat soldier. They will never be worn again. They will never lead the men of Team Three into combat. They will never again step foot on American soil. To the men, soldiers, and friends who followed those boots, I salute you. I know that you will never forget your squad leader—a part of him will forevermore live in your hearts. To all of us Assassins—one more brother has fallen, and now it is up to all of us to make sure his legacy and that of other brave soldiers is never lost. Their lives are gone, but "WE WHO DO NOT DIE" press on in their memory, and because of that, they live on. [NOTE: the slogan "We Who Do Not Die" was passed down from Vietnam as the slogan given to the Assassins, 3-21 "GIMLETS," and we proudly bore that slogan on our hearts and sleeves during OIF III while serving to protect our American way of life.

Corporal Aaron Baily pulls security

Getting ready to train with the 160th
SPC Cullen, SGT Wells, SPC Johnson

SFC Mack with 160th SOAR

SSG MesMer, Stryker Combat Vehicle

Author holding a rocket propelled grenade launcher

SSG MesMer, sniper over-watch

Front Row: "Stevo", SSG Mike MesMer, SGT Matt Schaffer,
Lieutenant Rob Decker, MSG Brian Mack. Second Row: SPC
David Oman, PFC John "Doc" Crawford. Third Row: SPC

David Solso. Fourth Row: SPC Emmett Cullen, SGT Ryan Wells.

SPC Cullen and SGT Wells sit and wait for a high-profile target

BE ALL THAT YOU CAN BE

Before there was an "Army of One" and after Uncle Sam declared that he wants you, there was a little jingle that rang out something like, "Be...all that you can be...in the...Army." Now the Marines have "a few good men" and the Navy is "full speed ahead" and of course the Air Force is "aiming high," so all in all the future appears to be bright regardless of which branch of the military someone might find themselves in. Anyway, my point to this is that in the military there are endless opportunities to serve one's country, and not just serve but also to gain a multitude of technical, educational, and cultural enlightenments that can only come from hands-on experiences. These things cannot be learned from the pages of textbooks.

In my past thirteen years serving in the Army I have learned a great deal in various subjects, including those previously mentioned: technical, educational, and cultural. I believe and have seen with my own two eyes how much one can grow by traveling the world, enduring rigorous training, and learning the values and customs of other peoples around the world. Here are just a few stories of those adventures that I would like to share with you. But first let's look at one person who personifies the "be all you can be" attitude.

Lance Armstrong, who overcame his bout with cancer to go on to win his seventh consecutive Tour de France in 2005, stated that if it were not for his cancer he might not have had the heart and soul to go out and win tour after tour after tour. "Be all that you can be"....YES... Lance Armstrong, hence the *strong* in his name, went out and won seven straight races and not just any old races but a grueling, 2,000-mile bike race that puts to shame the average Sunday stroll down memory lane. In addition, Armstrong had to battle the biggest race of his life, the race to cure or end his cancer.

I think to myself that on any given day of the week I defeat myself by thinking that life may be too difficult at times. I wonder if at times during a race Armstrong would think the next mile to come was too far out of reach or that the next hilltop was too steep to climb. What is it that burns inside of a man to accomplish what no other man has ever done and to be the very best at it for so many years? Lance said in an interview before the 2004 tour that he was afraid of two things: dying and losing and that, to him, both were one and the same. If I die then I lose and I hate to lose, or something along those terms. It was his great determination not to lose that kept him peddling along. I salute you, Lance Armstrong, for your competitive spirit, your unyielding dedication to your passion, and of course your drive to "Be All That You Can BE."

Although I have never raced on a bike for 2,000 miles, I can be almost certain that Lance Armstrong never strapped a seventy-five pound "rock" to his back and humped up the Kahuku Mountains in Hawaii or conducted a twelve-mile foot march in the Egyptian desert, and I don't believe he ever tried out for Special Forces either. Nonetheless, the infantry soldier is like no other soldier in the Army. Regardless of what any other MOS (Military Occupational Specialty) says of his or her job, the infantry soldier is the hardest, dirtiest, and toughest job in the military. Now of course each MOS has its jokes, and the Army is by far more sophisticated than your average "Jar Head," can out-run and out-maneuver any "Fly Boy," and can out-swim almost the entire Navy—except for the elite "Seals" of course. Keep in mind, my opinions here are based on my sincere love for the Army and in no way am I downgrading the abilities of the other branches of service. If you were to ask a Marine if boot camp or basic training was harder, he would fight to the death and tell you that Marine boot camp is definitely harder than Army basic training. Anyway, the life of an infantry soldier differs from any other job in the Army. We are the front line... period.

My adventures in the infantry began in the 25th Infantry Division (L) in Schofield Barracks, Hawaii. I was in Alpha Company, 5th Battalion 14th Infantry, a "Golden Dragon." Interestingly enough, this was the same division and same brigade that Oliver Stone served in and was the backdrop for the popular movie "Platoon" staring Charlie Sheen. In fact, Stone was a "Gimlet," a fact known to those who belong to the "3-21 Infantry Battalion," the same battalion I am a part of this very moment.

Every MOS in the Army needs to be ready for combat and they all have their respective battle drills; however, the infantry soldier has a multitude of skills that encompass a wide variety of different abilities. For example, not only did I posses the abilities of an infantry soldier, who starts out as a basic rifleman learning the eight basic battle drills found in FM 7-8, but I was also picked to be a dragon gunner. A dragon gunner is a certified ground-pounding grunt ready to kill tanks using a shoulder-fired, anti-tank, wire-guided missile. To start out, the life expectancy of a dragon gunner on the modern battle field is approximately nine seconds, as that is about the average time in seconds it takes for the tank-killing, shoulder-fired rocket to hit its target at the maximum effective range of 1,000 meters. After the projectile leaves the launch tube, it ejects a cloud of white smoke visible to the eyes of the enemy. If perhaps the gunner is off target and misses, the enemy has time to pick up the hostile smoke signal and return fire in that immediate direction. Now, we as dragon gunners have our own battle drills to counter such an enemy reaction, i.e., false smoke signals and coordinated fires. Trying to dodge or outrun a bullet that can chop a tree in half, however, is no fun at all. There is more to being a dragon gunner than merely pulling the trigger, for we undergo quarterly training and testing that is very intense.

First we had to know everything technical about the missile itself and then be able to commit that to memory for future tests. After eight years of moving on to other positions in my career, I can still recall that it takes about seven pounds of pressure per square inch inside the gyro to snap the three restraining pins that hold the rocket in place inside of the launch tube before it can be propelled out of the tube. Sounds like senseless knowledge, but it serves a purpose as our dragon team won first place three years running in the all-around division dragon competition, which included Marine Corps dragon gunners. The competition lasted three days and included everything from written and hands-on tests, dragon firing tables, and probably the hardest test of them all: knowing every Warsaw Pack and NATO allied tank, APC, anti-aircraft gun system, and enemy aircraft, including fast movers and rotary winged aircraft. Let me not forget that the final test in the competition was the twelve-mile foot march with full combat gear and complete dragon system, which included the dragon missile, day optic sight and night thermal vision sight, extra batteries, and pressurized cooling bottles. Each team consisted of two dragon teams of three men plus a squad leader, and each team had to divide two dragon systems between them for the duration of the twelve miles. Now that's walking twelve miles in the Hawaiian heat with at least seventy pounds strapped to your back. When we were not engaged in a dragon mission, we provided local security for our headquarters element.

As I mentioned above, I learned a lot of technical things in the Army and being a dragon gunner was just the start. I have received training in secure computer and radio operations, highly technical weapons and thermal imagery, combat tactics, rappelling and rock climbing, and my favorite of them all, helicopter operations. Forget the county fair with its Zipper ride or the Egg Beater, because once you have skimmed the treetops sitting in the "hell-hole" of a Black Hawk helicopter, nothing else compares. As far as my educational experiences in the Army, nothing can compare to physically being present in some of the most spectacular places on earth. As an elementary school student I learned about the world's civilizations and how those civilizations helped shape our present culture; however, learning from a text book is significantly different from actually stepping foot on places like the Great Pyramid, Mount Sinai, or the Sea of Galilee. They say a picture is worth a million words and yet seeing someone eye to eye creates a memory that will follow you to your grave. Listen to some of these stories that were left out of the history books and that have touched me in a way that helps me truly appreciate my freedom. In 1993 I deployed from Hawaii to the Multi-National Force and Observers in Sharm El Sheikh, Egypt, which is located near the tip of the Sinai Peninsula and is about a day's drive from Cairo. The operation is run by eleven host nations, including the United States, Italy, France, Norway, Uruguay, New Zealand, Canada, Colombia, the Netherlands, Australia, and last, but definitely not least, the island nation of Fiji. Now for a farm boy from Kansas who had never seen the ocean, getting his first military duty station on the Hawaiian Islands and then in a country on the other side of the planet, getting a chance to see all these new and exciting cultures was in a way a culture shock to my system. The reasoning behind the Multi-National Force came about in 1979 with the signing of the Camp David Peace Accords that ended the war between Egypt and Israel. Our primary mission was to observe the truths of each nation not to enter each others' border space. Anyway, this was the chance of a lifetime for me to go and see the pyramids, the Red Sea, Israel, and climb the stone steps leading to the top of Mount Sinai. For each twenty-one day rotation that we spent out in the desert on our remote sites, some accessible only via helicopter and some riddled with old landmines from past wars, we would come back to South Camp for a week of R&R. I was ready for my first trip to see Cairo, the Great Pyramid, and the Sphinx. We set out on our tour bus with approximately forty U.S. soldiers, headed for a combined trip to Cairo and then off to Tel Aviv, Israel.

On the way I encountered several interesting and somewhat disturbing cultural ways of life. I experienced a country that by far has less income per capita, per person, than I had ever seen or truly knew existed in a world of such supreme power. This became relevant when our bus blew a rear inside tire, and we cruised steadfastly to the nearest town to find someone to fix it.

Our South American bus driver was a regular driver from South Camp and thus knew the geography of the area and how to deal with the locals, so as the bus pulled up to a garage that was an obvious workshop, we could either stay on while the flat was being fixed or get out to stretch our tired legs. I opted to get out and watch, but what I saw before my eyes blew me away. Now remember, here I was just eighteen years old, a young man who had just graduated from high school and who was seeing for the first time in his life what life was like on the other side of the earth. The apparent owner of the shop—or perhaps it was his son, a young Egyptian man of about thirty years of age or so— spoke directly to our bus driver to negotiate a set price for fixing our tire. It does not matter if the price is fair for the work to be done or not, because it will not be the older gentleman doing the hard labor in the hot desert sun. [NOTE: As is customary in many other cultures, whatever the father dealt his hands in as a business was the trade the son also would pick up, thus keeping the family business alive.] No, it would definitely be his two young sons doing the labor.

Now, I was a mere onlooker to the whole charade, for I could not predict what was to come of the whole matter. I only knew that two men spoke broken Arabic, exchanged several hand gestures, and the apparent owner left and walked back inside the garage. Moments later two boys came out with several tools in their hands. I recognized one as a large steel pry bar and a smaller one to break the seal on the rim. The older of the two boys must have been around thirteen years of age but the smaller boy was, to my amazement, only about six years old. Both boys scurried along, set the wheel blocks down, put the tire jack in the proper place, and began the process of raising the bus up high enough to be able to pull the old tire off and put on the new one. Keep in mind that it was the rear inside tire that blew, so they had to remove the first tire to get to the inside tire. In reality they were having to remove two large heavy bus tires while outside in the 103 degree heat, and the boys were not wearing any shoes either. I stood there in silence as I watched these boys work and many thoughts ran through my mind as I remembered the time I had to help replace the tire on my combine, in the machine shed, in the shade, with my work boots on and with the proper tools and clothing to get the job done right. Even with all of that it still had been no piece of cake. Then I wondered—what if the tire slipped off the rim after all the lugs were removed and slammed on the foot of the youngest boy, or what if the large pry bar happened to fall on a foot or a little toe?

I have not told you the worst part of the story yet. The little boy, who was about six years old and probably will never go to school and will never learn of our way of life and who will someday be the man who walks out to negotiate the price for someone else who happens to have a flat tire, had an apparent skin infection on his scalp that caused large chunks of his hair to fall out. On top of that, large bumps were visible where the hair was missing, making his head appear oddly-shaped and disfigured. It was gruesome to see and it made me angry, yet there was nothing I could do but feel pity in my heart for the little boy.

The two worked hard until the job was done, and done right it was. As I mentioned before, the price had been set but the payment was not delivered until the work was complete. Our bus driver reached into his pocket at the same time that the older gentlemen from the start of the whole ordeal came out. As the two young boys, by this time dirty and greasy, looked on in anticipation of receiving some of the profit, the owner pushed the two aside, said some words in Arabic, and then pocketed the money himself. As we left the roadside garage, I looked at the two boys standing there as if someone had stolen some candy straight out of their tiny little fingers. My heart was sad and angry, and I almost threw ten Egyptian pounds out the window to show my appreciation for the work they had done. They were outright blindsided and were left standing, watching our bus leave with only dirty hands and hot, dirty feet, waiting for the next order of work to be done.

On another occasion as we were traveling north to the boarder of Israel, I noticed a little farm house made of dirt sod with rusty tin flaps for a roof. The father was tending to his field on an old tractor with his eldest son following behind on foot, while his youngest son played barefooted in the front yard, kicking a small ball. As our bus curved around on the road, the smallest boy looked up, held his little hand above his eyebrows to shield his eyes from the bright sun, squinted his eyes, and noticed the big orange Multi-National Force symbol pasted on the side of the bus. The symbol represents peace in the form of a white dove with an olive branch in the background. It is both highly visible from great distances and also means a free handout of candy or the sharing of an occasional box lunch that accompanied us as we left South Camp. Dropping his ball on the ground at his feet, the little boy started at a dead sprint, racing for the bus with his hands waving in the air as if somehow, magically, the bus would come to a screeching stop. You see, he was hoping that by chance a soldier would see him running and drop some food out of the window, for that is what often happened when we toured around the desert and made necessary pit stops. Kids see the bus stop and naturally come up to us, waiting with great expectations for a healthy handout. Well, the bus didn't stop this time. The little boy soon ran out of speed and watched us as we drove on into the distant desert sands.

On yet another assignment, as we maneuvered into a sector control center for one of our twenty-one day rotations, we had no choice but to drive through a small town that was literally a trash heap with unpaved streets, rickety old buildings, goats that had nothing better to do than to rummage through the piles of trash, and an occasional pack of dogs that roamed free, doing whatever their dirty dog minds decided to do. As I sat there in the truck looking at all that, I wondered how on earth anyone could tolerate that kind of public filth and garbage and yet do absolutely nothing about it. The truck came to an abrupt stop, and standing in front of us was a human chain comprised of little kids linked together hand in hand, some naked, some more dirty than others, and none wearing any shoes. They were only doing what they knew how to do in order to survive: taking extreme measures, putting their little bodies in harm's way in hopes of getting something to eat. The children had in fact made a human road block, forcing the truck to stop dead in the middle of the street. At the same time, other children not directly involved in the human chain surrounded the truck and did two things: one, they begged for food by speaking Arabic, which none of us could understand. Instead they put their fingers up to their mouths and tapped their lips. Second, if they were not actively begging for food, they grabbed anything that was not tied or bolted down.

It was just a way to survive and complete the cycle that the animal kingdom calls the "survival of the fittest." The biggest and strongest animals survive the harshest of elements and live on to populate the herd in order to ensure a strong bloodline. The fact remains that these kids just wanted something to eat. It broke my heart when I saw a soldier throw an MRE (Meal Ready to Eat) out into the street. He didn't just do it to see a bunch of little kids scramble to get at the one MRE but rather as a gesture of sorrow and a heartfelt desire to help someone who had nothing. As the MRE hit the pavement, it landed at the feet of a little girl with wavy brown hair, no shoes on her feet, and no one to protect her from what was about to happen. Just as she picked up the food packet and looked in the direction of the moving truck as if to say thank you, a bigger and stronger boy ran up behind her. With a mighty push, he let her have it in the back. The little girl went flying and the MRE was cast out of her hands like a football tossed by a quarterback. Then the boy picked it up and scampered like a running back across the trash-filled street, not looking back because he instinctively knew that others would soon pick up the chase. What would you do if that happened on your street today? That is why I thank God for having what I have today, and by the world's standards, that is a lot.

On my trip into Israel I found that the Bible was accurate when it declared that Egypt would be a land of eternal waste because of the manner in which it treated the Israelites. There is no OSHA or safety committee designated to ensure their safety at the workplace. Trash is customarily thrown out into the street, and as for properly disposing of deceased animals... Letting them lie right where they bit the dust, so to speak, was, I guess, their way of handling business.

Once as we were conducting a training mission, we walked into a quaint town and were not so pleasantly greeted with a smell that overcame us with such a powerful stench that it almost made us turn back and find an alternate route. A dead camel that had been baking in the hot, hot Egyptian sun for days and was foul, disgusting, maggot ridden, and stomach turning, just lay there on the side of the street like it was nothing to raise an eyebrow over. Even the dogs would not bother with it! All we could do to keep from losing our breakfast was to pull our sweaty T-shirts up over our mouths and noses as a kind of air purifier and hope that the wind would blow the foul stench away from us. All in a day's training? Yes. It makes me have a whole new appreciation for the trash man who picks up my dirty garbage every week.

Now getting back to entering Israel: We had been traveling down a long and bumpy road cratered with potholes when we finally came to the border checkpoint. It was not much to see and the order of procedure was to step off the bus, form a single-file line, and wait to advance into the one-room control center. A very interesting thing occurred as we all stood in line. A car with young Egyptian men came whizzing by us and screeched to a halt. One young gentleman stepped out of the car and approached some soldiers at the end of the long line. The men in my part of the line could not hear what words were being exchanged, but we imagined that he was asking politely for a handout.

It was only a short while before he made his way to me, and I found out that he was asking to buy a pair of sneakers from anyone who would be willing to part with theirs. The man stood in front of me and said, "Sir, would you like to sell your shoes?" As politely as I could, I said, "No, thank you." He countered that with, "Sir, if you were to sell them to me...how much then?" I paused for a moment and thought to myself, "These are top of the line Nike basketball shoes that are fairly expensive." I replied with, "Well, if I were to sell them, then I would ask maybe twenty dollars or so." As we both stood there, I could see the disappointment in his eyes. Twenty dollars in American money was beyond what he had and beyond what he could ever afford for a pair of shoes, and he was asking for a pair of used shoes at that. The man had great persistence though, and he kept going up the line in hopes of getting lucky. As I watched him, I remembered that in my closet at home I had at least five pairs of shoes. To me that is normal, but to someone who probably has never had a new pair of anything in his life, a good used pair was just as nice as a brand new pair.

The line slowly but surely dwindled down until I was about to enter the control center with my Egyptian identification card in hand. What I was to witness is again a representation of how desolate and behind the times this desert wasteland is. Inside the one-room control center and behind a wooden desk, an Egyptian customs agent sat in a wooden chair with a wooden ruler, blank sheet of paper, and a No. 2 yellow pencil. As each American soldier passed by his workstation, we gave him our I.D. cards. He meticulously recorded our names and the identification numbers while using the ruler to keep everything in a uniform straight line. I was bewildered at the sight, and to make things more amusing the man behind the desk had caught a small brown and yellow sparrow which he kept in a little cardboard box sitting on the edge of his desk, only taking it out for his amusement if time permitted. Back on the bus, we were ready to do this entire process over again as soon as we crossed the border and entered Israel.

As I mentioned before, the Bible describes the lands of Egypt as an eternal wasteland. That could be taken literally or figuratively, but I saw for myself that Israel was a land of milk and honey. That was the report given by Joshua to Moses after he sent spies into Israel. If I may recount for you, the Israelites had roamed aimlessly in the deserts of Egypt for some forty years before God allowed them to enter His Promised Land. That was kind of what we were about to do except that we had only been driving in the desert for a matter of hours. In addition, we did not need to send spies, for we were welcome to visit.

My point is that as soon as we crossed the border, we were astonished as our eyes caught sight of green grass, flowers with gorgeous blossoms, palm trees, and birds, bees, and insects of all kinds flying about in the fresh air. As we entered the air-conditioned control center of the I.D.F (Israeli Defense Force), there was a soldier sitting behind a desk working at a computer. Like his Egyptian counterpart, the Israeli soldier took our information, but entered it into their central computer system. It is hard to think that two totally different technologies, two lifestyles with different cultures and religions, can live so close to each other and yet be so incredibly different.

Although cultures can be significantly different, man's heart and condition is just about the same wherever you go. There was poverty in Egypt, and we saw some poverty in Israel. One particular day we were visiting Nazareth, the home of Jesus' parents, Joseph and Mary, when at one point a man stood on the street corner, hanging his head down, while at the same time holding his hand out for all to see. Nothing was wrong with his hand, he was just waiting and hoping for someone to stroll by and perhaps drop some coins into it. Maybe someone might even give him some food to eat. As I walked along the sidewalk, I had plenty of coins in my pocket left over from souvenir shopping the day before. (The American dollar gets a good exchange rate, so for about every one dollar we can expect about nine Egyptian pounds or about five Israeli shillings in return.)

I approached the man on the corner, and just as I dropped several coins into his hand, my eyes caught sight of his real problem. Was he poor and dirty and presumably hungry? YES. But somehow he had incurred an injury to his foot that had in fact become infected, developed gangrene and had swollen to the size of a football. I will not describe its grotesque condition but it bothered me very much in my heart.

At another point in our travels I came across several young women who were pregnant yet had no husbands. The only hope they had was to beg on the side of the street. In some cultures if a girl becomes pregnant out of wedlock she is indeed deemed impure and either alienated or worse, stoned to death. That is correct, that in the twenty-first century people in the world are being stoned to their deaths. These women hung their heads down in shame, and like the older man they too hoped for a handout from a kind passerby.

There are many more stories I could tell, but the fact remains that until I had actually stepped foot into countries like Egypt, Israel, Kuwait, Iraq, and Korea, I had no idea what life in these countries was actually like. Pages on a textbook can only create a mere image, but to walk, breathe, and live history is worth more than any amount of money because it cannot be adequately described on the pages in a textbook. I will carry these images and experiences with me for the rest of my life, and I hope to some day share them with my children.

If someone were to ask me if I feel that I have been all that I can be, I would respond that up to this point in my life I have. Nevertheless, I still have a full life ahead of me to explore new beginnings and experience new ways of life. Some people stay in their present situations until their deaths. For me, however, I can remember that as a little boy my imagination took me places that I never knew existed. One day I was exploring the Colorado mountainsides searching for Indian arrowheads and looking for evidence of dinosaur bones, and the next day I was certain that when I grew up I would dedicate my life to finding the real Big Foot! Now I am thirtyish and there is still a smidgen of imagination living inside of me that believes a large, hairy creature of the deep dark forest roams around eluding any and all contact with the human race. Just as there could be—and I stress *could be*—life on some other planet beyond our solar system, I won't be the one to say, "That's absurd and the most crazy idea I have ever heard." God said that he created the heavens and the earth so the possibility of other life forms, in outer space, is perhaps a reality and not some crazy fairy tale after all! Well, it is fun to dream and have crazy ideas at times, and as I look at my life, I realize that I have already done more than most of your average American folk. Don't get me wrong. I am not trying to brag or show off all that I have done and insist that I am better than most. It is a true fact, however, that as a soldier in the United States military we do more before 9:00 a.m. than most people do all day. In one of the songs Tim McGraw sings, part of the lyrics says that, "In my next thirty years I'm going...." As I look back for a moment at my last thirty years, I have lived some of my dreams. I am thankful for my service to my country because if it were not for the Army, some of those experiences would have never happened. At age nineteen I stepped foot in the Egyptian sands and toured the ancient cities of Jerusalem and Bethlehem. I have dipped my hand in the waters of the Jordan River and the Sea of Galilee and walked on top of Mount Tabor. I have seen with my own eyes the olive trees where Jesus of Nazareth might have prayed to the almighty God and Father. I have been to the Dome of the Rock and the Wailing Wall where I witnessed Jewish men and women praying. I have dived in the Red Sea with blue-spotted rays, sea horses, large parrotfish, and the infamous, aggressive barracuda. I have seen the all-natural rock formation outside of Sharm El Sheikh that amazingly depicts the profile of John F. Kennedy. I lived in tropical Hawaii for three years and would go back there in a heartbeat. I have seen three of the world's space needles in Seoul, Kuwait City, and Seattle. I have flown in helicopters and been bounced around inside a tank. I have rappelled from rooftops and sixty-foot towers, and I have had the opportunity to blow stuff up and shoot some of the most powerful weapons in the world. I have competed in races big and small, and I took sixth place in my first and last body-building competition. All in all, I have done a lot of fun stuff, yet I look forward to more years of fun and adventure. The point to all of this is that I have lived my life so far to the fullest. As I said in the very beginning of this book, Dr. Martin Luther King, Jr. said it best when he said, "I have a dream..." and then I said, "Now live it!"

Anyone can have a dream, but if you fail to put your heart's desires into action, then perhaps your dream will fade away and never be fulfilled. Speaking of dreams, at this very moment that I am writing these words there are Olympic athletes from all over the world living their dreams in Athens, Greece. They have spent countless hours training and preparing for the moment to compete for a gold medal and to be able to stand next to some of the most dedicated and professional athletes, Olympians, in the world. To be all that you can be and so much more is the continuing quest to reach for new heights, and in the end it shouldn't be all for the gold but rather for the chance to share in the spirit of what the world games are all about: FREEDOM. YES, *freedom* to compete in a sport you love and hold dear to your heart without fear of gunfire or mortar attack, or without having to run from building to building dodging sniper fire, and without having to see your child get on a bus and think that maybe the bus won't make it this time. It is about freedom to laugh and cry and hold each other with victorious glory for winning the race. It is about freedom to look another Olympian in the eyes and see one heart even if you speak a different language.

Last but not least, it is about having the freedom to see all nations rise and pay tribute to each others' nationalities without holding grudges or having bad attitudes. If there are bad attitudes, and who doesn't have them, they come from within and do not hold true to that for which the spirit of the Olympic games really represents. I hold sorrow in my heart for the Iranian wrestler who forfeited his match just because his first opponent was from Israel. The government of Iran has not formally acknowledged Israel as being a state, and thus holds ill feelings toward them. The two wrestlers, however, even though they are direct representatives of their countries and their peoples, shouldn't see a government but rather an Olympic opponent ready to defend the mat. Matching muscle against muscle, strength against strength, and talent against talent, taken to the mat in an all-out battle for victory should be the goal. There is no place for national pride and arrogance defeating the mind into thinking that competing with an Israeli would be a disgrace.

Soon the games will be over and all the athletes will return home and the world will continue to function as it has and as it will, but for one moment in time as the Olympic flame is ceremonially called into a retreat, may all who watch be reminded that for all mankind the true race is for Peace, Liberty...and Justice for all.

As I close this last chapter in my book, I would like to reflect on the closing of a chapter of another kind. Mr. Rulon Gardner faced his last wrestling match on an Olympic mat in Greece, although he has many more chapters of his life yet to live. Four years earlier I watched Gardner defeat his Russian friend, and I rose to acknowledge his victory in my living room as if I had just won. I love competition for it puts me at the edge of my seat, and I was proud of him for winning the gold medal. I could see the victory in Gardner's eyes as he danced around the mat with an unbelievable yet humble prance as he truly realized that the gold was his.

As I watched him wrestle again this year, I was just as much on the edge of my seat as the last time and was sure he would make us all proud by bringing home another gold medal. I remember a reporter asking him if he was confident that the gold would be his, and Rulon answered something like this, "Anything can happen. I am just going to go out there and give it my best." Anything can happen no matter how much you have trained and prepared. You see, it was the spirit of giving his best that got him to where he is today—an Olympic athlete. He will be that for the rest of his life, and every time I hear his name I will immediately remember the feeling he gave me as I watched him win his first gold. It was a feeling of pride and happiness and patriotism. Unfortunately this was Rulon Gardner's last match in Olympic competition, and we were all witnesses to his final chapter in the world of Greco-Roman wrestling. We were also witnesses to a ceremonial ending of a wrestler's career. Gardner sat in the middle of the mat with tears slowly falling from his cheeks, the American flag draped across his wide shoulders caressing him while he unlaced his shoes. It was finished, and he placed his shoes in the middle of the mat as if to say goodbye to an old friend.

-It is finished — It is done-
-The Alpha and The Omega-

Figuratively Rulon was saying, I have come and conquered and now I say goodbye. With that he faced the world and raised his hands and arms high with the strength of a gentle giant letting go of his beloved sport. I salute you, Rulon Gardner, and you are the kind of athlete that I admire and respect. You are a man who has faced many challenges, yet they did not stop you from living your dreams. In some ways those very challenges gave you strength to fight on and shout in victory.

In the same way that Gardner left his shoes in the middle of the mat, there is a ceremonial salute to fallen soldiers who perish in the realms of combat. It is a sight that automatically brings tears to my eyes, for it is a sight that means only one thing and that no parent wants to see of his or her son or daughter. It is a sight that brings grown men to their knees, men who served alongside and perhaps in the same firefight as the one who is being honored. Along with that sight is the sound of the saddest melody in the world, the playing of "Taps."

With the sound of the trumpet, "Taps" is played and all behold the sight of a pair of empty combat boots that once held the swift feet of a combat soldier, a soldier who volunteered to risk his life for the freedom of other Americans in order for that freedom to see another day. Those are boots that will never be worn again and that no man can replace, for the one who wore them is the only one who knew the risk it took to lace them up in the first place. They are the boots of a soldier who believed that freedom is worth fighting for. [And like the words that have been spoken before, "Give me Liberty or Give me Death," it comes one with the other...Liberty and Death...]

Death is not something that I wish upon any man, and death is something in which God himself is the final referee, but the soldier is the one who does not think about death. No, the soldier thinks of victory, and of winning the battle, and of fighting to save his comrades in order to preserve the very nature of the greatest country in the world—his country. The soldier is the one who focuses on accomplishing his mission with great faith, knowing that sometimes what he does as a soldier deserves no recognition.

Like I stated above, the games have come to an end and the world goes on, yet the soldier is the one who will stay awake late at night guarding his post. He will walk a thousand miles at night and fight his enemy all day long. He will carry his comrade's gear and think nothing of it and he will sleep on the ground, in the rain and snow, in the jungle, and in grassy fields just to get up and march onward until his mission is done. There is no gold medal in the end, and the only hope that keeps the soldier alive is coming home to rest his weary head...safe and sound...quiet and restless...waiting for the next set of orders to go. It is the soldier who has shed his blood for all to see so that we can live and breathe and have our being. Remember that "amber waves of grain" keep swaying in the breeze, and the flag of the United States of America is right there waving her stars and strips across this nation "from sea to shining sea." Each star represents each individual state and there are thirteen stripes honoring our thirteen original colonies. The white stripes represent our peace and the red stands for the valorous blood of patriots who died fighting for her. They were soldiers, minutemen, statesmen, fathers, husbands, sons, and friends. Lest we should forget them, in honor we should keep remembering them, that they paid with their lives the ultimate sacrifice. To you VETERANS, you PATRIOTS, you SOLDIERS....I SALUTE YOU!

IN MEMORY OF ALL WHO SERVED

This is a book like no other. It is my book, written simply from the heart and is dedicated to the men and women who have served as part of our Armed Forces. The words are simple and the meaning is whatever you make of it, yet this book stands for what I believe to be a blessed nation. Just as it is printed on our own money, let us never forget:

-IN GOD WE TRUST-

Those are the words on which this country was founded and to anyone who believes in them, then to God be the glory....

FAMOUS QUOTES

Some famous and not so famous quotes...
"Americans never quit."
GEN. DOUGLAS MACARTHUR
WWII Commander
1880-1964
"Americans are a free people, who know that freedom is
the right of every person...it is God's gift to humanity."
GEORGE W. BUSH
Union Address 2003
"We need men who can dream of things that never were."
John F. Kennedy
"Let's Roll."
TODD BEAMER
Flight 93
9/11/01
"I think a hero is someone who understands the degree of
responsibility that comes with his freedom."
BOB DYLAN
Rock-n-Roll icon
"Knowledge speaks, but wisdom listens."
JIMI HENDRIX
Rock Legend
1942-1970
"Obstacles are those frightful things you see when you
take your eyes off your goal."
HENRY FORD
1803-1947
"In the end, we will remember the words not of our
enemies, but the silence of our friends."
DR. MARTIN LUTHER KING, JR.

CIVIL RIGHTS ADVOCATE

1928-1968

"The true measure of a man is how he treats someone who can do him absolutely no good."

SAMUEL JOHNSON

1709-1784

"If a man does his best, what else is there?"

"The object of war is not to die for your country, but to make the other poor bastard die for his."

GENERAL GEORGE S. PATTON

1885-1945

"It's not the size of the dog in the fight; it's the size of the fight in the dog."

MARK TWAIN

1835-1910

"'Tis better to be silent and thought a fool, than to speak and remove all doubt."

ABRAHAM LINCOLN

1809-1865

"Even a fool seems wise if he keeps silent."

PROVERBS 17:28

"I have seen enough of one war never to wish to see another."

"The tree of liberty must be refreshed from time to time with the blood of patriots and tyrants."

THOMAS JEFFERSON

"You cannot teach a man anything; you can only help him find it within himself."

GALILEO

"More history is made with secret handshakes than by battles."

JOHN BARTH

"Histories make men wise."

FRANCIS BACON

1561-1626

"The way of a fool seems right to him, but a wise man listens to advice."
PROVERBS 12:15
"One is none...and two is one."
"Don't be late, Don't be light, and Be in the right uniform."
SSG STRONG
SSG HALL
US ARMY SPECIAL FORCES
"The past is a source of knowledge, and the future is a source of hope."
STEPHEN E. AMBROSE
1936-2002
"Cowards die many times before their deaths; the valiant never taste of death but once."
WILLIAM SHAKESPEARE
"Go confidently in the direction of your dreams. Live the life you have imagined."
"Men are born to succeed, not fail."
HENRY DAVID THOREAU
"Real integrity is doing the right thing."
"The biggest adventure you can ever take is to live the life of your dreams."
OPRAH WINFREY
"The eyes of the Lord are everywhere, keeping watch on the wicked and the good."
PROVERBS 15:3
"Speak softly but carry a big stick."
THEODORE ROSEVELT
"Go ahead...make my day...punk."
CLINT EASTWOOD...a.k.a.
DIRTY HARRY
"We're here to...*pump...you up.*"
HANS & FRANZ
"May the force...be with you."
YODA
"Join the dark side."

DARTH VADER

"I pity the fool."

MR. "T"

"Fire your Guns."

AC/DC

"You can't handle the truth."

JACK NICOLSON

"A FEW GOOD MEN"

"The prayers, the training, the vitamins."

"What are you going to do when the largest arms in the universe...crush you?"

HULK HOGAN

WWF CHAMPION

"Yapple Dapple"

Joe Thomas

BSA

"Momma says, life is like a box of chocolates."

FOREST GUMP

"Top of the morning to ya,' girls..."

"You gotta test yourselves everyday, gentlemen..."

"That's the test of all tests if ya' ask me..."

"Well...I shall finish the game..."

BILLY THE KID

"YOUNG GUNS"

"I'm your huckleberry."

DOC HOLIDAY

"TOMBSTONE"

"The name's Bond, James Bond."

007

"We're not worthy, We're not worthy."

WAYNE & GARTH

"Take me to your leader."

MARTIAN

"Na nu, Na nu."

MORK

"Live from New York...it's Saturday Night."

SNL

"Farmers are comedians. This is no special news, because
if you're into farming, you can't afford the blues."
STEVE TREMBLEY
Abbyville, KS
"Really living, ain't it?"
GARY FOSTER
Abbyville, KS
"Today we're going on a cosmic death run; we're gonna
run so hard you see stars."
"Today we're going on a plaid run; we're gonna run so hard
you see plaid."
SSG BRIAN T. NORTON
1/503RD Camp Casey, Korea
"That's all, folks."
PORKY PIG

For Elaine

Everything that follows is my view of the universe.
You are welcome to have a different view.

What Do I Do Now?

Chapter 5 – Or Not.

But suppose you don't want to fight cancer? There are several other alternatives. There are in fact many people living with cancer.

Chapter 6 -- Who Should I Tell?

One of the members of my group had a cancer that she believed would cause shame in her family, so she didn't tell anyone. Cancer is harder to cope with alone, but who do you tell, and how much? Do you tell a waiter at your favorite restaurant? How about family members?

Chapter 7 – Make a Decision

Perhaps the most important thing you can do for yourself is make decisions -- about your doctor, your care, your life. Some say decisions are hard. Suppose I make the wrong decision? What then?

Chapter 8 – What Game?

What game is your favorite? How do you apply the rules of your favorite game to your disease? In tennis, the game isn't over as long as you continue to hit the ball over the net. In football, the game is over when the clock says it's over. If a medical professional tells you that you are terminal, would you rather use the rules of tennis or football?

Chapter 9 – Dark Night.

No matter how philosophical I am, there are always times when I get caught up in my own thoughts, particularly late at night in a hospital. Here are some ways to get back to sleep.

Chapter 10 – Your Provider

Everyone will talk about your provider, but how much control do you have over "Your" provider? More than you might think.

Chapter 11 – Control of Life

Does anyone really have control over his or her life? Do you always do exactly what you plan? Or, like most of us, do plans change? In cancer treatment, make plans and expect changes.

Chapter 12 – What is Normal?

Is it normal to have a headache? What about tingley feet? Before I had cancer I had headaches. After diagnosis I still got headaches. Is that usual or part of the cancer?

Chapter 13 – Support Group

I relied on my support group. It is one of the best things that happened during cancer treatment. Here's how to find one.

Chapter 14 – Quality of Life

A decade ago, my mother called the family into her room and told us that she wasn't doing Chemotherapy again. She'd had enough and she was going home. We didn't like it much, but that was her right. Yours and mine too.

Chapter 15 – Health Crisis

Our nation is in the middle of a health crisis. A political solution probably won't work. Maybe we should be looking at other options.

Chapter 16 – What Works?

How do I know if the chemotherapy is working? Or acupuncture? Or herbs? I don't. Sometimes I have to trust, (and verify).

Chapter 17 -- Now What?

So now I'm finished with the treatments, will the cancer come back? How long have I got? What should I do now?

Preface

I have cancer.

The minute I was diagnosed with Stage Four Colon Cancer, and announced to others that I had cancer I became inundated with information. My doctors and medical professionals wanted to tell me things. Friends had advice. Other people who were being treated for cancer or who have survived cancer wanted to encourage me. People I don't even know wanted to tell me stories about family members with cancer.

Sometimes the stories went like this; "My brother-in-law had colon cancer, he had surgery and radiation and died." What useful information that is! Not one of these people was trying to hurt me, in fact they were all trying to help. But what each of them was actually doing was filling the space with words. And at that moment I had more to process than I could even think about.

Now you are beginning the cancer process (I assume). You are about to be inundated. Even reading this book will contribute to the clutter. I thought about this while I was writing. I hope this book is filled with useful information and not just more words. Nobody with cancer (or anyone supporting someone with cancer) needs someone else pouring more words into their heads. If you can't take any more words right now put this book down (for a while) and take a walk. I won't be upset. If you have decided to continue reading, good for you. I hope all this will be useful to you.

I have cancer. Not in the past tense, not "I had cancer," or perhaps "I'm a cancer survivor," although from the time I received the diagnosis I became a cancer survivor (from minute to minute). I have cancer right now. Even though my body is apparently free of detectable cancer cells (for the moment), cancer is one of those words, for me anyway, that is always in the present tense, always in this moment.

This is not to say that some people don't have cancer in the future tense. If your mother and all your aunts died of ovarian cancer or breast cancer, or your father and all your uncles died of prostate cancer, you have a right to think about cancer in the future. You should do everything you deem prudent to avoid getting the disease. Testing has come a long way in the recent past. Get tested.

But don't get into a rut. Don't say, for instance, "My mother died of cancer, my father died of cancer, my brother has cancer, and I'm going to die of cancer. I probably have it now, they just can't find it." I call this the "future insane" tense. If you don't believe me, change the word "cancer" to "automobile accident" and see how it sounds.

I want to be clear. I'm not suffering from cancer and I'm definitely not dying of cancer. If you are suffering or dying, you should skip the first part of the book and go directly to the chapter on "Making a Decision." Anyone can have cancer. Some people can have the disease without suffering. Some people live with cancer. Although everyone dies eventually, you don't have to live your life as if you were dying of cancer. It's possible to live life and have cancer.

I am also a student of Taoism, the philosophy not the religion. And I am a Christian. I tell you this not because I want to convert you, which I don't, but because although the stories I am using are Taoist stories, many of them have counterparts in Christian, Moslem, and Jewish traditions. Most good moral stories have counterparts in many traditions. I don't think you have to believe in God in order to survive cancer, but I think it helps to have a "higher power" as the twelve-step programs say. More on this later.

I have studied Taoist philosophy for almost forty years, and I have never found any contradiction between the study of Tao and my Christian faith. Taoist friends tell me that there is no real contradiction between Taoism and any of the major religions. I haven't studied all of the major religions, so I can't say for certain that this is true. But for me, Taoism explains some of the inconsistencies in Christianity.

To some people, the word Taoism sounds like an airy-fairy, West-Coast kind of new age philosophy. It's not. Taoism is a Chinese philosophy that has roots as old as 4000 BCE, so it's certainly not new age. And it's not West Coast because China doesn't have a West Coast. It's not, at least in my case, a religion; my Taoist teachers didn't try to substitute Tao for anything I've been taught since I was a child. (My mother raised me a Presbyterian.) Taoism is a complement to everything I learned in Sunday school, church, and everything I've learned since.

Taoism is definitely not Buddhism, although the two share several things in common. In China, the two philosophies split many hundreds of years ago. Buddhists are pacifists, they won't hit back. If you attack a Taoist you're liable to get into a fight that you can't win. Buddhist priests don't have sex, Taoists priests do. The major difference, however, is that Buddhists are looking for Nirvana, something that exists somewhere in the future, and Taoists are living moment by moment, right now, without looking for anything in the future at all. What will happen after we die? We don't know, and we can't know, it is un-knowable, so why worry about it?

One of the principle concepts of Taoism (according to my view of the universe) is this: if we realized that everything is part of one whole we could stop being afraid of everything. If we weren't terrified of life we could accomplish more, be happier. We might write more books, play more music, save more people from starvation, do more good in the world, (if this is your idea of a good time) and be happier.

I used to say to people; "Stop being afraid," but that isn't right. Fear exists because fearlessness exists. Think of a stick. If you like one end and hate the other end, you might try cutting off the end you don't like. But all you would really end up with is two sticks, each with two ends. As long as the stick exists it will have two ends. This is the nature of sticks.

Fear can sometimes be a useful thing, a motivator, something that makes me get things done that need to be done

12

(if anything really needs to be done). But it isn't necessary to be terrified. Terror (in this case) means fear taken to the level where I can't move. Terror keeps me from moving forward, back, or sideways. . Consider this from poem 73.

"He who is fearless in being bold will meet with his death. He who is fearless in being timid will stay alive." (Dim Cheuk Lau's translation of Tao Te Ching)

Another translation reads: "Brave daring leads to death. Brave caution leads to life. The choice can be the right one or the wrong one. (Translated by Ursula K. Le Guin)

Who has correctly translated this verse? I can't say. Both translations have good and bad points. This is the nature of Tao. Every time I think I have the exact meaning of anything I find someone who has something to add.

When I found out I had cancer, several people thought I should become a victim, to *suffer from cancer.* They were not bad people; they were just reflecting what they had been taught. If you have a fatal disease you suffer. But suffering just is not necessary. It is not necessary for you or I to suffer from anything. I had pain, I was sick, but it is not necessary to suffer from pain or sickness. The Buddhists believe that suffering exists in the world. The Buddha said

13

so. It's one of the great truths. But many Taoists believe (or at least the ones I know believe) that suffering is unnecessary anywhere at any time.

I think suffering comes from comparing what you feel now to what you used to feel, or comparing what you feel now to what you believe you should feel. It can also come from comparing what you have now to what you had or to what you think you should have. Suffering, to my way of thinking, is always a comparison.

If my cat is hungry, she's hungry. She doesn't suffer from hunger. Instead she goes looking for something to eat. Cats are very much creatures of this moment, they don't worry about what happened in Europe last week, or what the stock market is going to do next month. If I can stay in this moment, and the next, and the next, only feeling what I feel right now, I don't suffer. To stay in this moment or not, to suffer or not, is always my choice.

Taoism is also a practical way of looking at the universe, my life, and the problems of the world. Practical is the key word here. Taoism asks us to look at the world as it is, not as it should be, or as we wish it were, or as it was or could be. Instead, we should look at the world as it really is. It's easier to make decisions based upon reality than on wishes, dreams, or hopes, no matter how well meaning they are.

As I said, the philosophy is Chinese, but I'm not. I took my first steps down the road of Taoism when I studied with Dr. Lee. (For those who are new to Taoism, this is kind of a joke: road, Tao, steps. Never mind. I'll try to explain later.) Dr. Lee is, was, and will always be in all ways Chinese. I met him when I was twenty-five and he was ninety-three. I'm nearly sixty now, so it is possible that he has gone on to the next part of his journey, whatever that is. But he is still very real to me and I will try and recreate him for you in parts of this book.

There are also many important people who have guided me in my steps throughout the years. Tao, in one way, can be described as a road, a path, or a way of being. Along the path of your life you may have seen or heard people who made important contributions to you, but they may not have even known it. Someone said something at just the right time or in just the right place, and your vision of life changed. Congratulations. That was a Tao moment.

I have been fortunate. Many people in my life were teachers, even if they didn't realize it. I've also learned that there are teachers who don't teach and road signs that don't point the way. These events only mean something because of the exact time and the exact place you are in. Carl Jung calls it synchronicity. I don't call it much of anything, but it is interesting

I expect that most of the people who have read this far in the book either have cancer or are living with someone close who has cancer. There could also be a group of practicing Taoists who want to know what I have to say, to listen to the student and make sure he doesn't make any mistakes. If I'm fortunate, there could also be a group of medical professionals who heard about this book and want to check it out. There might even be some people who don't know exactly why they are still reading. These are the most interesting to me. Taoism teaches us to follow our inspiration, our inner voice. So if you are inspired to read this, good for you. All are welcome.

I've learned that each person brings his or her own experience into every situation. Individual experiences have created a path beginning at whatever place that person started and leading to here and now. Because I don't know your path, I can't be sure what you will get out of this book. I can only hope it points in a comforting direction.

Don't be put off by the lack of detail: the exact number of days I spent in the hospital, exact number of staples I had taken out, exactly where and when I heard some of these stories, who said what to whom, etc. Information like this isn't really useful, and may just be more clutter in an already cluttered world. The stories in these chapters are my own interpretation of some much more ancient stories; Taoist, Buddhist, Judeo-Christian, Moslem, Hindu, Sikh, but mainly from the poems of Lao Tze, a poet and philosopher of Taoism, and Chuang Tze the story teller. If you are interested, the poems are collected in a book called Tao Te Ching, or the Book of Tao. Some of the stories were written by the philosopher Chuang Tze are also available in translation. The book is usually just called "Chuang Tze."

You may have heard some of these stories before in other contexts or at other times. They survive because they are good stories and they allow us to think about things we might not be able to think about without them. Good stories remove us from the hurt and effort of daily life into a place where we can examine problems and ideas without applying the morals to ourselves. Unless we want to, of course.

You may want to read this book all the way through from cover to cover. Or you might want to read the chapters

17

that sound interesting to you right now and save the rest for later. It really doesn't matter how you read this book, follow your inspiration, your own inner voice. You will get out of it what you are supposed to get out of it. Do what feels right to you.

There are some conventions in this book that you should know about. When Bill W. started the AA program he set down some rules. One of them was "What happens in the group stays in the group." I belong to five different groups and I believe in this rule. It's important that the members of a group feel safe in talking about how they feel, and believe that their innermost feelings aren't being shared with the world. If they wanted their feelings shared they would write their own books.

But some of the things said in one or more of my groups might be of value to you. Here's what I've done. I combined all the groups into "my support group," and changed several of the names. Please know that all the things referenced were said in one or another of my groups, perhaps not necessarily by the names attributed. Names are just labels anyway. Names, in and of themselves, have no real power unless we give a specific name power.

Now you are part of my group. If you see me, let me know how you are *really* doing. What happens in our group stays in our group. I believe that. It's the only way a support group can be open and honest.

Dale Grothmann October 2008

Chapter One

How do you feel?

When I began to think about writing this book I had this question in mind: "What would I want to say to a relative or a friend who had just been diagnosed with cancer?" What could I tell them that would be of any value? What do I know that might be helpful? What advice can I give? There isn't any advice. For reasons I will explain later I have stopped giving advice. But there is still information that might be helpful for you if you are recently diagnosed, if you are the family or support person for someone with cancer, if you are still fighting cancer, even if you have completed your treatments. That is what this book is about.

There are five things that I would want a friend to know right off the bat. First, this is not your fault. You didn't do anything or neglect to do anything that caused this. Cancer doesn't take sides. The righteous and the sinful get cancer. Rich Americans and poor Indonesians get cancer.

It's a disease. It's not a respecter of age, race, national origin, sex, political affiliation, belief or lack of belief, or any other human thought. It isn't your fault.

Secondly, you are about to receive more advice, information, opinions and comments that any one person can possibly process. Friends will have advice; people where you work, people in your clubs and organizations, even people you don't know will have something to say about cancer, or recovery from cancer. I usually ignore most of it. It's noise. You are free to do the same.

There is a difference between information and advice. Information is just something that is available, take it or leave it. For instance, the neuropathy in my hands seems to feel better when I keep my fingers warm. Someone else told me she has more success with ice packs than with warming gloves. This is information.

Advice is different. People who give advice usually believe they have answers. Their advice will solve your problems. I think advice is usually offered because people think they can live my life better than I can. (That shows my arrogance. I think I know what they think.) There have been people telling me how to live my life since I can remember. I have made an attempt through out this book to avoid giving advice. You are the expert on you, or at least you could be. Unless you live in some bad sixties science fiction movie, nobody knows what's going on inside your skin better than you do. (If you are living in a bad sixties science fiction movie, the "pod people" know all!) I have a hard time recommending restaurants to people without knowing them very well. What I like might taste vile to you. How can I know? Here's my advice: don't take anybody's advice unless you want to, not even mine.

Opinions are usually easily spotted. Opinions usually start, "I think…" or "If you want my advice…" But they can also sound like; "My father's friend, who is a doctor, told me…" Most opinions are truly useless. The only opinions I listen to are from my oncologist. I chose him for his informed opinions. (But it doesn't always make him right.)

The comments you will get are truly amazing. Someone said to me, "My sister's husband had colon cancer. He went through the chemotherapy and he died in the hospital." Wonderful. That kind of comment will certainly help me in my recovery and lift my spirits at the same time. Worse are the ones which start out, "I read on the internet…" People who have no experience with cancer read something on the internet or in magazines at the dentists office or in the daily newspaper or see it on television and assume you haven't read or seen it, especially if it is bad. They are really not trying to hurt you; in fact most of them think they are helping. Comments are just that, comments. Something to say.

The third thing is this; your doctor is about to become as close to you as one person can be to another. He or she will know things about you that your spouse might not know. Spend some time thinking and doing research before you settle on a doctor. Talk to him or her. Make sure that he can listen to you and that he can communicate with you. My oncologist is great. He will explain a thing to me three or four times if it is necessary, which it sometimes is. He listens to my questions and answers them in words I can understand. I never lie to my doctor intentionally. What good would that do either of us? (Sometimes I may mis-state a fact because I think is true.)

I will never understand why a person would take whatever oncologist was assigned to them, go through a life and death treatment, and never understanding what the treatment is about, how long it will last, or what the results should be. All this because their doctor couldn't explain it to them simply and clearly.

Fourth: never let anyone tell you how you are supposed to feel. They, whoever they are, are not you. Feel the way you feel. I repeat, you are the universe's expert on you, or you can become the universe's expert on you, if you will start listening to your body. Nobody else can know what you know about you. Most of the health professionals would warn me about the POSSIBLE effects of certain drugs and treatments, but I don't remember one of them telling me how I would feel after taking this or doing that. I am unique. You are unique. Different from anyone else in this universe. Why should you feel like someone else?

Lastly, you are not alone. Whatever thoughts you've had or will have, whatever feelings come up for you during this process, I can almost guarantee that someone has had this thought before, someone has felt this way before. There is the real advantage in being part of a support group. In my group I found people who were experiencing exactly what I was experiencing. People who had the same thoughts, the same feelings, the same ups and downs I was going through. Sometimes it is good just knowing that there are others who share in the joys and distresses of life.

I might also tell my newly diagnosed friend about Taoism and what it has done for me during this process.

Taoism is an ancient philosophy, perhaps older than any currently being practiced. It is also eclectic; Taoists will borrow from almost anyone as long as the underlying understanding of the world doesn't change. At one time in China, Taoists and Buddhists were nearly the same thing, but hundreds of years ago there was a split.

The accepted story goes like this. A man named Bodhi Dharma came from the west to visit the Taoist monks and see how they were progressing. He found them hiding behind their monastery walls. "Why are you hiding here?" he asked, "Why aren't you out helping the people and teaching, as you should?" Most Taoists consider teaching others good for the soul.

"We are afraid," they answered. "Every time we leave the temple, robbers attack us and steal our food and our clothing."

Bodhi Dharma was so shocked at this report that he went to live in a cave and meditate about the problem. The monks were not only afraid, they were fat and out of shape from sitting in the temples. So he devised an exercise program. When it is done as exercise (slowly) it stretches the muscles and sinus, and is called Tai Chi. When it is practiced as self-defense (quickly) to strengthen the senses and give confidence it is called Chi Gung, or in the west, Kung Fu.

So Bodhi Dharma taught his new exercises to the monks. He also reminded them of the underlying premise of Taoism: we are all part of the same thing, the same universe. I am part of the same stuff as the robbers, the ocean, tigers, and cancer. It seems simple enough, but it is more complex than you might think.

When a baby is born it begins to explore. You might have seen a small baby put its foot in its mouth and bite down. This is because the baby doesn't realize that the foot is part of itself. But we can see that the foot, the mouth, and the baby are the same thing. Once the baby figures out that the foot is part of itself, it doesn't chew on the foot any more, or at least it doesn't bite hard.

So it is with me. I'm not afraid that my hand is suddenly going to attack my stomach. That's just silly. Why would I attack myself? And if I really am part of the same whole as the tiger, why would the tiger attack me?

Lao Tze says:

"One who is filled with the harmony of Tao is like a newborn baby, snakes will not bite him, tigers will not claw him. His bones are soft and his grip is strong, even though his body is supple. His mind is innocent but his body is vigorous and his strength seems endless. Like a baby he can scream all day without loosing his voice.

Unfortunately studying harmony creates abstractions, and following abstractions creates rituals. Trying to become more than ones nature leads to misery and trying to control nature creates violence."

(Tao Te Ching, Chapter 55)

When I first heard this I thought, "Great. But suppose the *tiger* doesn't know it's part of me? What then? I'm enlightened, but who is enlightening the tigers?" No matter how much my upper rational mind knows, there is still that reptile brain underneath which is afraid that the tiger won't have taken up Taoism, and I'll end up being the one who is eaten.

The truth is the monks weren't afraid of robbers because the robbers took their food and clothing. They were afraid the robbers would kill them. And they were afraid of tigers. And cancer. One of the first thoughts I had when I got the cancer diagnosis is, "I'm going to die. Cancer is going to

27

kill me." This is not a high minded philosophical thought, but it's the truth. Cancer could still kill me. If deep down inside you don't fear that cancer will kill you, you are either much braver than I am, or you don't understand the disease.

Or, perhaps, you are no longer afraid. This is the underlying secret of Taoism, in my opinion. I am going to stop saying that now. Everything in this book, from now on is *my opinion.*

Stop being "afraid of dying" and you might stop being afraid altogether. Easy to say, hard to do. I can think I'm not going to be afraid and still be afraid. It's not a matter of thinking it's a matter of knowing. Deep down inside, no matter what your religious faith tradition or rational philosophy is, there is usually a little voice that says, "Suppose I'm wrong? What then?"

I don't know. There's no way to be sure of anything about death. I think, I believe, but I can't know. Neither can anybody else. So we all go about living as if we know. We have to. The alternative is to lock myself inside my bedroom, pull the sheets over my head and stay there, safely, until I die.

So now I have a choice; I can be afraid of dying and do nothing useful with my life, or I can get out there and do all the things I know I ought to do, feed the poor, visit people in jail, teach what I know. This was the split the ancient Taoists had with the Buddhists.

There's an old story. A Taoist monk is walking along a road in the country when he sees a young Buddhist monk sitting at a crossroad meditating. So the Taoist monk sits down next to the Buddhist. "Younger brother, what are you doing here?" asks the Taoist monk.

"I am meditating to become Buddha," replies the younger monk, obviously annoyed by the question.

"Oh," says the Taoist monk, and sits for a while saying nothing.

Time passes. Then the Taoist monk picks up two rocks and begins rubbing them together.

"What are you doing?" asks the Buddhist monk.

"I am rubbing these two rocks together to make a mirror," replies the Taoist monk.

The Buddhist opens his eyes and looks at the Taoist monk for a moment. Then he says, "You can not make a mirror by rubbing those two rocks together. You are wasting your time."

"Excellent," laughed the Taoist monk, throwing away the rocks. "Then we have both learned something today, because you can not become Buddha by meditating alone."

Everyone has choices every day. I can either stay home and worry about dying from cancer or I can go out into the world and do whatever it is that I would have done if I'd never heard the word cancer, or some third thing I haven't even thought of. Many people helped me when I was diagnosed, now I'm writing this book to try and help others.

I have cancer. It's mine. It's part of me. It belongs to me as much as anything can belong to me. When I talk about it, I try to remember that it belongs to me. I don't always remember, but I try. I do this intentionally. Some people talk about their cancers as if the cancer wasn't actually in their bodies. They talk about "The Cancer" as if it were something foreign. Listen to the people around you. In fact, listen to yourself. How do you talk about cancer? I think it's important to own my cancer. There's a reason.

The people in my neighborhood are usually good about keeping up the appearance of their front lawns. Most of us try and cut them every week, weed, water all the things that are required to make the lawn look good. But there's one person who didn't. He's moved now, but while he lived here his lawn was usually a mess. Sometimes it looked alright, at least it was cut, but there were usually weeds growing in it, dandelions flowering, bare patches, grass intruding on the sidewalk.

I don't really care. Down deep inside me it doesn't matter enough to say something to this man about his lawn. After all, it is his lawn and he can keep it anyway he wants. His lawn is not my responsibility, so there's really nothing I can do about it. My lawn is my responsibility. I own my lawn and I can keep mine anyway I want. If my lawn doesn't look the way I want it, I either call someone to mow it or mow it myself. I can apply water and fertilizer to make it as green as I think it should be. It belongs to me, so I can do something about it.

The same is true of my cancer. It's mine, I own it, and it's my responsibility. Not that I created it, I didn't, or wanted it, I don't. But when I am standing in the rain, I didn't create the rain, and I have to decide what to do about it. Once I found out about this cancer it became mine, a part of me. If I don't like it (and I don't), I can do something about it. This is my cancer, my treatment, and the doctors' work for me. I'm in charge, as much as I can be in charge of anything in this life. Sometimes is doesn't feel like it, but I'm the one who makes the final decisions.

How do you speak about your cancer? Words have meaning and they have power. Listen to the people around you. Start listening to yourself. Change the words and change the situation. It's your life. It may feel like life is out of control, but you get to be in control of it if you want to be.

This book is about many things; cancer, surgery, chemotherapy, doctors, attitudes. But much of it is about feelings. Lenny Bruce (the comedian) once said "If a man falls off a fifty story building and hits the pavement, thud, some reporter will stick a microphone in his face and ask, "How do you feel?"

Americans are obsessed with asking, "How are you feeling?" The truth is most people don't want to know. They're just asking. They expect me to say something like, "Oh, I'm feeling better, thanks." If I say more than that, most people will get a glazed look on their face and nod their heads. But they won't listen because we (I do it too) don't really want to know details. We are always asking, "How do you feel?" but we don't really want an explanation.

One of my *Two AM Quandaries* was, "Why do we ask what we don't want to know?" There are more *Two AM Quandaries* later in the book. In fact, this book was written, at least in part, to get my mind out of the *Two AM Quandary* rut and into something that was at least useful and finite. *Two AM Quandaries* are not useful, they are unending, and they won't go away so I can get back to sleep.

Another thing I wanted to explore in this book is, "Am I normal? Is this normal? What is normal?" In fact there is a chapter on *Normal* later in the book. All through this treatment I have been asking, "Is this normal? Is my feeling about this normal? Are my fears normal? Is this pain part of the treatment or is it another cancer? Is it normal to think about cancer all the time? Or is it just me?"

It's not just me. That is one of the things I learned in my support group. And it's not just you either. There are thousands of people going through cancer treatment. Many of them have the same thoughts and concerns you have. You are not alone, although you can feel like you are alone if you choose to. You can think about cancer all the time if you choose. Or you can try and think about something else.

My friend Bill Clarkson said, "When you first start out, you will think about cancer all the time. After a while you might get down to once a day, then once every day or two. Maybe you will have a week where you don't think about cancer. But it will always be there. Something in the newspaper, or on television, or on the computer will remind you that you are a cancer survivor. The objective is to recognize that this is just a thought and let it go. If you know the thoughts are coming, it's easier to recognize them and let them go. They are just thoughts."

He's right. It's easier to let go of a thought if you know it's coming. But there will be times, mine are usually at *Two AM*, when my mind won't let go. The little voice in my head just keeps thinking, it won't let go, and I can't make it shut up. It's frustrating. I have some tips and tricks that worked for me in times like this. One of them is this; write your own book. I'm serious. Keep a journal. Write everything down. Let the thoughts keep the debate going in a book while you sleep. At the very least a journal is a place to put unwanted thoughts so you don't have to keep them in your head.

I have no proof of this, but I think Lao Tze wrote the Tao Te Ching just to clear his head of all the stuff inside it. He went so far as making all his thoughts into poems. Try it. The next time you get an unwanted thought, try making it into a poem. Poetry isn't easy. Poems have to rhyme, the lines have to be about the same length, and the ideas have to make some sense. Since your mind can't think of two things at once, you can either debate an unwanted idea, or compose the poem. The harder the poem, the less room there is for the unwanted idea. Try a sonnet or a haiku.

The advantage of poetry is it can be finished. Once you write something down you can go back to sleep. If you let the "unwanted idea" debate go in your head you could be up all night.

Sleeping became very important to me during my treatment. I was tired most of the time. I even got to the point where I was asking myself, "Is any of this treatment worth it?" Part of the problem with chemotherapy, radiation, and surgery is that I could never tell if they were working. Everything looks like failure until we succeed. Edison found thousands of ways not to make a light bulb until he finally succeeded in making one.

Half way through chemotherapy or radiation treatments is not the time to ask if it is going to work. Maybe you will see some results, but maybe not. "So," my group's facilitator asked, "Why keep going? If you can't know if this is working or not, why keep doing it?"

Great question. I'm not sure I have an answer for anyone but myself. I kept going because of my wife Elaine. She's important to me. And I kept going because I trusted my doctor. I had several recommendations about my Oncologist before I met him. When we met, I knew I trusted him. I had to. Although I have always believed *anything someone can do I can eventually do*, cancer is not a field that I could become expert in soon enough to make a difference. So I let my doctor guide me through the treatment and trusted him to know if it was working.

But did he really know? I don't think so. He had statistics that indicated the most likely treatment for the majority of people, but statistics don't apply to individuals. He was guessing. He had a very educated guess, he's seen a lot of cancers, done a lot of treatments, and seen the results. So his guess is really better than mine would have been but it's a guess never the less. Sometimes it's better to be lucky that smart. My doctor is both lucky and smart.

Which brings us to another point. Most cancer patients are more attuned to their bodies and their treatments than most other people. Even if you are not now, you can become the expert in you. You should expect to begin to recognize small differences in the way you feel. You may see differences the medications are making, or you might see a difference if you change medications. Cancer forces you pay attention. This is where a journal comes in handy. It's hard to remember exactly what I was feeling yesterday, much less

36

three weeks ago. So how can I compare how I'm feeling now with how I felt before the cancer? Unless I write it down, of course. Like Lao Tze, I can clear my head of all the unnecessary junk by writing it down.

"On a scale of one to ten, how is your pain?" I got to hate that question. Every time I saw a doctor or nurse they asked the same question, "On a scale of one to ten…" I found out why. They, medical professionals, are required to ask. It's the law. It is still annoying. On a "scale of one to ten" I had days where the pain was a twelve and days where the pain was a one. I guess. I don't really know what this scale of pain means. But, and I'm guessing here, the medical community has adopted this scale because it works. Somehow my brain can analyze my pain level and put it on this scale. But answering that question every time I have an appointment was tiring.

Oh, by the way, congratulations. You are a cancer survivor. From the minute cancer was detected you became a cancer survivor. You, me, Lance Armstrong, Elizabeth Edwards, and hundreds of millions of others. We are all living with cancer.

Whatever else you might think, it's not your fault. You are not being punished; you didn't do anything to deserve this. Nothing you could have done in the past has any bearing on your condition now. It is a waste of time and energy thinking about what might have been in the past. "Don't *should* on yourself," someone once told me. It's easier to go into should've could've would've. But it isn't useful. Write it in your journal and leave it there.

Someone once said, "All the past is prologue." I think it was Shakespeare, but I can't find any reference on the Internet. Which brings up this point; I have a lot of quotations in this text. If I can remember who said what, I will tell you. But much of the time over the last year I have had a condition called "Chemo-Brain." It is a real thing. The chemicals in chemotherapy work on the fast growing cells in my body, and it affects short-term memory. I'd forget things I should have remembered. (Should have. There I go again.) You will probably forget things, in fact, you probably already have. We all do, it's part of the human condition. Sorry about that. If you are fortunate and never forget anything, give yourself credit. Most humans forget things and chemo-brain makes it seem much worse.

I was lucky. My wife is one of those organized people who can take in information and keep it on a calendar, which makes sense to her. Otherwise I fear that I would have missed several of my appointments. Some days I woke up and asked her, "What day is it?" I wasn't being funny. I really didn't know.

The chemicals and radiation are messing with your short-term memory. Don't get into a depression about it. Don't get into a depression about anything if you can possibly avoid it. How you feel really does effect the working of the chemotherapy and/or radiation treatments. If this book is depressing you, put it away, or throw it away. (Or better yet, give it away.) But I hope you don't. I hope it helps. One thing I found out during this process, I couldn't control what other people think, or feel, or say. I never could really, although I sometimes thought I could.

If you do get depressed, tell your doctor. There are drugs that can help. Don't be afraid of chemical help. This process is giving you enough grief. If you need chemical help to keep your head on straight, get help.

At one point my oncologist told me I was depressed. "No, I'm not," I said, thinking I was toughing it out.

"You are. You have cancer. Everyone who has cancer is depressed. If they aren't, they don't understand the disease." He wasn't casting aspersions of cancer survivors; he was trying to make me feel better about antidepressants.

Let yourself feel exactly the way you feel, begin to recognize what you feel, and don't ever let anyone tell you what you should feel. Lao Tze says we should look inside ourselves for answers. This is especially true of cancer.

Lastly, I have found comfort in a book called Tao Te Ching, which means "The book of Tao." A man called Lao Tze wrote it. Lao Tze translates into "The Old Man." *The Book of Tao by the Old Man.* It is a book of poetry written originally in Chinese. Taoism is a philosophy and/or a religion depending on what you need from it. I have a religion; I was raised in the Presbyterian Church, so I only use the philosophical Taoism. Many of the words have been comforting to me through this process.

Lao Tze asks: "Why did the ancient masters respect the Tao? Because once you are one with the Tao, what you seek you find and if you make a mistake you are forgiven. This is why everyone who finds it respects the Tao."

(Tao Te Ching Chapter 62)

Chapter Two

Chinese Language and Tao

The Chinese character, or hanzi, which represent "Tao" can be translated as Way, or Path, or perhaps Way of Being (although I am reminded that there is no capitalization in Chinese, no difference between nouns.) I sometimes use *way of being* as an English translation of the Chinese concept, although this translation won't work much of the time. There is a problem in trying to explain a Chinese concept to someone whose primary language is English (or Spanish, or any other language that uses letters instead of concept diagrams, which is what a pictogram is.)

Each Chinese character, or pictogram, can have several meanings depending on what character it is associated with, put next to, or combined with. The other problem with explaining Tao is that Tao isn't a thing.

The master Lee was walking with his students one night when he stopped and pointed his finger. "Look at that," he said. All of his students concentrated their gaze on his finger. "Not at the finger," he said, "Look where the finger is pointing. If you concentrate on the finger you will miss the glory that is the moon." Some of the students looked at the moon, some continued to study the finger intently.

Taoism has some important concepts for me in my cancer treatment. But they are only concepts, not great truths. They are fingers pointing at the moon.

One of these concepts is Wu-Wei, which is sometimes translated as "doing without doing." What does this mean? I don't know. But I heard a master describe Wu-Wei as doing what is appropriate without thinking about it. I like that better.

Wu-Wei is looking at the universe exactly the way it is, instead of as I want it to be or as it "should" be. I have thoughts about cancer. I find that, when I listen to my thoughts about cancer, or chemotherapy, or radiation, or my situation, I suffer. When I ignore my thoughts about cancer and just accept the cancer for what it is, I don't suffer. There are religious people around me who think suffering is good or necessary. I believe suffering harms the soul, so I try not to suffer.

Barbara was a friend of mine and a member of my group. She had been under chemotherapy treatment for eight years, and had tried almost every combination of drugs available for her cancer. She was also a diehard Oakland A's fan and went to every home game.

One morning in our group she announced that she was stopping her chemotherapy. It wasn't a question, it was a statement. She didn't want our opinions; she was just informing us of what she had decided. It was a brave decision and, for me, an expression of Wu-Wei. She had had enough. She had that right. So do I. And so do you. You have the right to feel exactly the way you feel and do what is appropriate for you to do. And nobody (not even me) has a right to tell you otherwise.

Having said that, there is nothing to lose and everything to gain by finding someone who will listen to you and help you find out why you feel the way you do. I did. I found a support group of people who also had cancer and also had some of the same feelings I had. I'm writing this today because I could tell them my truth and listen to their truths without changing who I was or who they are. There is nothing wrong with taking drugs to help clear your mind of chemical imbalances that distract from seeing the universe more clearly. Depression is a filter on the universe. It is unnecessary and distraction. Anti-depressants helped me. If your doctor recommends them, consider it carefully and do what is appropriate. Wu-Wei.

Another concept in Tao is P'u (the sound a child makes trying to keep a feather from falling without touching it.) This is usually translated as "the un-carved block" whatever that means. I don't know any wood carvers, but the idea of an un-carved block is interesting. It is simple, real, meaningful without trying to be meaningful, without thinking about it. Wu-Wei and P'u are mastery of life.

I learned P'u from my cat. Try telling a cat what to do. See how well that works. When the cat is hungry it looks for something to eat. When it is tired it finds a place to sleep. When it is lonely it climbs on my lap and tries to put it's head on my keyboard (like now). Every cat I have ever met is a master of "catness." Eating is good. Naps are wonderful. Resting on my keyboard is not appropriate. Stupid cat.

There have been many human "masters" in the past. Many of them are quoted regularly in religious institutions. Steven Mitchel said, "There's nothing mystical or lofty about the Master. He (or she) is simply someone who knows the difference between reality and his thoughts about reality."

Seeing the universe without any preconceptions, without fears, without preconditions. Simply. P'u.

In his book, The Tao of Pooh, Benjamin Hoff says "the essential principle of the Uncarved Block is that things in their original simplicity contain their own natural power, power that is easily spoiled and lost when that simplicity is changed." (Tao of Pooh, page 10) Another person's finger pointing at the moon.

My doctor and I decided on my treatment. He didn't tell me what to do, he asked. My wife sometimes tells me what she wants me to do, but she knows better. My group listened to me and told me exactly what they thought. On the other hand, I am surrounded by people trying to give me advice. And all of them have reasons.

I worked with a man who sold Investment Real Estate, apartment buildings and office buildings worth millions of dollars. Occasionally I'd ask him, "Where should we go to lunch?"

"I don't know. Where do you want to go?"

So I would choose a place. Once I'd chosen a lunch spot, he would have a list of reasons why this wouldn't work; it's too expensive, it's too far, the food isn't great, too crowded, etc. If I suggested another place he'd have reasons why this second place wouldn't work. We usually started to lunch at 11:30 and finally got to eat after one. Imagine what he would think of a cancer diagnosis and all the choices we survivors have to make. In a state of P'u choices become easier to make. This doesn't mean you will not have a fight on your hands once you've made a choice.

I met an oncology nurse who has breast cancer. Her surgeons suggested radical mastectomy. It didn't seem right to her, so she refused. She didn't have a medical reason. She said it just "felt wrong" to her. (Good for her. This is her body, her cancer, and her treatment. It should be the right treatment for her, not just what works statistically for the doctors.) She had to change doctors three times and fight every step of the way to get her HMO to provide the treatment she felt was the best for her. But the decision to have this treatment was clear to her. She made a decision by looking at the situation as it really was. She was in a state of P'u. What her outcome will be is still in doubt, but she is happy with her treatment.

Someone in its truly natural state might see a cancer diagnosis for what it is, just one more thing in a long string of things that make up life so far. Not a pleasant thing, but not a horrible thing either, and certainly not a death sentence.

The idea of Tao might also be understood as a very low-key, normal, natural state of being, the being that we actually are and have no control over changing. So I have a way of being *me,* I don't have to add anything or get rid of anything to be me.   You have a way of being *you*. This computer has a way of being, not just a computer, but being this computer. The cat is a cat. The universe is the universe.

I could no more be you than I could be this computer, or the cat, or the universe, no matter how much I want to or try to change. Each person, each animal, each thing in the universe has a way of being, a Tao, separate and unique from every other thing.

Put another way, the treatments which are keeping me alive might kill you. So, as I said, don't expect specific remedies or treatments to be mentioned here. For instance, I take several supplements and rub a homeopathic remedy on my feet. If you used these, they might or might not work for you. And what's keeping you alive might kill me.

Those of us who aren't you can suggest, or ask, but we can't know what's inside you, not the way *You* should know. You are really the expert on *You*, or at least you should be. In my way of looking at the universe, this expertise is very important in cancer treatment. You already

47

know what you think, how you feel, what you want and need, and what assumptions you have made about life. All of us outside have to ask, "How do you feel?" You already know. If you aren't already the expert on yourself, I suggest you become the expert. It's just easier to live that way. It's also easier to talk to your doctors about your cancer and its treatment.

So what does this have to do with Cancer? One of the things cancer can create is fear. Fear is created in the brain. The brain creates an un-natural story of the future, a future where things are worse than now, and convinces me that this un-natural future will be true. My brain says "Cancer will kill me," or "The chemotherapy will make me so sick that I won't be able to continue it. I will loose all my hair. My nose will fall off. Everything is going to be terrible. Woe is me."

Any of these things might be true at some time in the future, but they aren't true now. And there isn't anything to be afraid of, not really. Why should I be afraid of something that might happen at some time in the future? I might get hit by a bus, but I'm not going to live my life in fear of busses.

Not living in fear is easier said than done, but it is possible. For me, the first step is to face my fears. I made a list of everything that could go wrong. Then I asked myself why I was afraid of each one of them. A good support group helps. Why might I be afraid of this drug but willing to take that one? Both are drugs, but my mind has heard something about one and not the other, and decided one is good and the other isn't. Facing my deepest fears was hard, but it was also worth doing.

About Tao itself; it's spelled Tao but it's pronounced Dow (like the Dow Jones Industrial Average.) You might ask why. The explanation is exceptionally long, boring, and, in my opinion, not worth the effort to explain. It has to do with the people who originally translated Chinese into English and what dialect of Chinese was being spoken in the location where they started their translations. If you really want to know, look on Wikipedia. Or just say "Dow" and everyone who's interested will know what you are talking about.

The major work of Taoism (the philosophy) is called Tao Te Ching, or "The Book of Tao." It was written in the 5th or 6th century BCE (depending on who's history you want to believe) by a man who's real name is lost to history. He's called Lao Tze, which means "The Old Man" in Chinese. Although Tao Te Ching is considered the first major compilation of Taoist thought, there is written reference from the court scribe to the court astrologer asking for an interpretation of the meaning of Tao as early as 4000 years BCE. Taoism has been part of the human condition for a very long time.

Taoism doesn't claim there is a God, it certainly doesn't claim to be God, but Lao Tze does refer to God several times in the Tao Te Ching.

"The Way is a void, used but never filled. A great space, like an ancestor, from which all things come. It blunts sharpness, resolves tangles, tempers light, subdues turmoil. A deep pool, it never runs dry! Whose child it may be I don't know. It is like a preface to God."

(Tao Te Ching: Chapter 4
Translated by R. B. Blakney)

About the Great Tao (or Great Path) Lao Tze says; "Look for it can't be seen. Listened for it can't be heard. Reached for it can't be grabbed. Above isn't brightly lit. Below isn't dark. Unnamable, it returns to the realm of nothing. Shape that includes all shapes, it is an image without an image, refined beyond all concepts.

Go toward it and there is no beginning, follow it and there is no end. You can't understand it, but you can be it, being at ease within your own life. Just realize where you come from, this is the basis of wisdom."

(Tao Te Ching Chapter 14)

Another finger pointing at the moon.

Lao Tze's book is written as a group of eighty-one poems in Chinese. Each of the poems is numbered and, because each was originally written in Chinese, there is a never-ending struggle with translations. Every scholar with a Chinese to English dictionary (including me) tries to translate a single, simple poem into something meaningful and useful about Taoism. Each scholar is sure he or she has the right translation and each is sure that everyone else is wrong. This kind of dichotomy (I'm right and you are wrong) is represented by the Yin and Yang symbol. It also makes Tao Te Ching one of the most translated books in the world. Somewhere Lao Tze is laughing.

In poem number 70, Lao Tze says: "My teachings are easy to understand and easy to put into practice. But intellectuals fail to grasp them, and when they try to practice these principles they fail. My teachings are older than the world. How can you get a hold of their meaning? If you want to know me, look inside your own heart."

I'm as guilty of mistranslating Lao Tze as anyone else. I have a Chinese-English dictionary, so the quotations you read in this book are mainly my own interpretations. They are what I have gleaned from Tao Te Ching in many translations, as well as in original Chinese. But I could be wrong. You will have to get a copy in translation and judge for yourself.

You probably already know several things about Taoism. Lao Tze's sayings have become part of every culture of earth. "A journey of a thousand miles begins with a single step." (Tao Te Ching, chapter 64) "If you don't trust people, you make them untrustworthy." (Tao Te Ching, chapter 17) "If you realize that all things change, there is nothing for you to hold on to" sometimes translated as, "The more things change, the more they stay the same." (Tao Te Ching, chapter 74)

Even before Lao Tze wrote his book, there was Taoism. The Yin and Yang, the circle that is half white and half black, was a Taoist symbol for the universe. Each thing in the universe is created by and creates its opposite, and each thing contains a small part of the opposite (the white dot in the black side, and the black dot in the white side.)

Even the most evil man in history might love his dog or his sons. Even the most righteous woman might have something that keeps her from being perfect. No one is completely evil and no one is completely righteous. Nothing can be completely good or evil. Even cancer, bad as it appears, is not completely evil. It may not be fun, it may not be particularly easy to deal with, but it is not evil. It is a disease, something to be dealt with, and nothing more (or not. See Chapters Three and Four.) Hating the cancer, for me, has no particular value in its treatment and it certainly isn't good for me, either emotionally or physically. When I let go of the emotion and saw cancer for what it is, a disease, I felt better and began to react better to the treatment.

When my niece was very young, she saw the Yin and Yang symbol and said, "It looks like two fish chasing each other." At the time I thought this was a cute, if not very accurate, view of the symbol. Now I'm older and I can see the fish. This is a Taoist thought; sometimes children see things as they are more accurately than adults do because they follow instinct instead of relying on their preconceptions.

Taoists also believe in an energy that flows through our bodies and through everything else in the universe. The energy is called Chi. Chinese doctors might tell you that disease is caused by an imbalance in the flow of Chi. In ancient China a doctor might prescribe a diet, acupuncture, or Chi Gung to balance the flow of Chi. Today some Chinese doctors still assess the flow of Chi before prescribing many of the same medications used in hospitals in the United States. The difference between modern Chinese medicine and modern Western medicine is usually in the assessment, not necessarily in the treatment. Chinese medicine looks at the whole person sometimes called a Holistic View, instead of a single part or disease. It happens that my Oncologist asked me about my lifestyle and general well being before we began treatment for my Cancer. It's one of the reasons I like him.

To keep the Chi flowing correctly the ancient monks developed Tai Chi and Chi Gung, a series of slow, rhythmic movements meant to encourage the flow of the Chi. The Taoists believe that the same Chi that flows throughout the universe flows through each of us. (Because we are part of the universe, not something separate from it.) They believe that, with practice, we can harness this Chi to use to help with everyday life stress, as well as in healing. (But we would need to practice.)

If nothing else, Tai Chi and Chi Gung are slow, rhythmic dances, which stretch the muscles, improve breathing, and relax the joints. They make me feel better. If you have a Tai Chi or Chi Gung class near you, you might think about joining. It is very relaxing, it raises the Chi, the healing energy in your body, and it is something to do to keep your mind and body engaged. Most cities have Tai Chi classes. Many have Chi Gung classes. Check your local YMCA or similar organization.

Acupuncture or acupressure are also ways of balancing the Chi within your body. Many health organizations are beginning to recognize acupuncture and acupressure for the relief and management of pain. If you are in pain, you might check this out. It can't hurt and it might help.

Lao Tze didn't want people to read his work and walk around like robots following his instructions. He believed in listening to your inner voice. Each of us has an inner voice, a basic understanding of ourselves and the universe. Each of us must make our own decisions based on our own inner voice.

Lao Tze was a true libertarian and Taoism is a very libertarian (with a small L) system. Consider Lao Tze's poem number sixty. "Governing a great country is like frying a small fish. You spoil it with too much poking." Truer words were never spoken. In chapter seventy-five Lao Tze says, "When taxes are too high, children go hungry. When the government is too intrusive, the people lose their spirit." This was written almost three thousand years ago. Some things don't change.

What does this have to do with my cancer? And what can I do about the cancer? Ignore it? Taoism teaches three important things which relate to cancer and its treatments. First, I don't have any idea what will happen tomorrow. I can't. I can guess, but that is all it is, a guess.

"When you realize that all things change, then there is nothing worth holding on to. If you aren't afraid of dying there is nothing you can not accomplish. Trying to control the future is like trying to replace a master carpenter. If you aren't sure what you are doing, when you grab the master carpenter's tools, chances are you will cut yourself."

(Tao Te Ching, chapter 74)

The future is uncertain. One day there was no vaccine for polio, the next day there was. One day there was no way to stop the AIDS virus from killing everyone who was infected, another day there was. Is there a cure for cancer? I don't know. I can't know what will happen tomorrow, I will just have to wait until tomorrow comes and find out.

The second thing Taoism tells us is this; I have (or soon will have), all the external information I will ever need. Lao Tze says: "The master observes the world and trusts his inner vision. He allows everything to come and go. His heart is as open as the sky."

(Tao Te Ching, Chapter 12)

Chapter Three

This Is Not Your Fault!

"Our lives are not determined by what happens to us but by how we react to what happens, not by what life brings to us, but by the attitude we bring to life. A positive attitude causes a chain reaction of positive thoughts, events, and outcomes. It is a catalyst, a spark that creates extraordinary results." –Anonymous

My first meeting with the oncologist went something like this. "You have a mass in your colon and we believe it is cancer." Then he said a lot of other things, but I missed most of them. Fortunately my wife was also there and she remembers them better than I do.

When my oncologist first said the word "cancer" it became real, a real thing, a threat, and I went into a kind of shock. My mind went into overdrive. Why did this happen to me? Did I cause the cancer? Am I being punished for something? Did I do something wrong? Suppose I'd done the colonoscopy at fifty when I was supposed to, would I have cancer now? Maybe I should have eaten more fruit, or less red meat, or taken more vitamins. It's my fault. It's got to be my fault. I should have taken better care of myself and now I have cancer.

There's an appropriate expression that involves a male cow and its excrement, but this is a civilized book, so I won't use it here. I didn't do anything to deserve cancer. Neither did you. Nobody deserves cancer. Cancer is a disease, it's not a sentence or punishment for past wrongdoing. I don't believe cancer is Karma from past lives either. People who are good and wonderful get cancer, people who are not so good or wonderful get cancer, and even evil people get cancer. Religious people get cancer, agnostics get cancer, and atheists get cancer. Rich Americans get cancer, middle class Europeans get cancer, and poor Chinese get cancer. This disease is not a respecter of race, color, gender, sexual orientation, political affiliation or much of anything else. It's a disease. It doesn't pick out individual people and say, "This is the one. I'll get this guy." It doesn't care. It doesn't think. It doesn't feel.

It took me a while to finally understand this. I didn't do anything. *I DIDN'T DO ANYTHING.* And I didn't neglect to do anything. I did exactly what I should have done and avoided doing exactly what I should have avoided doing. I lived my life and I am exactly where I am right now because of the way I lived it. Regret has no value and the past is the past. Nothing I can do now will change anything in the past, and it's a waste of time and energy to keep repeating it in my head. You too. So stop it. (I know. This sounds like advice. I'm sorry.)

There is another point here. If you are like me, you have read or will read things about cancer in a magazine, newspaper, or on the Internet. I actually went looking for things to read. I went to WebMD and looked up my kind of cancer. There were articles there about stages, tumor size and location, and survival rates. I have Stage Four colon cancer. But knowing that I have Stage Four cancer is meaningless in and of itself. What does Stage Four cancer mean? What is Stage One cancer?

Doctors routinely use these staging systems, but they scare the heck out of patients like me. For us, there is a problem. There isn't just one staging system, there are at least two. (Actually there are several stage systems currently in use: TNM and MAC are two of them.)   The "stage system" is used by the medical community to relay information about a patient's cancer to other doctors and cancer boards, and suggest to your doctor a specific treatment. It's medical shorthand, a jargon. Here is an example of what one of the stage systems means. (I assembled it from information on the Internet, particularly WebMD and the American Cancer Society.)

Stage Zero is "Carcinoma in situ," (In Latin "carcinoma" means cancer and "in situ" means "in its place".) This is an early form of carcinoma without invasion of surrounding tissues. For instance, "Carcinoma in situ" of the skin (called Bowen's disease) is the accumulation of cancerous cells within the epidermis (top layer of skin) only.

Generally Stage One cancers are small, localized tumors that are usually curable in a normal course of treatment. They can be removed, or treated with radiation or chemotherapy and they go away. Non-tumor cancers like Leukemia, don't have the same staging definitions as most cancers with tumors. This makes sense, it's hard to tell what the cancer is like if it is in your blood.

Stages Two and Three cancers are usually locally advanced (they have grown, but only in one place) and may now involve a local lymph nodes. A local lymph node is one close to the cancer. If the cancer grew in your foot, "local" wouldn't be the lymph node in your neck. Lymph nodes are part of a system your body uses to get rid of harmful things, like cancer cells. Although the lymph nodes may not be directly next to whatever organ has the cancer, they can still become infected because the loose cancer cells are flushed into your lymphatic system.

If you had a cancer that started small and grew before you found it, it might be Stage Two. If it grew into another organ close to its original location, but it didn't go anywhere else, that's Stage Three.

Stage Four usually represents inoperable or metastatic cancer (cancer that is so near an important part of the body that it can't be removed with surgery, or it has spread to an organ which is not adjacent to the original organ.) Notice that there are two different Stage Four cancers. I have Stage Four cancer because it started in my colon and spread into my liver, but not into the lymph nodes. Different types of cancers spread to different parts of the body. Check with your oncologist if you want to know more about this.

The medical community precisely defines each stage, however the definitions are different for each kind and location of the cancer cells. Also the diagnosis indicates to the doctor a specific treatment for a given stage also depends on what kind of cancer it is, so a Stage Two Non-Small Cell Lung Cancer has a different treatment than a Stage Two Cervical Cancer, and a different statistical recovery rate. (We'll go to statistical recovery rates later.)

When I read this on the Internet, I asked the doctor what stage cancer I had. And he told me. "Stage four. It has spread to your liver." Stage Four?

Stage Four is the worst, I thought. Maybe he made a mistake and it's actually stage one and just looks like stage four. But no. The PET scan told him that it had started in my colon and moved to my liver. "But the stage isn't really that important," he said, trying to sound assuring.

What?? After all I'd read? It sounds terrible. Stage Four is the highest, there is no Stage Five, and that sounds important to me! How can it not mean anything? Does this mean I have Colon Cancer and Liver Cancer? What are my chances of survival? For the second time since I'd had the diagnosis my mind was shouting so loudly that I couldn't hear the doctor.

A short bit of history. "Doc" Holliday contracted consumption in the 1860's. Consumption is what we would now call Tuberculosis. It is not cancer, but like cancer (and many other diseases of that time), doctors could diagnosis the disease, but there wasn't anything anyone could do about them. These were terminal diseases that killed everyone who contracted them, if they didn't die of something else (such as gunshot wounds).

Cancer has been described in medical literature as early as the time of Hypocrites, the ancient Greek physician. The Scottish surgeon John Hunter (1728-1793) suggested that some cancers might be cured by surgery, if the tumor had not invaded nearby tissue and was "removable." Doctors had been trying various medical procedures for centuries, but the first effective treatments were discovered in the 1940's. For the convenience of the doctors, cancers were usually described by their location. So a person might have colon cancer, leukemia (blood cancer), or skin cancer. Women might have "Female Problems," because even doctors wouldn't discuss certain parts of the anatomy with anyone but another doctor. In fact, two of my great aunts died of "Female Problems." That's how it was listed on the death certificate in Nebraska at the turn of the last century.

Back to "Doc." It didn't really matter what doctors called these terminal diseases if medical science doesn't know enough to cure them. "Doc" was told that he might live longer in a warmer, dryer climate. (He was also told to take a form of morphine called laudanum.) That's how he ended up in the southwest.

Time passes. In the 1930's and 40's, medical science learns more about cancer and the ways to treat it, first using nitrogen mustards (a form of Mustard Gas) and folic acid. But, even as treatments began to show signs of working, we were still stuck with the description "Colon Cancer" even though there are several kinds of cancer that can occur in the colon. The only way my doctor can determine exactly which cancer I had was to examine a biopsy under a microscope.

The medical community still uses a stage system to describe cancer. Some cancers are fast growing and move to adjacent organs or the lymphatic system, and some move more naturally to non-adjacent organs. Exactly what kind of cancer I had and where it had moved made a difference to the oncology department in fixing an exact treatment, but the stage of my cancer didn't really affect me directly.

I got on WebMD and looked up the information I had about the cancer. Please be *VERY CAREFUL* about what you read. All sorts of information is floating around, lots of statistical information is available, and most of it will have nothing to do with you.

To make matters worse, in our society there are fictional numbers, statistics that people made up! A commercial on television says, "Ninety percent of statistics can be used to prove anything fifty percent of the time." I love that because it is true. People make up numbers to prove all kinds of things all the time.

I was listening to a presentation on domestic violence when the presenter said, "Fifty percent of domestic violence is never reported." Really? Then how, if it is never reported, do you know it is fifty percent?

"There are twelve million illegal aliens in the United States." I've heard this repeated by congressmen several times. How do they know? Did they go and interview all twelve million? Did they count them? And if they did, then the government ought to know where the illegals are right now, and we can ask them to leave.

So what is the survival rate for colorectal cancer? Here are the average five-year survival rates as they appear on the Internet as of October 13, 2008:

* Rectum: 59%

* Right colon: 59%

* Transverse colon: 59%

 * Rectosigmoid junction: 62%

 * Ascending colon: 63%

 * Left colon: 65%

* Descending colon: 66%

It's important to notice that all the different tumor stages are combined in these survival statistics, says the Internet. So, if a tumor is diagnosed at an early stage (Stage One), the survival rate is likely to be higher than what's shown here. If a tumor is diagnosed at a later stage, like Stage Four, the survival rate will likely be lower than shown here. It would have been good to have my cancer diagnosis earlier than later, not that I can do anything about that now.

These survival statistics come from a study published in the European Journal of Cancer. The data is from approximately 54,000 cancer patients who are registered in SEER, a database maintained by the National Cancer Institute. This data covers cancers which were treated between 1985 and 1989, so this is really old data. Colorectal Cancer treatments have improved since then and survival rates are more likely to have improved.

That's what is on the web. If you want to check it our, this is the address:

(http://coloncancer.about.com/od/cancerstatistics/a/US
_Cancer_Site.htm)
And here is one for information on staging:

(http://www.taxotere.com/consumer/about_cancer/
Screening.aspx)

Is this information any good? Yes, as I write this, it is statistically accurate. Does it apply to me? It's hard to say. Does any of this really matter? Statistics on approximately 54,000 people won't apply directly to me. I am unique and individual. If I am unique, my cancer and its effects should be unique also. So is yours. If you want to read numbers, there are lots of them out there. Every organization involved in cancer research and treatment publishes numbers. My advice? For what it's worth, look for the numbers which support your treatment and recovery and leave the ones which make you sicker sooner. Or, to say it another way, keep the good numbers close at hand and leave the bad numbers on the Internet where they belong. (I know, I promised not to give advice, but there it is.)

Or you could just forget the numbers altogether. They don't apply to us anyway. All the numbers on the Internet, all the numbers in medical journals, all published numbers everywhere have one thing in common. They are all old. By the time something has been collected, written, edited, and published it has taken weeks, if not years to reach the light of day. New things are found in the field of cancer almost every week. New things may be found in the middle of your treatment. Then it will be up to you and your oncologist to decide if you want to change treatments based upon the new information or continue with the treatment you started.

I finally gave up trying to decipher the numbers and just did the chemotherapy. It has been a lot easier on me. Besides, every time I came into my oncologist's office with something I'd read in the newspaper, he'd say something like, "Yes, I read that in the British Medical Journal last week. Now they have revised it, and next week there is a new study due out which may make this obsolete."

Lao Tze says; "The follower of knowledge learns as much as he can every day. The follower of Tao forgets as much as he can every day, eventually learning not to rely on facts. Then nothing is done and nothing is left undone. The world can only be controlled by letting things unfold naturally. It cannot be controlled by meddling."

Chapter Four

At War with Cancer

How do you think about your cancer? Stop just for a moment and remember the words that you used the last time you talked about your cancer. Is cancer your friend or are you at war with your cancer? Do you want to destroy it, to kill it, and win the battle against cancer? The American Cancer Society says "The American Cancer Society is the nationwide community-based voluntary health organization dedicated to eliminating cancer as a major health problem by preventing cancer, saving lives, and diminishing suffering from cancer, through research, education, advocacy, and service." This is their mission statement: they want to *eliminate cancer*. They certainly aren't friends of cancer. I don't try and eliminate my friends.

If you are the caregiver for someone who has cancer, how do you think of the disease itself? What words do you use to describe it? Listen to how you speak and listen to the little voice inside your head. Listen to the people around you, listen carefully to their words. Do you think of beating cancer? Eliminating cancer?

If so, can cancer be your friend? Do you fight against your friends? Do you talk about killing your friends? I don't think so. If you are fighting against cancer, then cancer is the enemy. There was a lady in my support group who was going to the hospital to "nuke" her cancer. What she was actually doing was going for a radiation treatment, but what she said was "nuke." If you are younger than I am, nuke might mean to stick in a microwave and heat, as in "I'm going to nuke lunch." But for those of us who grew up in the fifties and sixties, nuke only has one meaning. Nuke means to drop an atomic bomb on. People talked about nuking North Korea or Viet Nam. It was the ultimate way to win a war.

I think that certain types of people have certain basic mindsets that dominate their lives. Warrior types tend to gravitate to certain jobs and professions because of how their minds' work. Warriors become soldiers (of course), but they also go into law enforcement, fire fighting, and missionary work. Some teachers are warriors. Crab fishermen in Alaska are warriors.

During some of the worst parts of my chemotherapy I would sit and watch "The Deadliest Catch" a television program about crab fishing in Alaska. Captain Sig, the Hansen brothers, and the Hilstrands are warriors. They go out in the Bering Sea, battle against the cold, exhaustion, wet clothing, huge rogue waves, and ice to fish for crab. Sure, the money is great, but if you don't have a "Winning is Everything" mind set, don't go crab fishing in Alaska.

What has all this got to do with cancer? The war analogy is a good for warriors. Cancer invaded your body. You didn't do anything to invite it in, and now you must fight it. And win. Winning is literally everything. In this fight you are the general, the one making the plans and strategies for the attacks, and the foot soldier, the one doing the actual fighting. You will have an army of people assisting you in the fight, but you are the one making the final decisions about your treatment.

There is good advice about fighting in Sun Tzu's book, "The Art of War." Sun Tzu was a general in 6th century China. Military officers have used his rules of warfare for centuries. Most of them still apply. You might want to read it, if you have time. Some of it is strictly military information and will not apply to your fight, but some of his thoughts do apply.

As the general you will need to do the things generals have done since before the time of Alexander the Great. Gather around you the best minds you can find. This would include your doctor, nurses, nutritionists, perhaps a support group. (My support group is an excellent information source, but more importantly they give me hope.)

Get as much intelligence about the enemy as you can. Sun Tzu says: "If you know the enemy and know yourself, you need not fear the result of a hundred battles. If you know yourself but not the enemy, for every victory gained you will also suffer a defeat."

Whatever information you gather should apply to your situation. Although it is interesting to find out that there is a clinical trial of a new cancer procedure for breast cancer, it's not useful information if you don't have breast cancer. You will need to find out not only where your cancer is located, I have colon cancer, but what kind of cancer it is. This will help you weed out information which is clutter and keep information which relates to your battle.

Stockpile your resources and prepare for battles, not one quick single battle, but as many battles as it takes to win the war. Sun Tzu said, "The good fighters of old first put themselves beyond the possibility of defeat, and then waited for an opportunity of defeating the enemy." Be prepared for whatever the cancer throws at you. Also be prepared for well meaning people to say inappropriate things.

I actually heard from someone, "My cousin had stomach cancer and he lasted for almost a year before he died." Wonderful. That kind of comment will certainly improve my chances of surviving as well as my moral. On the other hand there are people around you who have either had cancer or have been a caretaker for someone who survived cancer. You will know them because they will give you relevant information; "There is a mouthwash I used and it helped with mouth sores. I will get you the name of it." They will also say things which will help your moral; "You might loose your hair, but it will grow back. Mine did."

As the general of your war, use your doctors and nurses as resources. Ask questions. They have information about your specific cancer that you might not have. Your oncologist can help you formulate a strategy for your war against cancer. And be prepared. Don't think of this as a short skirmish. Prepare yourself for the long haul. You are in it to win it, however long that takes.

As a foot soldier you will want to do the things soldiers have done since war was invented. Eat things that will promote your ability to fight. Rest when you have the chance. Exercise to prepare your body for battle. Don't be afraid to fight. And stay alive at all costs.

Napoleon said, "An army travels on its stomach." He wasn't wrong. Eating is one of the most important things your army against cancer will do. Before you had cancer, empty calories, alcohol, candies, sweetened drinks, were something you shouldn't eat because they tended to make you fat. Now empty calories can get in the way of eating nutritious foods, and nutrition is important in this fight.

One of the things I had to get used to when I went into the Oncology department was their obsession with my weight. They were much more worried about it than I ever had been. They had me on a scale every time I went in. And they kept records, something I've never done. I know approximately how much I weigh at any given time, but not exactly, and certainly not from day to day.

But my weight seemed to be very important to my oncologist. It is one of the ways he judged my general health. It was also important because my weight determined the amounts and strengths of the chemicals he was using in my

76

chemotherapy. If you are loosing weight your doctor will know, but if you just can't eat, make sure you tell him or her. There are things that can be done to help you keep up your weight without candy bingeing.

There is actually a medical specialty called Oncological Nutritionist, it's that important. If you are at war with cancer, you need to find the best foods to support your fight.

Don't forget about drinking, and I do not mean alcohol. Every soldier knows the amount of fluids or lack of fluids will eventually affect his thinking ability. Water is your friend. So are fruit and vegetable juices. On the other hand, the armies of the world, or at least the armies who win wars, don't issue alcohol to soldiers in the field. Alcohol depletes the fluids in your body. Alcohol is a diuretic. And alcohol clouds your judgement. You must be able to think clearly during this battle. Save the celebrations until after you've won.

Any good Force Recon Marine (that's redundant. There are no bad Force Recon Marines) knows that during a battle you rest when you can. It's important to your survival. Sleep is important to you in your battles against cancer. Cancer will try to keep you from sleeping. Cancer will intrude on your thoughts when you go to bed. Don't let this happen. These thoughts aren't useful, they are enemy propaganda meant to frighten you and keep you from sleeping. If you can't sleep, or you don't feel rested when you wake up, tell your doctor. There are things he or she can do to help.

The Spartans had a great reputation as warriors. They made it a ritual to exercising every day in preparation for fighting. You might adopt a similar ritual. Exercise will help you sleep and will also prepare your body for the onslaught of surgeries, radiations and chemotherapies you will have to go through to win. Exercise will not only help you bounce back more quickly from the various attacks on your system, it also make you feel better.

If you are one of those people committed to an exercise program, keep doing it. You already know how it makes you feel, and you already know it's good for you. But if you are like me and don't exercise on a regular basis, or if you have never exercised before, take a walk. Really. Put this book down and walk around the block. The book will be here when you get back. Walk around the house, outside if the weather's good or inside if you feel better doing that. Or, if you are still in the hospital, walk around the hospital wing.

Wherever you are, if you are able to stand up and walk, walk. No matter how short the walk is, it's a hundred percent better than not walking at all.

Che Guivara, the revolutionary, literally wrote the book on guerilla warfare. Whether or not you agree with his politics, his book is an excellent guide for fighting an enemy from a weakened position. Two of his rules are "never fight a battle you can not win," and "the guerilla army must always fight." It may sound contradictory, but it isn't really.

What does this have to do with cancer? If you are going to war against cancer, be prepared to fight it at every opportunity, and never, *under any circumstances*, accept losing. Look for ways to fight against cancer; clinical trials, nutrition, exercise, rest. If radiation therapy isn't going to produce the results you need, think about changing battlegrounds. A holistic approach might be a new way of fighting.

Join a support group. In any war we need as many allies as we can get. A good support group should help you in your fight against cancer. It doesn't really matter what the support group "does" as much as what it is doing for you. I know a lady who is in a knitting support group, a group of cancer survivors who knit. That's not my idea of fun, but it works for her. I knew a lady who went to baseball games. She had season tickets and went to every A's home game she could. This doesn't sound like a support group, but she was surrounded by other season ticket holders, other people who were as passionate about the Oakland Athletics baseball team as she was.

I've heard of Pilaties cancer support groups, Tai Chi and Yoga groups, groups of people who exercise together. Groups are an excellent way to get additional information about cancer in general and your specific treatment as well. Having many pairs of eyes and ears is better than just having one or two pairs of eyes and ears. A good support group also gives you hope. You are not alone in this fight, nor are you unique in fighting against cancer. There are people who have beaten cancer. There are some people who have been fighting cancer long before you were diagnosed and are still fighting it.

A good group should also relieve stress. Stress is as much your enemy in this fight as the cancer is. There is a field of study called Psychoneuroimmunology. It's easier to explain this word than to spelling it. Your brain talks to your immune system. When you are depressed or under stress your immune system doesn't work as well. This is why your doctor may recommend antidepressants as part of your treatment. If your doctor recommends antidepressants, he or she is not implying that you're crazy. You have cancer. Your immune system needs all the help it can get. If you don't feel good it affects how your immune system works. In my opinion, anyone who is fighting cancer and "feels great" about it doesn't really understand what's going on. If your doctor is prescribing pills that are supposed to help you in your fight against cancer, why would you not take them?

Also, put your money and time where your fight is. Go to the walks against cancer. Support organizations in your area that fight cancer. Read books about cancer survivors (especially Lance Armstrong's book.) Sun Tzu says, "To secure ourselves against defeat lies in our own hands, but the opportunity of defeating the enemy is provided by the enemy itself. Thus the good fighter is able to secure himself against defeat, even if he cannot make certain of defeating the enemy."

This is not a fight of half measures. This is literally the fight of your life. Assume you are going to win and act like a winner. Celebrate your victories (but not with alcohol). On days when you have received radiation go out and enjoy lunch or dinner with your loved ones. On days after chemotherapy go to a movie or visit with friends. Never accept defeat. Get mad. Anger can be your friend if you use it to fight your cancer.

A wise man once said, "whether you think you can or you think you can not, you are right."

But suppose you are not at war with your cancer? Some people aren't you know.

Chapter Five

Or not…

There is absolutely nothing wrong with going to war with cancer. If it helps you to think of your treatment in this way, go for it. Being at war brings the "fight or flight" mechanisms into play. Your body will bring all your defenses up to meet this challenge; your adrenaline comes up, your blood cells will reproduce, endorphins will make you feel better and your thoughts become clearer.

But I don't believe I could have sustained this level of energy output over the long haul, and for me having cancer has been a long process. Like any peoples at war, eventually you might become tired of fighting. It takes a lot out of you to keep fighting, physically, spiritually, and emotionally. If you decide this is your best path, don't become a fanatic in your fight against cancer.

I actually heard someone in my group say: "Logically, if I wanted to kill the entire cancer all I would have to do is find a big enough microwave and climb in. That would kill all the cancer." It would, but the side effects are undesirable. This kind of thinking leads people to drive a carload of explosives into a crowded market and set it off.

Suppose you don't want to go to war with your cancer? Is there another way of thinking about treatment? Or suppose you are a caregiver and the person who has the cancer is at war with it? Do you have to be at war with the cancer too? If I'm at war with someone, I am usually afraid of them. This is logical. They might attack me at any time and without any reason.

The sage Lao-Tze has said, "There is no greater delusion than fear, no bigger mistake than preparing to defend yourself, no greater tragedy than having an enemy. Whoever can see through fear will always be safe."

(Tao Te Ching chapter #46)

Most religions, cultures, and philosophies divide people into "Us," those who are right and righteous, and "Them," those who aren't. So, for Heideggerians, people who follow the philosophies of Martin Heidegger, there are those who are living an authentic life and those who are not. For Catholics the world is divided into those who can take communion and those who can't. For Jews there are God's people and the rest of the world. For Moslems there are those who have understood God's word, the Quran, and those who either haven't read it or haven't understood it. Buddhists understand the world to be divided into enlightened and unenlightened. For some the world is divided into "Straight" or heterosexual, and "Gay" or homosexual. The problem with this view is that "They" might go crazy at any moment and attack "Us" for no reason.

Chen Tze the philosopher asks, "Will my feet suddenly go crazy and attack me? Do I have to fear them? No. My feet are a part of me. I would never attack myself, unless I was completely out of my mind." So the Taoists began to understand that the Chinese were "Us" and the non-Chinese were also "Us." The Catholics, Jews, and Moslems are "Us" too. Gay and Straight are all "Us."

The sage goes even farther. He asks, "If I am walking through a forest and see a Tiger, should I be afraid of it? Not if I realize that it is part of me and I am a part of it." My feet won't attack me because they are a part of me. The Tiger won't attack me because it is a part of me. Catholics,

Jews, Moslems, Gays, and Straight are all part of me. Even cancer is a part of me.

When I knew that this was true, not just saying it, but knew down deep inside myself that it was true, I stopped being afraid of the cancer. War becomes an insane idea in the face of the knowledge that we are "Us" and they are "Us" too. How can we go to war if they are all part of us? We shouldn't be afraid of each other, or tigers, or cancer. But we are. This is the world the way it is.

When I stopped being afraid of cancer I realized there was something I could do about it.

"But suppose the cancer doesn't know it is part of you? Suppose it kills you?" one of my friends asked. It very well could. Even now when there is no evidence of disease detected, cancer could still kill me. This is a fact. So is this; I could be killed by a passing truck, or a Catholic, Jew, Moslem, or a tiger who doesn't realize that he is a part of me, or a falling bit or space junk. In all cases, as far as I know, I will die sometime. Everybody dies. It's not about how I die, it's about how I live.

So I don't go to war with my foot. Do you? The cancer is part of my body, even if it is a part I would rather not keep. How I think about my cancer will influence what I do about it. Is there another way of dealing with it, of thinking about cancer? What would happen if you didn't go to war with your cancer? I wasn't. For me, cancer is like a cockroach.

Now let me say that my wife will not like the idea of my implying that there has ever been a cockroach in our home, and there hasn't. She is a magnificent housekeeper, especially when I was undergoing cancer treatments, and I appreciated it. However, when I was going to college I lived in a house with five other guys, and on occasion we were not as neat and tidy as we might have been. This is where I learned about bugs in a house.

So cancer is like a cockroach. It's disgusting. It might indicate lapses in my personal behavior (like missing my colonoscopy appointments for several years). And seeing one roach or finding one cancer tumor indicates the possibility of more. In fact I had active cancer in more than one place (metastasis) but it took a PET scan to find the secondary location.

I don't necessarily want to kill the roaches or the cancer cells, I just wanted them to go away. Neither roaches nor cancer is an enemy, but each is a problem, something that needed a solution.

I talked in the last chapter about the warrior mentality. I'm not a warrior. I'm an engineer. Engineers tend to work in media, computers, design, jobs that involve problem solving. I think that deep down in every engineer's mind is the idea that for every problem there must have a solution. I may not have the technology to find the solution, I may not have the education to find it, it might be that the solution is so dangerous or vile that I don't want to implement the solution, but deep down engineers have this idea that if we work on the problem from every angle, from every side, eventually we will find the solution. Then we can go on to the next problem.

The very worst time I had during my entire cancer treatment was the period from the colonoscopy, when the radiologist told me there was a mass and I should see an oncologist, to the time I actually saw my oncologist. It was excruciating. I couldn't define the problem, I didn't know exactly what it was or where it was, so I couldn't work on a solution. All I could do is sit and wait. I don't know about you, but I hate waiting. God grant me patience, and I want it right now.

Once I'd seen Dr. Butani, my oncologist, and he had explained where the cancer was and his suggested method of treating it, I could approach this problem the same way I have approached problems all my life. I found the best people I could find, got all the relevant information I could acquire about colon cancer, made an action plan, and proceeded.

It sounds much easier than it was. Between the time the radiologist told me there was a mass in my colon that might be cancer, that he had scheduled me for an Oncology appointment, and the time of the actual appointment I was confused and angry. Not just angry, furious. It was an unfocused anger. Not angry at a specific person or thing, not angry at the cancer exactly, certainly not my wife or myself, just angry at life and the universe in general. This wasn't fair. Why did I have cancer? What did I do?

Logically I know that cancer has a genetic component, that it runs in some families. My mother died of cancer, as did my father, so there was a good chance that I had the genetic makeup to get the disease. And, again logically, there is an environmental component to cancer. I live in a society which generates toxic waste and disposes of it in the air, in the water, and in the soil, so we are more prone to getting cancer than people who live in a cleaner environment. Also logically there is a mental component, people who are under a lot of stress are more likely to contract cancer than people who are not. Stress can be situational; that is, someone near to you might have died, you might have stress at work, or there might be other temporary stress in your life. Or the stress can be chemical; you might have a chemical imbalance that can be corrected chemically, if it is diagnosed properly.

But logic has nothing to do with how I felt. Feelings aren't necessarily logical. Feelings aren't usually logical. It didn't matter what I thought, I was angry. My wife caught the brunt of my anger. It wasn't fair, but it was true. She is the closest person for me to vent to. I know she was afraid of the cancer and I think she had some of the same anger I had, she just didn't share these feelings with me. I think she believed that expressing her anger to me would make me feel worse, so we didn't talk about it. She's right about this, when she's upset it usually upsets me. I knew I was getting better when she yelled at me for the first time after the chemotherapy.

Several people I've talked to have had the same sort of reaction to a cancer diagnosis: *anger*. Not aimed at anything or anyone, just unreasonably, illogical angry. I couldn't be angry with the radiologist for finding the cancer. That certainly wouldn't be reasonable. I wasn't even angry at the cancer. After all cancer is a disease, not some malevolent monster. Besides, being angry at the cancer wouldn't help.

I was angry at the uncertainty, the lack of knowing. I didn't know anything about cancer or the treatment. I didn't know if I would survive or even if I could survive. I didn't know what was going to happen. And I was afraid. Ron, the facilitator for my cancer support group, and someone who has studied such things, says anger can sometimes mask fear.

So before I met Dr. Butani I was afraid. Where did that fear come from? And where did it go, because I'm not as afraid now as I was then. I'm also not as angry. In fact, as soon as I met with my Oncologist I stopped being afraid. He had a plan. We had a plan, a way to deal with the problem of cancer. There was a clear path to be taken, a way to go with reasonable expectations and, perhaps, measurable results along the way. Engineers like measurable results.

The plan included surgery, which removed part of my colon and the cancer it contained, and chemotherapy to remove any unattached cancer cells in my body. I've finished the treatments, but I'm not exactly sure the original cancer is dead.

After the surgery, my surgeon came in and asked me how I was feeling. Now you need to understand that certain anesthetics, certain painkillers, and certain alcoholic drinks make my sense of humor darker that it usually is. So I said to the surgeon, "I'm fine. Do I get the parts back?"

He looked confused. "What would you do with them?" he asked.

"I don't know, but if I went to have the shocks in my car changed (in California) I'd get the old parts back. I suppose I'd do the same thing with these parts I do with the old shocks, throw them away."

He said something about biological hazard and toxic waste and that I was not going to get the parts back. So I don't know exactly what he did with them, and I'm not entirely sure the original cancer is dead. It could still be out there somewhere growing in someone's lab experiment. I don't care. Cockroaches, remember? It's not in me anymore and that's all I wanted. I assume the original cancer is dead, but I don't know that it is. And I don't really care. I am at this moment disease free and that is in accord with the plan. The plan worked. I'm happy.

If I had been at war with the cancer I would have had to know it was dead in order for the war to be over. The most illogical notion I've ever heard was "Well, if I die, at least the cancer will die too." You would have to have a real hatred for cancer to even think something like that. It would have to be the most implacable enemy anyone could ever think of. Something to be destroyed at all costs.

Really? Some people think that? Because part of my doctor's plan was to get me back into my life as soon and as painlessly as possible. During one of the most depressing parts of my treatment my doctor asked, "Where would you be if you were not here?"

"Disneyland," I said, knowing that Disneyland is exactly the wrong place for cancer patients undergoing chemotherapy. It's full of children carrying germs, the foods are full of sugars and fats, and it takes a massive amount of energy to spend a day there.

"Then go," he said.

I was confused. "What about germs? What about nutrition? What about all the things I learned in the cancer classes?"

"Germs are everywhere. If you get sick, we'll deal with it. What's the point of all this cancer treatment if you aren't able to live your life?"

Eventually I ended up in Disneyland. And I had a good time. I didn't get sick, although I did get very tired and had to rest more often than I would have liked.

What is the point of your treatment? What do you need to get you back into the game of life? If you have to fight, then fight. If you have to solve the problem, work on the solution.

I know a couple of business people who are treating their cancer as their job. They read the latest journals on cancer treatments, look for clinical studies of the specific disease they have, enlist the aid of the people around them to accomplish the task at hand. They are making their treatment a profession. They work at it every day. When they are not working on cancer, they are thinking of ways to work on the cancer.

I've heard of another alternative; people who aren't fighting cancer or solving the problem of cancer. I've now heard of certain people who just want to understand their cancer. The Zen Buddhist master I was privileged to speak with isn't fighting. He expressed it this way; "The cancer cells are a part of me." Can he hate a part of himself? Can he be at war with a part of himself? Why would part of him cause a problem for the rest of him? (He sounds a lot like Lao Tze. There's a reason for that. At one time, the Chinese Buddhists and the Taoists were essentially the same thing.)

The Zen master believes he should be able to understand his disease. He spends time every day sending love to the cancer cells in his body, hoping they will respond and join with him again. He also believes that this is not the only time he will live, so he isn't as concerned with existing now for the sole purpose of existing. He believes he will reincarnate, and will have gained from his experience of cancer.

It's not that he doesn't care. He cares about life and he cares about his cancer, but he's not concerned. He cares about `how he lives, what he does to improve the condition of the people around him, what light he can bring into the world, but he's not concerned about struggling to continue to exist for the sake of existing.

I can't do that. It's too much for me. I can understand how he arrived at his conclusions rationally, but I could never live that way, which is why I am not a Buddhist. It is also why I am a Taoist student instead of a master. I know that there is a line or reasoning that says death is not the end of life, but I'm not willing to give up on this life just yet. I still have some things I want to do. Lao Tze says:

"The Tao (Way of Being) is forever nameless.

If powerful people could remain centered in The Way of Being all things would be in harmony. The world would become a paradise and all peoples could be at peace. Laws would be unnecessary because justice would be written in the hearts of the people.

But in order to govern things are divided into groups by name. These divisions aren't real. When you look at things and see only the names, stop and think. This way you will avoid danger.

All things end in The Way of Being (Tao) just as the small streams form the largest rivers. In the end, all flow through the valleys and into the sea."

(Tao Te Ching Chapter 32)

Chapter Six

Who should I tell, and when?

Cancer has been a real learning experience, although not one I would want anyone else to have to experience. When I got my cancer diagnosis, I told anyone who would listen or who asked. I never had any thought of hiding my disease from anyone. But apparently there are people who have cancer and keep it a secret, who don't want anyone else to know. They want to keep it a secret. I guess this is all right, I just never considered it.

I know cancer is a disease, something I got from my genetic predisposition, the pollution of the atmosphere around me, perhaps a virus I contracted at some point in my life. It is definitely not some lapse in either my character or my personal life style.

I know, there are people who insist on smoking cigarettes, and there is certainly a statistical probability of these people getting lung cancer. But what about the people who smoke all their lives and don't get lung cancer? What about children who develop lung cancer having never smoked a day in their lives, and who have lived in households without smokers present? If cancer was a result of bad habits or bad lifestyle, people with bad habits who lived an exceedingly bad lifestyle would always get cancer and people who didn't have bad habits, who lived an exceedingly good lifestyle would always be free of it. That's not how cancer works.

There are many prejudices in our society. One of them is against people with disease. Some people make assumptions about how and why disease happens. I know a lady who has cervical cancer and is afraid to tell her extended family because she believes they will judge her morally deficient because of where the cancer is located. Medical science is now certain that a virus causes many types of cervical cancer. There is even a vaccine to prevent some kinds of cervical cancer. It doesn't matter. People make judgements. She is afraid her family will make judgements about her. So they won't find out something important about her, probably until after she is dead.

Telling people can also cause the problem of overload. People think, "If I tell everyone, everyone is going to have an opinion which they'll want to share with me." This is true. Everyone has something they will want to share with you, and some of the junk people shared with me were of no help whatsoever. Someone said to me, "I had an uncle who died of colon cancer." They weren't trying to ruin my day, but the comment certainly didn't help with either my treatment or my attitude.

One of my friends rides motorcycles. He loves long rides with his friends. He also has colon cancer. Someone told him that motorcycle riding caused colon cancer. A motorcycle rider sits just above the electromagnetic parts of the engine and the Electro-Magnetic radiation causes the cancer. This is what he was told.

He worked as an Information Technology professional for much of his life. That is, he worked in and around computers. The EM radiation coming off computers that are directly in front of you is significantly more than the EM radiation coming from a motorcycle engine under your seat. In fact, as far as I can tell, getting your teeth x-rayed generates more EM radiation than a functioning motorcycle. But his "friend" didn't consider this. His "friend" just wanted to explain where the cancer came from.

Someone told me that eating red meat caused the cancer. "Red meat," he said, "sits in your gut rotting for months and eventually causes the cells to mutate." Since then

I have found that oncologists suggest cutting back on red meat, not because it sits in my gut, rots, and causes cancer, but because statistically it is related to colon cancer diagnosis.

Of course my friend was a vegan and a member of PETA, so I had to take his comments with a grain of salt. I ate my steak at dinner with a grain of salt also. I have never found any reference to a healthy adult being found with rotting meat in their intestinal tract. This is apparently an urban myth.

What if you decided not to tell anybody about your cancer? Some of your friends will be hurt when they find out (and they will find out eventually). "Why didn't you tell me?" they will ask. They will ask your significant other why he or she didn't tell them if you aren't around. If you don't tell anyone you are withholding a secret from everyone. Holding a secret takes a lot of energy, at least for me.

If you tell some people and not others it could be worse. First, you will have to decide who to tell and who to keep from telling. Next, you are making the people you have told responsible for not telling the people you are keeping the secret from. Eventually the people you are keeping the news from will find out. Either they will find out about your illness, or they will find out that they are being kept out of the loop. Either way they will want to know. It's human nature. We all want to know what we don't know. The universe being the way it is, they will usually find out in the middle of your treatment when you really don't need the aggravation. Then they will want an explanation; they will want to know why you didn't tell them.

What about children? I had to think about this for a long time. I have nieces and nephews who have graduated from college, and some who are still in elementary schools. Some of them I can talk to like adults and some of them are too young to really understand. I think the hardest group was eleven through fourteen. The younger ones know that I am sick, but don't really know why. The older ones can go on the Internet and know more about my disease than I want to know.

The middle group was hardest. They have all come in contact with death, their grandfather, my father, died a couple of years ago, so they know what death means. But how could I tell them that I might die, but I might not? This is what I decided. I would be as open with them as I could, that is, I would tell all those who were interested and were able to hear and understand what I have. I would talk about how I felt, good or bad, if they wanted to know. I would be more open with them than I planned to be with most people. I did this because I wanted them to see how I dealt with cancer, good and bad, because some day they might have to deal with it. It wasn't always easy. Eleven-year-olds can ask difficult questions, and they will know if I was keeping something from them. They might not say it to my face, but they understand it. But if they were ready to hear about cancer and me I told them.

Some people will actually want to know about your cancer and some won't. With the exception of very small children, I decided not to make that choice for anybody else. Anybody who asked, even marginally, I told. This created some unusual situations.

In our society, people ask, "How are you?" as a social question. They ask in elevators, on the street corner, on the way into church, at meetings, at lunch. The proper response is, "I'm fine, how are you?" They can say, "Fine." The social obligations are met and everyone can go on their way.

When someone asked me, "How are you?" I would answer, "I have cancer." This usually stopped the conversation for several seconds. Several people got a blank look on their faces and wandered away without another word. Some people said something like, "I'm so sorry," and walked away. But some people advanced to the next question, "Is there anything I can do?" These are the people who really wanted to know how I was, and if there was anything they could do to help. Good for them. My attitude has become; if you don't really want to know, don't ask.

Which leads me to another point. Some people around you will really want to help you. You should think about ways people can help you. Bring a meal, get gas in your car, fix a running toilet if they are so inclined, or watch your pet while you are in the hospital.

My father was a professional Boy Scout executive for many years. One day, at our summer camp, he sat on the ground with two big boxes of pipe. One box was filled with nipples, short pipes threaded on the outside of each end, and one box with sleeves, pipes threaded on the inside of both ends. He would pick up a nipple and thread it into a sleeve, then another nipple and another sleeve.

One of the Scout Masters, who happened to be a plumber, walked by. "What are you doing," he asked.

"I have to connect the water supply up there to the toilet down here," my father answered, pointing to the water supply sticking out of the wall.

"Why are you using all those little pieces of pipe," the plumber asked, "Why not just get the correct sized piece and make the connection? You have a pipe threader in the warehouse, I saw it last week."

"But I'm not sure I know how to use that thing. Besides, this is faster and easier."

"Let me take care of this," the plumber said, grabbing the connected pipes from my father.

The plumber did. The toilet was installed in less than twenty minutes, the plumber was happy to have been able to help, and my father got back to his job of running the camp. That night I asked him about it.

"People want to help," he said, "They just don't want to admit it. All I did is give the plumber the opportunity to do what he wanted to do anyway. People won't volunteer unless they are given the opportunity."

Cancer can give some of the people you know the opportunity to help, if you will let them. People who love to cook might never think to volunteer to bring a meal unless you suggest it. Retired people who still drive can take you to and from appointments sometimes, if you ask. I'm not suggesting you ask everyone to do everything for you, but leave some room for people to help. It's really all they can do for you.

You also have an opportunity to help others with cancer. When I started in my support group I was new to having cancer, scared, and lonely. There were people in my group who understood exactly what I was going through and how I felt. They had all been scared of cancer. Each of them had started out new to the cancer experience.

Most of us are lonely at one time or another. In a world full of people it is possible to feel completely alone. In this case, how you feel is the truth, whether it is rational and reasonable or not. Don't let anybody tell you how you feel.

Only one thing in my life had changed. I had cancer. That was all. I still had a family, friends, acquaintances, and people I worked with. I was still working, going to church, having dinner in restaurants, putting gas in my car, living a normal life. But cancer made me feel removed, even from my wife and my family.

Now I have been through chemotherapy and I am still a part of my support group. Sometimes I feel my life isn't necessarily about me. Sometimes my life is about supporting other people. When I arrived, there were people in the group who were in the position I am in now, and they helped me

105

understand what was going on. Now the newest person in the group can see that I survived, I continue with my life. Maybe I can do for them what the original people in the group did for me. One day I will be so far removed from my treatment that I will move on, but for now this is my group, my friends. So for now I am still in the recovery support group.

There are other things you can do. There are walks against cancer. You can walk, or, if you can't walk, make a donation. If money is a problem, volunteer to hand out water or sandwiches. There are telethons. You can answer the phone. Or do accounting. There are lots of things to do. Pick something. If nothing else you will feel better being around people. Or at least I did.

The sage Lao Tze says:

True goodness is like water, it gives to everyone freely without making distinctions or competing. People hate the lowest places, but water seeks them out. So does Tao. Accept the nature of the world and join in it with compassion. Be generous to everyone. When you speak, speak sincerely. Treat others with fairness. Concentrate so that you are competent in whatever you decide to do and in every aspect of your daily life find true contentment. Work in harmony and with opportunity.

Most importantly, if you do not fight against anything then you can never be at fault.

(Tao Te Ching Chapter 8)

Chapter Seven

Make a Decision

I like steaks, particularly medium rare with potato and steamed vegetable on the side. I know this goes against some of my Taoist teachings, but I like steaks anyway. When, during my treatment, I found out that many oncologists believe that red meat is detrimental to people with cancer, especially colon cancer, and usually recommend less (or no) red meat to colon cancer patients, I felt deprived. Why was the world punishing me?

Which, of course, it wasn't. The universe is neutral. It doesn't reward good nor punish bad. The Christian bible says: "He causes his sun to rise on the evil and the good, and sends rain on the righteous and the unrighteous."

(Matthew 5:45)

Lao Tze says: "The great Tao (path) flows everywhere. All things come from it, yet it doesn't create them. It pours itself into everything and yet it makes no claims on anything. It feeds all the world, but doesn't grab hold of anything in the world. Since it is part of everything and works unseen by anyone, it can be called humble. All things eventually disappear into the Great Path and it alone endures. It isn't aware of its own greatness so it is truly great."

(Tao Te Ching, Chapter 34)

I am responsible for my cancer. When I said this to my group they had questions. "If you are responsible," they asked, "why have the cancer at all? Why not just get rid of it right now?"

I'm responsible for my cancer, but I didn't create it. I didn't make it happen, but now that it has, I must be as responsible for it as I am for anything that happens in my life. This way I have choices about it. I can make decisions about it.

If I am responsible for my cancer, then I must be responsible for the choices I make about the cancer, its treatment, and my diet. I am the one who decided to eat less red meat, not the doctor, certainly not the cancer. Why would I deprive myself? I wouldn't. I wouldn't like myself very much if I did. I want me to be happy. I really like me, and I want me to live as long as possible. That's why I decided to eat less red meat and more fish. So, I must not be deprived.

Could I have chosen never to have had cancer in the first place? No. I'm not prescient, I can't see into the future. Can I choose not to have cancer ever again? Not if I want to continue living. I can do things that help promote health, but I can't choose to never have cancers as long as I am still alive. I can't choose to have it never rain on me, not if I want to go outside into the world. But I can choose how I feel about the rain falling on me, and what I do when it starts to rain. And I can choose how I feel about the cancer, I can choose what I do about it, and I can choose who I tell about it (or withhold it from). I have choices.

Think of it this way: parents are responsible for their children. They can't (and shouldn't) meddle in every moment of the child's life, or micromanage the child, but they have overall responsibility for that child and the child's actions, health, and wellbeing. So every day I make choices about cancer, even when I've finished treatment. I still choose.

Every day, each person on earth makes choices, decisions, usually without thinking. This is because most people don't know what a decision really is. Many

Americans don't like to make decisions; we like to keep our options open, which is, of course, making a decision. You decided to read this paragraph. Maybe you thought about it before you began it, or maybe you just began to read because it's the next thing in this book, but either way you decided.

I once heard a famous motion picture director give a lecture to a group of film students. After he was finished, someone asked him why Hollywood made so many bad movies. This is approximately what he said. Nobody starts out saying, "Let's make the worst movie ever made." The writer has an idea and he thinks it might make a good movie. So he writes it down and shows it to somebody, usually a producer. The producer thinks it might make a good film, with a few changes, so he hires a director and actors. The director thinks it's a good project, with a few changes, of course, and the actors can see good parts, with a few changes. The little changes begin to add up, and suddenly the movie isn't what the writer, producer, director, or actors envisioned. It's terrible. None of these people set out to make a bad movie. Everyone connected with the project made the best decisions they could, based upon what they knew, thought, or thought they knew at the time.

I don't believe anyone has ever sat down to make a bad decision. I'm not sure there is any such thing as a bad decision. Bad consequences can come from perfectly good decisions. Bad things can happen even when you decide not to make a decision. Bad things can happen specifically because you decide not to make any decision. Each person makes the best decisions they can with the information they have at the time.

As I've said, I'm an engineer by training and engineers like to know things. (Actually, engineers like to believe we know everything. It must be annoying for the rest of you, being so slow.) So I went to find out about the word "decide". Decide is a strange word. It is made up of two parts; "De" and "Cide." "Cide" is part of many other words; suicide, insecticide, homicide, herbicide, etc. "Cide" means to kill off. Insecticide -- to kill off insects. Homicide -- to kill off humans. Suicide is to kill off yourself (Su means "you" in Spanish the same as it does in Latin).

"De" is a root word that means "everything," so *decide* means, literally, to kill off everything else, every other choice. If you decided to read this book, you decided not to go out for a walk or watch television. If you decide to go out the door of a room, you kill off the possibility of staying in

112

the room or going out of a window or another door. To decide means to make this choice and not any other choice. And every one on earth makes choices every day.

Here is a joke from my friend Ed Slott. Three frogs on a log. One decides to jump off. How many frogs are left on the log? Three. The one frog only decided to jump off. If the frog took no action, nothing changed. Making a decision, for me, has to include taking action.

I was talking about this with a group of friends. They didn't agree with me. One of them said, "What about the poor children of Africa. They don't have choices. They didn't choose to be poor or starving."

True. I doubt anyone would choose to be poor and starve in a refugee camp. But I repeat; in my opinion everybody on earth makes choices every day. Even the refugee children in Africa decide whether to get out of bed in the morning or not, to drink the water that's available or not, to eat what little food is given them or steal from others, stay put or leave. The difference between the choices in their lives and the choices in mine are not in number of choices. The difference is in the consequence of being wrong. It is a matter of degree.

If I make what turns out to be a terrible choice I might end up eating a fatty hamburger for lunch instead of having the salad. Or I might see a terrible movie instead of reading a good book. If the refugee in Africa makes a bad choice he or she might not wake up tomorrow. Every choice for a starving refugee is a life or death choice. None of my choices today will be, at least none of the ones I know about. Except where cancer is concerned. Cancer treatment choices might be life and death. I think refugees might be more equipped to make these choices than I was. I wasn't ready to make life and death choices.

But no one makes a bad decision. I will repeat that. No one makes a bad decision. No one sits down and says to themselves, "What's the worst thing I could do in this situation?" I might say to myself "What's the worst that could happen?" in order to eliminate a particular choice, but no one in their right mind would choose the worst possible thing.

There can be bad consequences to making a decision, the ending may not be what we would like, but nobody intentionally chooses the bad course. Each of us takes whatever information we have and makes a choice. Beating yourself up about the results of a decision is

114

counterproductive. There's nothing you can do about it now. You made the best choices you could, given the information you had at the time. Then we live with whatever comes of this choice. It's the only thing we can do.

One of the worst things you can do is put off a choice. Eventually the choice will be made, either by you or by your circumstances. Either you will move forward or, eventually (but hopefully not right away), you will die. Your choice.

The problem isn't making a decision if the choices are "yes or no." A computer can make yes and no decisions, either the switch is on or it is off. The problem is Baskin and Robbins. Don't get me wrong, all ice cream is good, (except the gummy worm ice cream. It is not one of my favorites). The problem is that all the ice cream is good. It's not a yes and no decision. The yes and no decision has already been made, I'm going to have ice cream. The problem is which one (or which ones) and with what topping (or toppings). I am definitely not going to have all thirty-one flavors with all the available toppings. (My doctor would have a fit.)

There are lots of ways of making a decision among several good things, but all of them come down to choosing one and not choosing all the rest.

What does this have to do with cancer? Many of the choices related to cancer are "Baskin-Robbins" decisions. Either all the choices are equally good, or all the choices are equally bad. For me, much of the time, the decisions were between three or four bad things. I got to choose which was the least bad.

I certainly didn't choose to have cancer. I don't think anyone chooses a bad situation. (There are no bad choices, remember?) We wouldn't choose to be in an earthquake, or a flood, or a hurricane, or to have any terminal disease. We don't have control of that choice. Things happen in our lives that we don't plan. There's a famous John Lennon quote; "Life is what happens while we are making other plans."

We always have a choice about how we will react to these events, how we feel about them. What do you do about the earthquake in California? Do you move to Iowa, or stay put? If a flood happens in Mississippi do you move away or go back and rebuild? If you live on the Gulf Coast, there will be hurricanes. Do you go someplace else or do you stay? And what do you do about your cancer? How will you think about it? Will you go to war, treat it as a problem, send it love, go about the business of getting rid of it, ignore it and

116

hopes it goes away, or something I haven't even considered? You always have choices and you decide. Your decision might be to do nothing. Doing nothing, putting the decision off until tomorrow, is still a decision.

When you have cancer, in addition to the way you think about it, there are two basic choices; are you a sick person trying to get well, or are you a healthy person who has a temporary, persistent illness called cancer? These may sound like the same thing but they aren't.

I don't know Donald Trump. I've read about him and heard him speak. He's rich. Or at least he seems rich to me.

As I said, I don't know Donald Trump but I would bet that he's never thought of himself as a poor person. If Donald Trump was alone in Manhattan at night, without his entourage or whatever bodyguards he has, and he was mugged; someone stole his wallet, credit cards, telephone, coat and shoes, I would bet money that his first thought would not be, "Well, I guess I'm poor now."

Not having cash or access to cash is one definition of poverty. But even without any of the trappings of his stature, I can't imagine Donald Trump thinking, "Well, I'm poor." If you are rich, you're rich. You might have a temporary cash flow problem but it doesn't change who or what you are.

Rich is a mindset, it is something you are, a way of being (a Tao). Cash flow is a temporary problem which, if you are rich, you can go about solving.

So is health. If you are a healthy person, you have temporary conditions called illnesses, something to be corrected. If you are a sick person, you are always sick, but sometimes you feel better than other times. Either way, health is always your choice. It can also makes a difference in how quickly you recover from a disease.

A sick person expects to be sick and might never really recover. He or she might feel better, but they are still essentially sick. A healthy person expects to be healthy. Any change in this condition is a temporary one, something for medical professionals to deal with. I decided that I am essentially healthy and I have an annoying condition called cancer. It's mainly annoying because of the time it is taking out of my life; time I think I could better use for other purposes, like writing this book. But I am, in the essence of my being, healthy. What about you?

I heard a story from one of my wife's cousins. He's worked in Hospice in Idaho for more than fifteen years. He said he met a man who had been misdiagnosed with terminal disease and went home to die. The man just gave up. The

118

doctor told him he was dying. That was it. He decided he was dying and became a sick person who was never going to get well. So he stayed in his bed for almost five years and finally died. What a waste.

Think of all the things he could have done in five years. Think of the books he could have written, the movies he could have watched, the people he could have inspired, the grandchildren he could have helped with homework. Instead he told people he was dying, he stayed in bed, and eventually he was proven correct. He died. Whether you think you can or whether you think you can't, you're right.

Now, you might say, "That was the doctor's fault for giving him the wrong diagnosis." You might be partially right, but not completely. Just because someone says something to you doesn't make it so, even if that person is a doctor. If a doctor tells you that you are anemic, he or she should be able to show you something, some laboratory information, another opinion, or a paper on the Internet that supports this diagnosis.

Ask! Doctors and nurses are people too, they are as prone to mistakes as the rest of us. If doctors were always right they would be richer than they are and not have to work at all anymore. It's your body and your life. You should be involved. In fact, according to the sage Lao Tze, you are involved in your life whether you want to be or not. You are the world's expert on you. You know what you think all the time. You don't have to guess how you feel, you know. Your doctor is guessing, based on the way you look and what you tell him or her. You actually know.

Now it's time for you to decide which you are; a well person or a sick person. Listen to how you talk about cancer to other people. Do you sound like someone who has the flu or a cold, or like someone who's been told they only have months to live? What do you say about cancer? Or are you afraid to talk about it at all, afraid to say the word?

How do the people around you talk to you? Do they make you a victim or do they know you are essentially a well person with a temporary condition? If your friends are making you a victim, get new friends. You are not a victim, you don't need this, and you deserve better friends.

How do you feel about the treatments you are getting? Have you heard horror stories about radiation or chemotherapy? Do you expect to get violently ill? Loose your hair? Be so tired you have to stay in bed for the rest of your treatment? Statistically some people do, but you are not a statistic. Why would you plan for the worst? To any consequence of this treatment, maybe you will and maybe you won't, but if you think you will, you definitely will.

Some people think, "making a decision" means looking back and judging if an action was good or bad. "If only I had just eaten more vegetables," or "if only I'd gone to the doctor sooner everything would have been so much better." There are no decisions to be made in the past. A wise man once said, "All the past is prologue." Worrying about the past just isn't worth the time and energy it takes, especially when you are fighting with cancer. No matter who you are, even if you knew exactly what changes to make, you can't change the past. Besides, you can't really tell if an action in the past is good or not.

Since all the information your medical professionals have about your disease and your treatment is statistical, even the best of them can't tell you for certain what caused your cancer or what exactly will happen during treatment. All the information is really a compilation of the results of hundreds of other people. You're not going to know anything until sometime after you've started. Even then, you won't know everything until after you've finished the treatments, and maybe not even then. Don't judge your decisions too soon.

There is an old story, probably told by Chen Tze. Once there was a farmer in China who had a horse. And he was considered rich because for most of the time in the history of China, there were whole villages that couldn't afford to keep horses, and this farmer had his own. A beautiful mare.

This farmer also had a fine wife and a son who was almost old enough to take care of some of the farm chores. This made the farmer the envy of the entire village. But he was also looked on as a fair and generous man. He'd loan his horse out to brides getting married, so they could ride to the wedding, and to families of the departed to take the body to the funeral. He also loaned the horse out to other farmers who needed more muscle that a man could produce.

One day there was a festival in the village, and the farmer told his son, "As soon as you have fed and watered the horse, you may join us at the festival."

The son wanted to go as quickly as possible. He knew that there would be food and fireworks at the festival, but more importantly, it was a way for him to meet young women. The farmer's son didn't go to school and so he didn't have much of a chance to meet girls.

So the young man fed and watered the mare as quickly as he could, but in his haste he didn't latch the gate and, during the night, the horse wandered off.

The next day, when the people of the village heard the news, they all came out to express their shock and grief at the loss of the horse. "What a tragedy. What a loss," they said. All but the Taoist monk who looked at the pen where the horse had been, then at the farmer's son, and asked, "How do you know this is a bad thing?"

The villagers muttered behind his back. "He's been living too long in the monastery. He's lost touch with reality," they muttered, although not loud enough for him to hear. Taoist monks are known to be touchy.

A week passed. The son cleaned the paddock and prepared it for pigs, you can't afford to waste pen space in China, even if you were rich and once had your own horse. One day, as he was cleaning, the horse wandered back into the paddock, followed by a fine Mongol stallion. The son closed and locked the gate and ran to tell his father.

Soon the entire village came to look at the two horses. "This is great good fortune," they said, knowing that each of them could one day have a horse, now that there was a male and female horse at the farmers'. All but the Taoist monk who looked at the horses and the son and said, "How do you all know this is a good thing?"

"He's lost his mind," the villagers said, not so softly. "How could this be anything but a good thing?"

Several weeks passed, and the son decided that having a second horse wasn't much use if the stallion couldn't be ridden, so he got a bit and put it on the horse. Then he grabbed the mane and climbed on. The horse bucked and through the son into a fence post, shattering his shoulder.

The farmer rushed him to the village doctor who set the bones and said, "He won't be able to do anything for at least six months."

"What a tragedy," the villagers said. All except the Taoist monk. "How do you know this is a bad thing?" he asked. The villagers didn't even respond. They all thought the monk was a nut. How could anybody not see how bad this was?

Weeks passed and one day General Sun Tze came to town and drafted all the young men into the army to fight against the Mongols. Seventy percent of the young men of the village died in the battle. Except for the farmer's son, who wasn't drafted because of his broken shoulder.

The Taoist question is; was the horse's walking away a good thing or a bad thing? And for who? (And the answer is: we don't know because the story isn't over.) Try not to judge the goodness or badness of any situation until you get to the end of the story, especially not chemotherapy, radiation, or cancer. (Yes, I know cancer looks like a definitive bad, but wait to judge the situation anyway.)

Chapter Eight

Make Sure You're Playing In The Right Game

If you're a football or basketball fan, or if you play golf or go bowling, you might be at a disadvantage in how you consider your cancer treatment. This may sound strange, but it isn't really. In football or basketball, as the clock winds down to the last minutes, a team, even a great team, can simply run out of time. Down 18 points with two minutes to go, even the mighty Michael Jordan Chicago Bulls would probably lose. There just isn't time left in the game to win.

Likewise, if Tiger Woods is down six strokes as he tees up for his eighteenth hole, unless this is a very unusual par seven hole, no matter what he does, he won't be able to win. Earl Anthony couldn't win in the last frame if he were down more than thirty pins. There just won't be enough pins left.

If you are a fisherman, you might have an advantage. Fishermen know that most of the time spent fishing is simply

126

waiting and, in my experience, they tend to be patient people. Likewise if you're a baseball fan you know that, even with two outs and down ten runs in the bottom of the ninth, as long as the batter is still standing at the plate and making contact with the ball, the game isn't over. No matter how much the Commissioner of Baseball tries to speed up the game, as long as Mike Piazza is swinging and makes contact with each pitch, nobody can make him sit down. The game isn't over until the third out of the ninth inning. As Curtis Granderson, center fielder for the Detroit Tigers says, "The game's not over until we come off that field."

In tennis or volleyball, as long as a team is hitting the ball over the net, the current score doesn't matter. It's not over until one team doesn't return the ball. They may not have the highest score at the moment, but neither team has won or lost as long as the ball is still in the air.

Another good thing about baseball; you don't have to hit a homerun every time at bat to win the game. If the Giants get the lead off batter to first base, then advances him around to second and to third and eventually home plate before the final out, the run counts when he scores exactly the same as if he'd hit a home run. In fact Runs Batted In (RBIs) are more significant in a players' career statistics than home runs. If a man legally crosses home plate during the game before the third out is made, the run counts, no matter how long the game has been going on. It's not over until it's over.

As far as I can tell, there's no time limit to the treatment of cancer and don't let anybody tell you there is. There isn't. That's all. I don't care if a hundred doctors and medical professionals say otherwise. (Which they won't. Most doctors know they aren't gods, even if some of their patients treat them as such. Usually it's non-medical people who talk about how long someone has to live. Like they know.) If you ask straight out, "How long have I got?" the doctor might give you a statistical answer, an answer based on hundreds or thousands of cancer patients with a similar situation. It doesn't mean anything to you specifically.

If we all reacted as the statistics say we should, there wouldn't be any childhood deaths at all, and men would die at age 72.2. Statistically, people die when they are older not in their younger years. Practically, people die when they die. There are children who die much too young and some of us plan to live long past 80. In fact, if you can just stay alive until you are 150 years old you will live forever because statistically nobody dies after age 150.

John Madden once said about statistics, "… if we ever got to the point where we knew what was going to happen, and it happened all the time, we wouldn't have to play the game." But the statistical team doesn't always win. Just ask the New York Yankees. For years George Steinbrenner has had consistently high payrolls, paying more money for the statistically best players, and yet the Yankees have only won the World Series occasionally. (The last was in 2000. They haven't won since.)

How does this relate to cancer? In truth, the universe is a strange and wonderful place. There can be a team that is in last place at mid-season but if they play hard and get a few good breaks they can still make it into the playoffs. People do win the lottery. And people recover from cancer. Sometimes cancer goes away and never comes back. As long as you are still making contact with the ball the game isn't over. Let the strange and wonderful universe work for you.

But what if it doesn't look like it's working out exactly the way you want it to? What then? Keep swinging. If you're not *officially* out, you're not out. And don't let anybody tell you how you feel. Keep trying. Curiously, in baseball, even if you swing at the third strike and miss you can still get on base. If the catcher drops the ball and you can make it to first base, you are considered safe. It doesn't happen often, but it does happen. Sometimes things just happen.

The Taoist master Chen Tze and his students were walking over a bridge, when Chen Tze saw some fish swimming in a stream. "Those are happy fish," said Chen Tze. "Swimming like that is happiness for fish."

"But you can't know that," said one of the students. "Not being a fish yourself."

"And you can not know that," said Chen Tze. "Not being me."

When I decided to release the news that I had cancer, I told the people closest to me. Then I decided to let whoever else asked know. This is a personal decision. But remember, keeping a secret, especially one as big as this takes energy, and you might want to use that energy for your treatment.

Again an aside. Several people in my support group have blogs, online information pages, which tell anybody who's interested about the cancer and treatments. A blog can help you with information dissemination. You don't have to keep repeating the same information over and over, and your friends don't have to feel left out of the information loop. All your friends have to do, if they are interested, is look on line.

The latest information about your treatments and your condition can be updated as you see fit.

After I released the information, I noticed that people treated me differently. Some would go out of their way to make contact, to say something, shake hands, make eye contact. They'd walk across the room and ask if I needed anything or how I was feeling. They were and are trying to help.

Others wanted to come up and express their sympathy, to tell me how sorry they were. They were, unintentionally, trying to make me the victim of the cancer, which I decided not to be. I had to get away from them. They were trying to help, to do what they thought I needed, but they weren't helping. It was very odd. There were also people who wanted to help directly, not only wanted to know how I felt, but wanted to know if they could do anything. It seemed like everybody was concerned with my feelings.

An hour after I saw the oncologist and the surgeon, physically I felt exactly the same as I did before anyone mentioned the word cancer. Since then I've been happy, sneezy, sleepy, lonely, hungry, dopey, grumpy and all the rest of the dwarfs, except Doc. I have a doc, but I never felt like Doc.

What I didn't feel was "different."

Some of the people around me, all well meaning people, all my friends, somehow had this idea that the use of the word cancer should change how I was feeling, how I related to the world, to them, to life. It didn't, at least not for me.

So here's what I have to say to you:

FEEL THE WAY YOU REALLY FEEL, AND DON'T LET ANYBODY TELL YOU WHAT THAT IS.

I've said this several times and in several different ways. I really mean it and I'm sorry if it sounds like advice. .

If you're happy, say to yourself, "I'm happy." Say it to yourself in a mirror, out loud if that makes you feel better. Tell the people around you that you're happy. They'll look at you strangely, but so what? If you feel wonderful, say that. Your friends will think you're a nut. "He says he feels wonderful, but he has cancer and he looks terrible." What are friends for anyway?

If you're hungry, tell the people that you're with that you are hungry and then get something to eat. Food usually makes me feel even better.

On the other hand, if you're lonely, sad, or depressed, tell the people around you. (Here's a hint: The reason most people ask how you feel is that they really don't know. Many of the people, not all of them, but many of them, really want to know how you feel.)

If someone bothers to ask, tell him or her exactly how you feel right now. But to do this, you have to know how you really feel right now, and most of us don't keep track from moment to moment. When someone asks, look inside and make an assessment. How do you feel, right now? Most of my friends can handle it. Lately most of the ones who can't handle my feelings won't ask.

Many, but not all of them. Some of my friends can't handle cancer as well as I do. You'll know who they are. (Another hint: if you have friends that get hysterical when the toilet paper runs out, don't tell them about your cancer, especially when you're not feeling good. They can't handle it.)

Cancer isn't just a word anymore. It's this thing that hides in dark places, with teeth and claws, ready to spring out, rip our flesh and tear us to death. Some people are so afraid of it that they won't even say the word. They make up names for it, as if saying the word will call it down on us. The Big C. People seem to be more afraid of the word than they are of the real thing.

Lao Tze says, "The thing that can be spoken aloud isn't the true thing." He was talking about the concept of Tao, but the idea applies to all names. The word "cancer" isn't the thing "cancer." If the word cancer were the thing cancer, then we could just take an eraser, remove the word from the language, and that would be the end of cancer. (I know this is stupid, but so is the fear of a word.)

I am not a victim. You are not a victim. Unless you want to be, of course. You and I do not have to be victims of the word cancer, or the thing cancer, or any of the well-meaning people who want us to feel afraid. You and I have some control of how we feel, if we want to take it. I mean this: you can feel any way you want, you can even think yourself into feeling lousy, and I can prove it.

Two hundred years ago an actor would stride out onto a stage, square his shoulders and, in his loudest voice, say, "I feel distraught, my father has died."

If an actor did that today he would be laughed off the stage. Today in movies, television, and stage we expect actors to express emotions, to look like they feel sad, happy, angry, whatever. Our expectations come from a man named Stanislavski. He was a director in the Russian theatre, and the inventor of modern acting.

Stanislavski told his actors how to act. "If you are going to portray sadness on stage," he said, "remember back to the most tragic thing that has ever happened in your life. Think about how your toes felt, how your face felt, how your shoulders and stomach felt. When your body feels the way you felt when you were sad, then you will be able to portray sadness."

The same is true of joy, excitement, or any other emotion. The great actors of our time, people like Jack Nicholson, Meryl Streep, or Denzel Washington can call up emotions to reflect the character's condition. The more accurately they "feel" the character's emotions, the more we believe them. But the truth of this is, they create how they feel in movies and on stage in order to act as if they are feeling these emotions.

If I've decided to call up the feeling "happiness," I would remember a time when I felt the happiest I have ever felt, then make my feet feel happy, my shoulders feel happy, and my face feels happy. If all of me is made to feel happy what is the difference between this and being happy? I can't find any difference between feeling happy because I feel happy, and feeling happy because I'm portraying happiness accurately.

Of course, there are chemical factors in my body that can cause depression. Chemical depression won't respond well to your mental control, although I know of some actors who can portray happiness on stage even when they are, in real life, depressed. I don't say you can think your way out of a chemically induced depression. If you are depressed all the time, or you stop doing the things that are a part of every day living, talk to your doctor. You should not continue to be depressed. It's not good for your recovery and there are things which can help. In the middle of my treatment my doctor prescribed an anti-depressant. I don't like taking pills, but in this case it worked. I felt better and I got better. What is inside is affected by what is outside, and what is outside also affects what is inside.

Lao Tze says, "Thirty spokes make up a wheel but it is the hole in the middle that makes it useful in moving the wagon. Shaped clay makes the pot but it is the space inside that makes it useful. Cut doors and windows for a room because without them the room isn't useable. Therefore purpose comes from what is there but usefulness from what is not there."

Chapter Nine

But in the Dark Reaches of the Night…

There is a difference between thinking about fear and having fearful thoughts. For me, thinking about fear sounds like this, "What am I afraid of? Why am I feeling so afraid?" Being afraid is different. When I am afraid, all I can think about is, well, whatever I am afraid of. Dying, losing a limb, losing my mind, whatever. It usually sounds like my mind screaming, "I'm going to die right now."

Some people advise me to "Buck up, stop being afraid." What does that mean? In my mind, fear and bravery are two ends of the same stick. If you have looked at a stick, it usually has two ends. If I want to get rid of one end I can cut it off, but what I have really done is create two sticks each with two ends. As long as there is still a stick it will have two ends. So "don't be afraid," doesn't seem like good advice. This is hiding the fear away, allowing it to fester and grow.

But what should I do? I find the best thing to do is stop, close my eyes, take a deep breath, and ask myself, "What am I afraid of? What is scaring me?" Now I am thinking about the fear instead of being afraid. Confronting the fear instead of hiding it away seems to make my life easier. But there are times when I can't seem to stop and think about the fear because I am too afraid.   And the fear doesn't have to be rational.

Someone once told me, "Your mind is a dark and scary neighborhood. Never go there alone." In my opinion, real terror is something I have to talk myself into, let into my mind. It comes from that little voice inside my head, the one that just said, "What little voice?" or "There's no little voice inside my head." The psycho-cybernetics people have a specific name for this voice. I just call it the little voice inside my head.   And I know I don't have to listen to this voice. I can train my listening.

We have a little cat, Katarina. (It's a cute name and she's a sweet cat.) We call her Rena. She has the sharpest ears of any animal I've ever had. She can be asleep in the back bedroom when I get out a can of tuna and by the time I have it open she will be rubbing against my legs. I don't give her tuna at the same time everyday, in fact some days I don't give her tuna at all. It can't be the smell of the tuna; she can't smell it if I haven't opened the can yet. And it's not just any can, not fruit or beans, just tuna. I don't know how she knows the difference, but she does. I believe that she has trained herself to listen for specific kinds of sounds. She knows what to listen for and what to ignore.

The little voice inside my head is there for a reason. It tells me, "If you grab that hot pan again, you will get burned AGAIN." It is there to protect me, but sometimes it goes too far. Many times, if I listen, it will keep me from doing things that I might enjoy. I have to keep training myself, know what to listen for and what to ignore. I have to work at screening out the unnecessary and harmful thoughts and fill my mind with pleasant thoughts. Sometimes this is referred to as visualizing. Thinking about being healthy and sound is good for my recovery. Bad thoughts and unfortunate visuals don't help at all. In fact thoughts of fear and illness can make us do things that, eventually, we will regret.

After nine-eleven, when the Twin Towers were attacked, the country was afraid. Not everyone, but many. The little voice inside our collective heads was coming out as conversation in the media. I could feel it in everyday conversations with friends; a real fear. The country was afraid and angry. We were angry. We were angry at the administration for not preventing the tragedy, at the CIA for not knowing about it in advance, at the FBI for not doing screenings so that it wouldn't have happened. But mostly we were afraid. The little voices inside our collective heads had convinced us that something like this could happen again. Without warning. And this time any one of us might be in the building.

Anger can mask fear. Anger and fear are sometimes linked together. When we are afraid and don't want to admit it even to ourselves we cover the fears by being angry. After nine-eleven we, the citizens of the United States, wanted something to be done. We wanted someone to pay. So we went to war. Although most people won't admit it now, the citizens of this country supported the war. "At least," we said to ourselves, "we are doing something."

But as time passed and nothing more happened, no more buildings were destroyed, no nuclear bombs exploded, no biological contamination, no plague, the people of the United States stopped being as afraid as we had been. Taking your shoes off in an airport was annoying. Lives had been disrupted for no good reason. Soldiers, our brothers and sisters, were dying in a foreign war. Now the mood of the country changed. Now most people were against the war. As long as we aren't afraid anymore, why were we at war anyway? So what has all this got to do with me? And what has nine-eleven got to do with cancer?

On the night after my surgery I was lying alone in bed thinking, listening to the little voice tell me all the things that could go wrong, things that had gone wrong, and things that would continue to go wrong. I know better, but I was coming out of anesthesia and moving on to power pain killers, trying to sleep in a hospital, starting the cancer treatment process, and generally feeling sorry for myself.

Thinking late at night is usually a bad idea, at least for me. Thinking late at night in a hospital bed is a disaster waiting to happen. If I can't sleep, I usually try doing something else (instead of worrying about sleeping). You might try turning on the television and watch something mindless on commercial TV, something socially meaningful on PBS, even something "Adult" on cable if you are able to. Listen to music on the radio or talk show pundits explaining what you should think about world issues. Write letters to friends. Do puzzles. Call people in the middle of the night just because you haven't talked to them in a long time.

On second thought, don't call people you haven't talked to in a long time from a hospital bed, especially if your friends know about your condition. It will freak them out. They will assume (naturally) that you are calling to say good-by. Even after you explain that you're not calling for any particular reason, your friends will always make the call something worse than it actually is if you let them. Their minds don't work any better than yours or mine.

In fact, if your friends are like mine, the more you insist that it's just a friendly call in the middle of the night the more meaning they will put into the conversation. I digress. Go for a walk instead of thinking. Walking is good for you. It loosens up the muscles and helps things fall into place better. If your surgeon allows it, walk every couple of hours. You will recover sooner. Besides, the pain will keep you from thinking, and too much thinking is detrimental to your recovery.

Anyway, on the third night after my surgery I couldn't do anything but think. I was stuck. I was lying in bed thinking. There are really only three things your mind can think about while lying in bed after surgery, and all three of them are bad. My mind wanders.

A famous football coach once said, "When you throw the ball there are only three things that can happen, and two of them are bad." My friend Ed Slott uses this quote in his financial planning seminars. If you were to use this quote in a room filled with a hundred people, you would get at least three people who will know exactly who said it. And each of them will have a completely different answer. Not only that, all three of them would likely be wrong. Ed knows the correct answer, because that's the sort of person he is. He likes to have correct information, and usually does. (So he Googled it). This thought takes my mind away from the surgery bed for a moment, then I'm back in the hospital.

I was trying to clear my mind. But all I could think about was this: eventually I would have to get out of bed and go to the bathroom (one), it was going to hurt so much that I would never be able to stand up by myself (two), I would die there on the floor with the bathroom in sight (three) and the nurse wouldn't find me until the shift change the next morning. I hit a Trifecta. I should have gotten an extra chocolate pudding for dessert.

I need to say here that none of these thoughts were true. One thing I have discovered is this, usually my most fearful thoughts aren't true. If I can think about why I am afraid I usually discover that it's really nonsense. This certainly was. I could have called a nurse to help me get up. People who become nurses usually do so because they want to help others, and I had a nurse assigned to me around the clock. (Not a nurse assigned to watch me specifically, she also had responsibility for the patients in the rooms adjacent to mine as well. But she was there to help me if I needed help.)

I had a plunger that would inject pain medication directly into my body. If that wasn't enough, I could get pills for pain, maybe even an additional IV if I needed more pain management immediately. My surgeon had prescribed some very good drugs, and besides, after spending all this money on me, my HMO wasn't about to let me die on the floor in the middle of the night. It looks bad in the papers.

But the pain I was worried about wasn't the pain I'd suffered the last time I'd gotten up, it wasn't *past pain*. Nobody suffers from past pain. And it wasn't the pain I was having at this moment, it wasn't *now pain*. It was pain in the future.

An aside here. I can only be worried about a pain in the future. I can't worry about pain now, all I can do is have pain now. Worry is thinking about something in the future that will be worse than things are now. But the truth is, there isn't any pain in the future. Pain is another word that only exists in the present, it's in the here and now, or it isn't. Any pain I can worry about in the future is all in my own head. I know this. I teach this. And there I was worrying about the pain that was GOING TO HAPPEN when I tried to get up.

Worrying about anything is ALWAYS bad for your recovery. It takes a lot of energy to worry. It takes a lot of energy to recover. You can't do both effectively, or at least I can't.

My friend Vic and I own an apartment building in Fresno. Actually, of the hundred units in the complex, he owns ninety-seven of the units and I own the other three, almost. (Don't laugh. At least I'm an investor.) Vic usually takes a lot of time checking out the renters. This means that the units are vacant and I'm not making any money. "Why take all that time?" I asked.

"Because," he said, "If I don't screen our tenants, we might get a bunch of undesirables, people who make noise at night and disturb the good tenants. If we allow a lot of bad tenants in eventually they will drive the good tenants out." This makes sense. The same is true of my thoughts. If I let the unwelcome ones in, eventually the good thoughts will leave.

I spent a miserable half-hour worrying, and by then I actually had to do something. My body told me I was either going to the bathroom or in the bed, my choice. So I reached up and hauled my tired and abused body out of bed. It wasn't nearly as painful as I'd thought it was going to be. Understand, it wasn't pleasant. It hurt. But I could stand up and get where I needed to go.

Now, having told you this story, any rational human being would think that the next time I needed to get up, I would just get up. After all, I had evidence that it wasn't as bad as I thought it was going to be. WRONG.

I slept until one in the morning and then spent another miserable half-hour anticipating getting out of bed. I thought about jumping out of bed quickly, before my body had time to adjust. This, I thought, will make the getting out of bed easier. I tried that approach once and nearly ripped out a stitch (or, in this case, a staple). The doctor wouldn't have been happy with this outcome. The floor nurses wouldn't be happy either. I wouldn't be happy. They, the medical staff, expected me to ask for help if I needed help.

Most people don't want to ask for help, especially male people. Taking painkillers might be okay, but asking cute young nurse to help me out of bed to go to the bathroom is embarrassing, especially since I am old enough to be her grandfather, and it would make me feel helpless and weak. Helpless and weak is not a description any male person would want applied to them. "You'll look foolish," my mind said. "You don't want to look foolish, You want to look strong and manly." Looking good is another bad approach to recovery. The reason my doctor prescribed pain medication was to prevent me from having more pain than I could deal with.

Lao Tze says: "Men are born supple and weak. When they are dead they become rigid and stiff. Plants grow soft and tender, when they die they become dry and stiff. Thus whoever tries to be inflexible and strong is a student of death, whoever is soft and asks for help is a disciple of life. The hard and stiff will break, where weak and flexible will succeed."

(Tao Te Ching, chapter 76)

There was no way I was going to die from getting out of bed in the middle of the night. And yet it was real to me.

147

This is real fear. I had to talk myself into it. I had to ignore logic in order to achieve it. Fear is one of the things Lao Tze tries to teach us to avoid.

"Hope is as hollow as fear.

What does it mean that hope is as hollow as fear? Hope and fear are both ghosts that arise from thinking about ourselves in the future. If we don't think of ourselves in the future, what do we have to fear? Think of the world as part of yourself. Have faith in the way things are."

(Tao Te Ching, chapter 13)

On the other hand, if you are walking down a dark trail in the woods and you turn and see a bear, or when you get to the top of a new roller coaster and realize that the bottom of the hill appears to be six miles away, you will probably be frightened. At least I usually am.

Your blood pressure will go up, your adrenaline levels will go up, your heart races, endorphins race into your bloodstream. Some people like this feeling. They go long distances to find the tallest roller coaster or to ski down an impossible slope. They say it makes them feel alive. I'm not one of those people. I don't particularly like to be frightened. When I'm frightened I usually don't have time to stop, take a breath, and ask myself why I'm frightened.

Now sometimes, usually in the middle of the night, when all I can hear is my wife breathing restfully on the other side of the bed, I wake up and find myself thinking, "I can't do this. (In the future) It's too much. Why is this happening to me? (again in the future.)" I'm talking myself into the fear again.

Why would I want to make myself afraid in the middle of the night? I know better.

For me, there is usually a simple physiological reason my brain would wake me up with these kinds of thoughts and questions. My brain is one of the major single consumers of calories in my body. But, you'll say, moving my little finger probably takes more energy than thinking. This might be true, but moving my finger requires more than one muscle.

When we run or exercise our muscles burn calories. When the muscles begin to run out of energy they send a signal to the brain, "We're tired. We're running out of things to burn." The brain then calls up stored calories and puts them into the blood system to replenish the calories needed by the muscles.

But when my brain begins to run out of energy there isn't any feedback system to call up additional calories, so my brain just cycles through thoughts one right after another. And I wake up. Lucky me.

If this happens to you, try this: drink a small glass of fruit juice. Any kind of natural fruit juice will work. Don't swish it in your mouth, your dentist won't like that. Just swallow it and go back to bed. It's simple; the juice is good for you, it will feed your brain, and it might help you sleep. It usually does for me.

But suppose juice doesn't work. What then?

Everyone I have ever met is searching for answers in the universe. If you are an engineer or a physicist, or a philosopher, your mind has been asking "Why?" most of your life. Why is the universe the way it is? Why is there starvation in a world of plenty? Why did the space shuttle fail? Why not have SIMM memory chips stacked one on top of another to increase capacity and speed? Why do good people die and bad people continue to exist? Why do I have cancer?

Searching for useful answers is a natural thing to do. But it's not very helpful in some situations. Engineers want reasons in order to prevent failure in the future; if we can find out why the space shuttle failed, we can build one that won't fail. Physicists and philosophers want reasons to advance their understanding of the universe. If a physicist can understand the nature of super-strings, he or she might be able to comprehend why light seems to behave in two contradictory ways.

Answers can be useful things if you are building another space shuttle or trying to figure out the nature of the universe. But every answer is not useful or worth spending the time looking for. Especially at two o'clock in the morning while sleeping in a hospital bed.

Suppose I could tell you the exact cause of the cancer in your body; every detail, exactly why and how it started, why it is located where it is, it's construction, cellular biology, genetic implications, every event and situation that went into its formation, down to the exact second it started. Would you really know anything more useful than you do now?

Really? Dr. Lee, the teacher who introduced me to Taoism, had a question that went like this. "Suppose I could give you the power from every nuclear plant, every gas and coal fired electrical generating facility, every wind turbine, everything on this planet that generates electricity. And suppose you could point your finger and apply all that power, as many times as you wanted, to any specific point on earth.

151

You could move mountains, change the seas, and affect the lives of every plant, animal and person on the earth. If I gave you this power you would be a powerful person."

"Now suppose I duplicated the wealth of the ten richest men in the world, not by taking their money, but by creating more wealth, and gave it all to you so that you could do anything that money can accomplish. You could change the course of the stock market, end poverty, feed the hungry, whatever you wanted. Then you would be not only powerful but also rich beyond the imaginings of men. If I did all of this for you, could you go back and change anything that happened three weeks ago? A year ago? An hour ago?"

No. No matter how rich or powerful you became, the past is the past. What happened in the world while you were reading the beginning of this chapter is gone. You can't change it. Neither can I. Neither can any person on this planet.

So what am I supposed to do in the middle of the night? What am I supposed to do with the speculations, the questions, the "If I had just ..." All the regrets, all the things I could have done, the changes I could have made in the past which might have prevented this cancer? What am I supposed to do with them?

Nothing. Leave the past in the past. Let them go. If you can, take a deep breath, close your eyes and recognize the thoughts in your head as thoughts. Concentrate on your breathing. Count the seconds it takes to breathe in? If a thought comes into your mind, recognize it as a thought and let it go. This is like "living in the moment," it is sometimes easier said than done. I'm great at giving advice, but not so great at taking it. (This is one of the reasons I have tried to stop giving advice.) But this is really all any of us can do, leave the past in the past and go forward.

Don't try to block the thoughts out of your mind, or hide them. It won't work. If the thoughts won't go away, concentrate on something else, something that makes you feel good. Something simple. Thinking about great sex, good food, exercise if that makes you happy, driving your car if you really enjoy it, people you know and love. Try to remember the best joke you've ever heard, or the worst joke. Things like this will drive the unwanted thoughts out of your mind. Usually.

While I was in the hospital, I kept a quacking duck by my bed. It was a little fuzzy toy that quacked when I pushed its flipper. My sister gave me one and my wife gave me another. It was a distraction. It was the silliest thing any of the nursing staff had ever seen, but it worked for me. When I woke up in the middle of the night I'd quack the duck, and laugh.

Dr. Edward DeBono, a professor at Oxford University, teaches thinking as a skill. In your free time, if you are interested, he has written more than sixty books about thinking, most available in bookstores. And he's a good storyteller, so his books aren't nearly as boring as they might sound. He's also an expert in thinking about thinking.

Dr. DeBono says laughter is a way of breaking up patterns of thought. Laughter keeps your mind from running down the same dark alleys of thoughts and opens your brain up to new thoughts, different ideas. He certainly knows more about this than I do. But, while I was in the hospital, I kept the duck near my bed and it worked for me. It made me laugh. In the middle of the dark night, when everything else was silent, the nurses must have heard the duck quacking. They never mentioned it, so I don't know what they thought.

Of course, it hasn't been nearly as effective since I've been home. My wife wouldn't understand the quacking duck in the middle of the night, or my laughing about it. So now, because I know what she would think, I don't have to make the duck quack. All I have to do is look at it or reach for it, and I laugh. I laugh and the fears go away.

"The person who is centered in his own way of being (Tao) can go anywhere he wants to go without being afraid. He knows that the universe is in harmony with itself, even in times of great pain and suffering. He is never alone because he has found peace in his heart."

(Tao Te Ching chapter 35)

What makes you laugh? What situations make you happiest? Family, children, pets, favorite sports teams, sky diving? Keep those thoughts close. Pictures can help. Something personal near you can help. Most hospitals recommend having familiar things around you. If you're a San Francisco 49ers fan, like I am, having the team win once in a while would help, but we can't have everything?

Or can we? Why not? Why can't we have everything? If you want to think about something, think about the Forty-niners going into the playoffs. That's an excellent thought for the middle of a dark night.

Chapter Ten

Choosing Your Provider

I heard a story about a man who, when he got a cancer diagnosis, fired his doctor. When the second doctor gave him the same diagnosis he fired that doctor. By the fourth doctor he began to realize that it wasn't the doctor, it might be him. There is nothing wrong with firing your doctor, but make sure you do it for the right reasons. The cancer really isn't your doctor's fault. He just found it and has to give you the bad news.

This is the way I found out I had cancer. I had a pain in my abdomen, not A PAIN, just a pain. It was below my belt line and felt like a small muscle pull, or appendicitis. My wife worries, so when I developed a temperature of 102, we went to the emergency room of our HMO. The doctors did some tests; a CAT scan, blood work and such, and decided I had an abscess. Something from my guts had leaked into my abdomen (Diverticulitis). The emergency room doctor decided to put me in the hospital under the care of a surgeon.

After a week in the hospital treating the abscess with antibiotics, my surgeon scheduled me with an Interventional Radiologist who took several CAT scans and pushed a needle into my abdomen to remove the abscess. I was getting better, but still had to have a colonoscopy before I left the hospital. It was during this examination that the radiologist told me he had found a mass in my colon and had made an appointment with an oncologist and my surgeon the following week.

At this point I should say that I am a member of a giant HMO in the western United States, but I won't use their name. Not because they aren't good. As far as I can tell, I had the best cancer care of anyone in the United States. They went farther and faster with my cancer treatment than I could have imagined such a big organization would be able to.

But I am not doing a commercial for anybody. There are lots of excellent treatment providers; skilled medical professionals, pharmacists, nutritionist, radiologists, oncologists and nurses. Some work for HMOs. Some with PPOs. Some work independently. I have experience with one group of people. Don't let my experiences, good or bad (but mainly good) keep you from moving forward with your own treatment.

Something else. Service providers. (I hate this. I want to say "Doctors" but I can't. Some of the service providers don't have a "doctor licenses." So I can't say "Doctor" unless I mean someone with a degree in medicine or a related field. Sorry.) Anyway, some of the service providers will try to explain your situation and the treatment options extensively, whether you want them to or not. It's the new trend in medical marketing. My HMO actually has a person who walks around with a clip board and interviews patients after the doctor has completed the first appointment to find out if everything has been explained clearly.

Most people won't have a choice of medical systems. You are probably already attached to an HMO, PPO, or some sort of insurance, and now is not the time to change. Most people aren't able to change systems anyway. Because of the insurance coverage mess we have in this country, once you have been diagnosed with cancer, it's almost impossible to change health plans. The new plan won't cover your cancer treatment, it's a pre-existing condition, and it's going to be expensive and time consuming for them as well as for you. Maybe one day we will have some kind of universal health care in this country, but that day isn't today, so now is definitely not the time for you to begin the process of changing health systems.

Within your system there are probably several choices of individual oncologists, clinics, laboratories, and radiologists. You need to choose the ones that are the best for you, for your care. Sometimes this means choosing the closest ones in location to where you live, but not always. Interviewing your doctors is like interviewing a prospective employee. In fact it is exactly like interviewing a prospective employee. You will be hiring that doctor to work on one of your most precious assets, your body.

One of the guides along my path in life is a man named Bill Bachrach. He has written several books and teaches financial planners to be Trusted Advisors (in his particular case, Trusted Financial Advisors). I mention him here because he's the one who gave me several of these ideas. He teaches these ideas to financial planners. I think he is short sighted. These ideas are just a basic understanding of the way things are (or perhaps the way things should be). I wish he would teach his course to doctors, nurses, auto mechanics, and anyone else whose opinion I have to listen to. It would certainly ease my way through life. On the other hand, there are already enough people who recognize the value of his teachings to keep him busy for the rest of this lifetime.

Bill teaches this: all the work and effort you are going to do in an effort to find someone who will advise you on any subject should go into the selection of your advisors. Whatever the field, if I know that my advisor understands me, that he is working for my benefit, that he is skilled in his or her field, everything from then on should be easy. He or she gives me the best advice based upon his or her skills, analysis, and understanding of my situation, and I take the advice based on my feelings at the time, what information I have retained about the subject, and what outcome I want. This last is the most important part. Why would anyone spend time and money finding and hiring an advisor they trust, someone that is an expert in a particular field, then question his or her advice?

Now I am not saying you shouldn't get a second opinion. In the medical realm, whether the news is good or bad, if it is an extreme change, get a second opinion. Remember, this is your body, your treatment. You must be your own advocate. As the old saw goes; if you don't blow your own horn, who will? To do this you must know what you want because in the original appointment, the one where you told your doctor what you wanted as an outcome for your treatment, you probably didn't tell him or her the exact truth.

My doctors are the most *Trusted Advisors* I will ever choose. By the time I started my treatment, all my decisions had already been made. (It's similar to the dialog in the movie The Matrix. The Oracle says, "You've already made the choice. Now you have to understand it.")

Choosing your *Doctor* is like choosing an *Auto Mechanic, Lawyer*, or a *Financial Planner*. The decision may seem more important right now, because of the urgency or the situation, but in the end the choosing is the same. We have to trust our advisors. If I wanted to, I could probably get a book or take a class on auto repair, I could go to law school and find out about the law, or I could go to courses on investing and become a CPA or a financial advisor. I could do lots of things if I had unlimited time and the interest to do so.

I could understand how the modern automotive engine works and, provided I had all the tools, I could fix it myself. I don't want to expend the time, energy, and money. Why do something when I can hire and expert to do it? But knowing as little as I do, having my auto mechanic try to explain the intricacies of an engine to me is useless. It wastes his time, which he is charging me for, and confuses me. I do want him to explain, in general terms, what is wrong, what caused it, and what he will be doing to fix it. I don't want a detailed explanation of the workings of the internal combustion engine.

The same is true for my financial planner and my lawyer. Either I trust each of them to do the best job they can do for the good for my future, or I don't. If I trust them why would I try to micro-manage every decision they make? If I don't trust them, does it make any difference what they tell me? I'm not going to take the advice anyway. The same is true of my doctors.

Once I knew that my doctors understood me and my situation, including what I really wanted from of my treatment, the explanation of the specifics of the treatment was a giant waste of his and my time. (Not that I am recommending signing your life away. If your doctor, financial planner, or auto mechanic or any other expert gives you something to look at, look at it. They probably gave you this information for a reason. If you really trust your advisor, why wouldn't you read the information they gave you?)

On the other hand, my friend Mikey (he's never been Miguel or Mike to me, he's always been Mikey) lives in Las Vegas. He's a professional is a gambler. For the last 30 years or so he has made his living at the sports book, either setting odds or betting on them. When he had a serious illness (cancer of the throat), he asked the doctor for the odds of his full recovery.

His first doctor wouldn't give him an answer. For most doctors this question sounds a lot like "How long have I got?" Doctors won't usually answer this one, they know better.

But Mikey wanted to know the odds so that he could ask the next question, "How do we rig the game? What can I do to make the odds better?" He wanted a doctor who could give him odds, and then rig the game (his treatment) in his favor whenever possible. He wanted a doctor who was a gambler. A gambler in Vegas, what are the odds?

He finally found one. His fourth doctor explained the odds and the things he could do to improve his odds. Mikey is still around and he and his doctor have been friends (and golfing buddies) ever since. Mikey is now in his ninth year of recovery and still betting the odds, although he does eat a lot more green vegetables than he used to, he makes it a point to get more sleep, and he's stopped smoking.

I digress.

What I needed for my treatment and recovery was a Surgeon and an Oncologist. (Not a small "s" surgeon and a small "o" oncologist, I wanted the best.) I asked a couple of nurses and some of the staff people I know who work within my HMO. Each of them recommended the same Oncologist. In fact, one of them called and made the appointment for me. You can't beat that.

I like my Oncologist. He cares about the general well being of his patients. We met him by accident in a restaurant between chemotherapy appointments. He came over to our table and asked how I was, even though he didn't have to. He could have waved across the room, picked up his food, and left, but he didn't.

I also like him because he thinks on paper. He sketches, draws, makes notes, and doodles. I keep the papers when he's done, so that I can look at the collection of lines and drawings to help me remember our conversations. Useful for me.

And I like my Surgeon. We like the same radio stations, the same kind of music. He tries to explain what he's going to do, uses charts and pictures of my insides, because it's required by the system, but he doesn't test me on the material at the end of the sessions. I listen, but we both know that he has the medical degree, so whatever he finds during the surgery he will have to deal with. But I also like him because I think he cares about me. He cares about my treatment. He has an investment, he wants to win. In order for a surgeon to win, he has to do the surgery and I have to recover. To misquote Chen Tze, "the patient's recovery is happiness for a surgeon."

I want people on my side who want to win for their own reasons, who want to solve my problems for their own piece of mind. When the situation looks the darkest, I want problem solvers on my team. Anyone can come up with a solution when the problem is easy. I want people who can come up with solutions when the problem looks impossible. I want people who talk TO me, not AT me. And I want people who listen to me, even when I'm not communicating very well.

Sometimes I want them to get my communications even when I don't talk. I want mind readers. I know this is unreasonable, but it's what I want. My oncologist came in during one appointment and said, "You're depressed. I am going to give you something for depression."

"I'm not depressed," I said. I was losing some weight, sleeping most of the day and didn't feel like going anywhere, but I'm a guy, and being a guy means never admitting you are anything but fine.

"Of course you are depressed," he said. "You have cancer. Everybody who has cancer is depressed. I am going to give you a prescription and we will see if you don't do better."

"I don't want to take any more pills."

He looked me in the eyes and said with a straight face, "Some men will do anything for their wives."

"He didn't really say that," I thought to myself. But he did. My doctor will use just about anything to get me to accomplish what I said I wanted to accomplish. He's a great coach. That's one of the reasons I like him.

"And so it is said, the path that leads into the light seems darkest, the path that leads forward seems to be going backward, the most direct path seems to be going the long way, and actual power seems like weakest."

(Tao Te Ching, chapter 41)

Chapter Eleven

Apparent of Loss of Control

"An object at rest tends to stay at rest and an object in motion tends to stay in motion with the same speed and in the same direction unless acted upon by an unbalanced force." Isaac Newton's First Law.

People are in motion all the time, it's what we do. Some of us are in a faster motion than others, but everyone is always headed somewhere. And we will continue in that direction unless we are acted on by an unbalanced force. Cancer is certainly an unbalanced force. It is also an unbalancing force. If you let it, cancer can throw you completely off kilter.

When I started the chemotherapy treatments it seemed like I had lost control of my time, my life, everything. People; doctors, nurses, other health professionals, family, friends, my wife, even people I didn't know were telling me where to go and when to go there, what I could and couldn't do, what I should and shouldn't eat and drink, what medications I should and shouldn't take, and when I should and shouldn't take them. All of them wanted me to follow their advice. I couldn't do all of it, and I didn't want to do most of it, but I didn't seem to have a choice about a lot of it. I felt like I'd lost control of everything.

Before cancer I always believed I had control of my life. I knew what I was doing, where I was going, and what I had left to do. I made plans. I worked. I went on vacations, had weekend plans, did things I wanted to do. I invested for retirement. Balanced my checkbook. I was in control of my life. I knew what the future was going to look like and what I was going to do in it. I was set. I was an expert in my field. People could depend on me and I delivered, on time and under budget. Then I got cancer and everything seemed to change.

Not only had I lost control of my life, I couldn't even make plans for the future. Not for certain anyway. I didn't know for sure what I would be able to do or not do. Whether I could work or not would all depend on how I reacted to the chemotherapy. I couldn't promise anyone that I would be at a certain place at a certain time and be sure I would be able to be there.

The uncertainty was terrible, especially for engineers. As I said, by training and inclination I'm an engineer. I like resolution and clarity. I like reservations to be kept, flights to be on time, things to begin when they are scheduled to begin and end when they are scheduled to end. And I expect the beginning and ending times to be arranged, and the specifications and goals to be set down before we start a project. Cancer has been a real lesson for me. Beginning with the diagnosis and continuing with chemotherapy I couldn't be sure of anything anymore.

Apparently I am not alone in this. The people in my support group have had the same feelings of loss of control of our lives. You might be feeling the same thing (or maybe you don't). Are we supposed to plan on a vacation or not? Can I volunteer for something or will I feel so drained that I can't make to whatever I volunteered for much of the time? Will I be able to drive to my appointments or will someone have to take me? Can I eat my favorite foods and what will they taste like after the chemicals have infused my body? What's the future going to be like? And what is my place in it? Or do I have a place in the future?

My oncologist was of no help. He's one of the nicest men I have ever met, a terrific oncologist, but he's a terrible psychic. He doesn't seem to know about the future at all. He couldn't tell me exactly how I would react to the chemotherapy chemicals, or how I would feel next week, let alone next month or a year from now. The only advice I could get from the people around me was "Try and live in the moment."

This advice has always struck me as fascinating. "Try and live in the moment." As if I could live anywhere else. What, exactly, are they (whoever they are) trying to tell me? Here's my idea. If I am concentrating on why I got cancer, my mind is living in the past. I got cancer in the past, and I can't change that. (I am wasting time now thinking about what happened a while ago.) If I'm worrying about the future, I'm missing out on what is happening now. My mind is living in the future. The past is over and the future hasn't happened yet. Right now is happening right now, so that's what I should concentrate on, according to some people.

But suppose right now isn't so good? Do I have to live in the moment if the moment is painful? That would be stupid. When I am in the middle of a CAT scan, and my shoulders are hurting from holding them in a certain position for what seems like hours at a time, I might want to be somewhere else. Maybe the past was better. Maybe the future is where I want to be. Living in the moment is not always such a great idea.

So what can I do? Do I make plans or not? And how far into the future can I plan? A week, a month, next year? And what about all this "live in the moment" stuff? Some "living in the moment" takes planning in the past, if you know what I mean. Airplane tickets are much more expensive if you try and buy them at the last minute. Some hotel reservations aren't available at the last minute. If I am not living in the moment in the middle of my root canal, am I in denial? In that situation, is denial a bad thing?

No. Denial is a defense mechanism human beings have developed over millions of years. Denial is a tool my mind uses to keep me from going crazy when everything around me is falling to pieces. It allows me to mentally go somewhere else in the worst of times. Living in the moment, at least for me, means concentrating on the best moments instead of thinking about cancer. I don't want to miss out on the experience of a trip to Disneyland because I'm thinking about the chemotherapy that won't happen until next week. It's terrible to be in the middle of a ride and discover that I'm missing all the fun because my mind is concentrating on how next month's CAT scan will make me feel, or what it will show.

But the truth is the thought of cancer will always intrude, even when I don't want it to. The reality is that I have cancer and I have decided to be treated for it. It takes time and energy, lots of time and a massive amount of energy. Even with this expenditure I may never be able to say that I have returned to "normal," whatever that was. I have a new "normal." In the future I hope to have another new "normal," one that is more like the normal I remember.

I don't have to think about the cancer all the time. Some whole hours go by when I don't think about it. My friend Bill, another cancer survivor, says he has whole weeks where it doesn't come into his mind. I hope to get to that point at sometime soon. (God give me patience, and I want it right now.)

The worst times for me have been the time between the CAT scans. The uncertainty was almost unbearable. I hate not knowing anything. I couldn't plan anything because I didn't have any information. I couldn't work because I couldn't concentrate on anything but the cancer. I hated the cancer for interrupting my life.

My first CAT scan was at three months after the end of my chemotherapy. My oncologist was looking for any change, any recurrence of the disease. I did the CAT scan and waited. I didn't get any information for several days. But I made myself busy. (Actually I was practicing the electric bass. I got a new bass guitar for Christmas. It's the first time I have played an instrument in public in forty years. But it was a distraction; something to worry about that had nothing to do with cancer. It was wonderful.)

I think that this may be the key to living with cancer. I know, this sounds like advice, but bear with me. Try to concentrate on the good times and ignore the bad times. Live in the present when the present is good and mentally duck out into the past when the present isn't so good. Don't miss out on opportunities to experience grandchildren, friends, places you have always wanted to go, or things you have always wanted to see when you are there, and when the bad moments come up, deny everything. At least until you have a plan for getting back to "normal," whatever that is.

On the old television show "Mash" there was a great line. A soldier who had seen terrible things in combat was in the hospital saying he was Jesus Christ. The doctors thought he was nuts, and he probably was. But his psychiatrist said,

"What's the harm? If I had a race horse who thought he was Man of War I'm not sure I'd want to convince him differently." Denial isn't always such a bad thing.

Some people are in denial most of the time. There are people who can't possibly finish, let alone win, the Hawaii Iron Man. They will go to Hawaii and try anyway. Each of them is sure that this time will be different. People who have no business singing try out for American Idol. People who shouldn't wear spandex clothing in public do. People who forget the punch lines try and tell jokes anyway. The chances of winning the Power-Ball Lottery are almost nonexistent, but people still buy tickets. Somebody has got to win sometime.

What has all this got to do with cancer? Somebody has got to be cured sometime or the medical people wouldn't bother with all the expensive treatment. If that's denial, so be it. Even if the odds are a million to one, somebody is winning against those odds, or the odds would be a million to zero. Why shouldn't the winner be me? Why not me? (My friend Mikey in Vegas pointed this out to me. He's an odds maker. He's right. Somebody has to win or there wouldn't be any odds.)

So do I make plans for the future? Sure. I assume that I will be able to go on vacation this summer just like every other year. Will I go? I can't know, yet. If I have to change the plans, I'll change the plans.

And that's the truth of the situation. I never actually had control of my life, not really. I appeared to have control, but I never really did. When things came up, I'd make changes in my vacation plans, and I said to myself, "Well, I guess I handled that." If I got the flu or a cold, I'd deal with it. If I got hit by a car or fell in a hole I'd change the plans. I only thought I had control of the future. I never really did. All the cancer diagnosis and treatment has done is point out my lack of control in my life. It puts this lack of control right up in my face. I can't ignore it.

So what should I do? Do nothing. Or do everything. Or something in between. Do what I might have done if I had never heard the word "Cancer." Nothing about my life has really changed, only the way I might look at the world has really changed. I will still go on vacation or not, go to lunch or not, drive to my appointments or not. Only now I realize that I may not really have control of my life.

My minister once said, "If you want to make God laugh, tell him your plans for the future." I guess this is true. So I am content making plans I might not be able to keep.

Lao Tze says, "Tao takes no action, but leaves nothing undone. When you accept this, your world will flourish in harmony with nature. Nature doesn't have desires. Without desires the heart becomes quiet. In this manner the whole world is made tranquil."

(Tao Te Ching, Chapter 37)

Chapter Twelve

Normal?

As soon as I began chemotherapy two things happened. First, I developed a monstrous sweet tooth. There couldn't be ice cream, cookies, or chocolate in the house. I would have to have some, sometimes a whole bag of cookies or carton of ice cream, even if I've just eaten a meal. The second is a pain in my left hip. Sometimes it still hurts and sometimes it doesn't. So I began to wonder, is the sweet tooth a result of the chemotherapy, or have I always had a sweet tooth? Is the pain in my hip a part of the cancer treatment or did it just happen? Or perhaps it was always there and I just noticed it because of all the other medical treatments. And what about the pain in my back? Is it because of the mattress I sleep on or is it part of the cancer?

Elizabeth Edwards, wife of presidential candidate John Edwards, and a cancer survivor once said, "You can't bang your hand against a door and get a bruise without wondering if it's the cancer coming back."

All through the process of surgery, recovery, chemotherapy, recovery, I've had the same question, "Is this normal?" Is it normal to be depressed? Is it normal to be sick during chemotherapy? Is it normal to lose hair? Is it normal to only want bland food, spicy food, or no food at all? Is it normal to have the tingling in my fingers and my toes? And the answer from the medical staff has usually been, "Yes, for some people, and no for others."

You and I are unique. According to Jerry Hirsh at the University of Illinois at Urbana-Champaign: "We estimated the probability that the second offspring born to parents will have exactly the same genotype as their firstborn to be less than one chance in over 70 trillion, because man, with twenty-three chromosome pairs, produces gametes with any of 8,388,608 alternative genomes."

(Uniqueness, Diversity, Similarity, Repeatability, and Heritability, page 127)

Genetically speaking, you are one out or 70 trillion unique combinations of genetic material even in your own family. So am I. Imagine the odds of two people who are not related being genetically the same. I have it on good

178

authority that there have not been 70 trillion people (Homo sapiens) who have ever lived on the earth cumulatively in the entire history of the earth. Not yet anyway. (We are headed that direction. There are six billion of us living here now.)

There are other scientists who dispute Dr. Hirsh's findings and there are historians and anthropologists who dispute the calculation of the number of people who have ever lived on earth. There are also people who think that cancer is nature's way of telling me that I'm boring and I should go away. I'm not really concerned with what any of these people think. I like Dr. Hirsh's number. It seems about right to me. What do I know? And I don't really care exactly how many have lived on the earth before me. Or how many will live here after I'm gone. I'm not leaving until I'm good and ready. This is my book and I can do what I want with it. But I digress.

Even if you are an identical twin, almost exactly genetically the same, your experiences, the things you know, the information you've retained would be different from anyone else, even your twin. Your fingerprints would be different, the people you like and the people you don't like would probably be different. Everything you've observed, touched, tasted, and come in contact with would be different than anyone else's experience, even a twin. Every feeling you have ever experienced, every notion you acted on, and every notion you didn't act on, all of these things make you unique.

So? What has any of this got to do with cancer?

If you and I really are this unique, one in seventy trillion, why wouldn't you and I have a unique and different reaction to chemotherapy, to radiation, or to the cancer itself? If each person has a different reaction, how can anything be normal? What is normal anyway? The next time my combination of genes comes around, in a couple of centuries or so there might be a "normal" for me, or maybe not. Besides, in a century or two, who is going to remember exactly what was normal for me?

So I might or might not become violently ill after chemotherapy or radiation. I might or might not have diarrhea, constipation, or both. (Isn't it exciting? I have a treatment that can give me constipation and diarrhea at the same time. There's an old curse: "May you live in exciting times." I'm beginning to understand why this is a curse.)

I might or might not lose my hair, (Actually, I didn't lose much hair, but I didn't have that much to lose) and it might or might not grow back exactly the way it looked before I started treatment. The color could be different, the texture will certainly be different, and it might or might not stay this way. The women in my group love this aspect of cancer treatment. The uncertainty of hair is more a problem for women I think. Men are usually aware that, if we live long enough, we will eventually lose our hair.

You might or might not be able to go back to work during your treatment. I couldn't. Some people in my group continue to work but most don't. For some people working is a form of therapy, something to take their minds off the treatment and give them a more normal life, whatever that is. For most of us the energy required to do the cancer treatment is what we would usually expend doing a job. Cancer becomes our job.

As far as I can determine, there is no exact standard from which to judge normal. Before the cancer diagnosis I hadn't ever considered this. I thought I was normal without ever having to consider what normal meant. Put another way, there is only a normal for you individually, something that you usually do or a way you usually feel. Your doctor isn't you, so he or she can't know exactly what's normal for you. When you ask if something is normal your doctor will probably give you an answer based on a statistical mid-point for the group called "cancer survivors." Statistics don't apply to individuals. Your doctor can't really tell you what's normal for you personally, only what usually happens in a large group of similar cases.

There are some things that are not normal. My chiropractor is fond of saying that continuing pain isn't normal. If you are in pain, and I mean any kind of pain that continues for more than one day, talk to your doctor. Your doctor wants this information. Besides, he or she may have something which will make the pain go away. I had several bouts of severe pain during my chemotherapy. It turned out that the port, the surgically implanted access to my blood system, may have caused blood clots to form. The clots were dangerous, they could have gone to my brain and caused a stroke or into my heart and lungs and killed me. And they hurt. This was something my oncologist wanted to know.

I had to go through another surgery to take out the old port and put in a new one. I also had to take a blood thinner, coumaden, to keep from getting the clots back. It's not something I liked doing, but it is something I needed to do. It made the pain go away. Fortunately, after the chemotherapy had ended, so did the coumaden.

There will be changes in your body and your habits. By definition, things that are changed are not the same as usual, out of the normal. This doesn't mean they are better or worse, just different. Make sure to tell you doctor about changes, especially any changes in your weight, eating habits, sleeping habits, or any different pains you experience. (Different pains, in this case, means pains that are new to you. If you've always had a pain in your shoulder when you garden, and you still have it, this isn't different.)

Half way through the chemotherapy treatments I began taking naps in the middle of the day. I had to, I was so tired I just couldn't stay awake. It was a choice of sleeping in a chair in the living room in front of the television or going into the bedroom and napping, and the bed's softer. It turns out my doctor expected me to take naps. He also expected me to take walks, but he didn't mention either of these things until he found out I was taking naps and not getting enough exercise.

You are going to change during this experience. Not just your habits, but also in your likes and dislikes. You might change what is normal for you. You might develop a new normal. You may also change what you believe about life and death. Cancer may bring up things you don't want to think about. That's the way it is. Sorry. Sometimes thinking about things we don't want to think about reinforces our attitudes, our religious beliefs get stronger, our relationships get better, our thoughts become clearer. Sometimes it makes bad things worse.

Either way, you are going to change. You can try to resist this, the change; act like everything is as it was. You can rail against the changes, complain to whoever will listen that it isn't fair that you have cancer and have to have surgery, chemotherapy, and or radiation. Or you can learn to expect changes and adapt to them as they happen. If I could tell you what was going to change I would, but nobody knows. Besides, what fun would that be?

Change happens. It always has. You may not have noticed it as much as you do now. Resistance is useless. Complaining won't help, it will just annoy your friends. As Plato the Greek Philosopher said, "When you fall into water over your head, whether by design or by accident, you will either swim or sink."

Cancer, among other things, brings clarity to many people. I've found this to be true in my support group. It made me think about what I really wanted and what I superficially wanted. Did I really want to go crab fishing in

Alaska, or was this one of those things that I'd thought about but was never actually going to do? What about sky diving? I'd talked about it, but did I really want to do it or not? Did I really want to spend the time to learn to play the electric guitar or was this just a fantasy?

Having the cancer diagnosis helped me cut through a lot of this "stuff." I have always kept a list of the things I've wanted to do, a kind of a life list. When I got the cancer diagnosis and thought I might die, I went through the list and crossed out those things that weren't that important. It was kind of like a closet cleaning. Most of the things on my list, things that were important before the cancer diagnosis, I now crossed off as unimportant.

Some of the results of the cancer diagnosis and treatment weren't bad. (This is sacrilege to those who are fighting cancer. For them, everything connected with cancer is evil.) Some of the results of the cancer treatment were good in fact. Certainly not as good as the cancer was bad, but the treatment did have some good side effects.

North Americans (and I mean Canadians and Mexicans as well as those of us in the United States) tend to "retain" things. Momentos, pictures, things we have collected, things we don't even need, gifts we've been given that we don't even like, but they were gifts, so we keep them. Clutter. My life was cluttered with stuff. Then I got a cancer diagnosis, and I started to unclutter my life. Uncluttering is good.

Lao Tze says: "It's easy to carry an empty a cup. It's harder to carry one that's all the way full. The sharper the knife is the easier it will be to make it dull. The more money you have the harder it is to protect. Pride brings on its own troubles.

When you complete your task, whatever it is, just walk away. This is the pathway to Heaven."

(Tao Te Ching: Chapter 9)

A good thing happened while I was on chemotherapy; my psoriases cleared up. I have always had itchy skin. Recently I found out psoriases is an autoimmune disease. When the chemotherapy suppressed my immune system the psoriasis went away. Of course when I stopped the chemo, it came back, but for a while I didn't have to worry about itchy skin. Some of the changes were good and some were bad.

Most of the good things are little things, but little things can make a big difference when you're dealing with cancer.

"Stop worrying so much and let your problems go. What difference does it really make if you answer a question yes or no? What difference does it make to your life if you succeed or a fail at a task? Must you have the same values as everyone else? Do you have to avoid everything other people avoid? That's ridiculous."

(Tao Te Ching, chapter 20)

Chapter Thirteen

Support Groups

I've mentioned my support group several times, but I haven't really explained what support is. My friend Bill Clarkson had a sign in his office: "Support is raising another person to the level of his or her own expectations." Sometimes support can be agreeing with someone, sometimes it is arguing against them, and sometimes it can be a swift kick in the butt. Most people don't really know what support is, so they don't know what to expect from a support group.

There are actually four support groups that I currently belong to. Two of them are cancer related, one is a group of writers who read and critiqued this book, and one is a youth group that I mentor at my church. The youth group is made up of teenagers who can spot a phony a mile away. They keep me honest.

The two cancer support groups are very different from the other groups, as well as different from each other.

One group, the colon cancer survivors group, is an informational group. All of us have a similar cancer and are getting a similar treatment. We talk about the latest treatments for colon cancer, the side effects of our particular chemotherapy, in my case Folfox Six and Avastin. We can talk about any new treatments we have seen or heard about, the various medical plans we belong to and the problems these programs can create, any clinical trials or other information that would be useful in our treatment.

My other group includes cancer survivors with several types of cancer. For some reason the Wellness Community refers to it as the Participants' Group. It is an emotional support group rather than an informational support group. I have always had a hard time opening up to anyone. Guys don't talk about their problems to other guys, or to anybody else. (See "Men are from Mars, Women are from Venus. It's a really good explanation of the differences.) But one of the problems I have in talking to people who are not currently involved in cancer, either as a survivor or as the support person for a survivor, is that most people don't know what to say.

"Well," they'll say after I tell them about the cancer, "you'll be okay." Really? My oncologist doesn't know that.

I don't know that. How can somebody else know that? I usually just walk away from this comment without saying anything. They mean well, but it is frustrating. Most of the people who have this kind of comment don't really want to know what I am going through.

Or someone will say something like, "I had an uncle that had the same kind of cancer you have and he died a painful and horrible death." (I've said this before, but it needs repeating.) Not in those words, of course, but this is the idea they communicated. Why do people outside of the cancer group think we need to hear the worst possible outcomes? Is this helpful? I'm already worried about what this will do to my life and they're contributing to the worry. (Worry is telling myself a story about the future that has a bad outcome. Worrying isn't helpful.)

Early on in my treatment my oncologist told me that there are several kinds of cancer that can be present in a colon. He said even he couldn't tell what kind of cancer I had without looking at it in a microscope. The problem is that "colon cancer" isn't a kind of cancer, it's a location where the cancer is. Before the 1930's, physicians could identify cancer, but they couldn't do much about it. There was no treatment, except for surgery, which only worked for some cancers and was always risky. So they identified the cancer by its location; colon cancer, breast cancer, liver cancer.

Now there are things that can be done for specific types of cancer located in parts of the body, but we still refer to it as "colon cancer." "What your uncle had may or may not have anything to do with what I have, other than location," I want to say to them. But I don't. It would be rude, and at least they are trying to connect with me.

To be fair, I never used to know what to say to someone who announces that he has had cancer either. What I'm thinking is, "I'm glad it's not me." But I couldn't say that. So I would usually say something like, "Is there anything I can do?"

People, we, don't know what to say, and it's not our fault. When I realized that they are as afraid of cancer as I am, I realized that they are doing the only thing they could to protect themselves. They are relating whatever story they have about cancer, and most of these stories don't have a happy ending.

Which brings up one of the questions my group has talked about since I have been a member. Who do you tell about your cancer, when do you tell them, and why? I don't want to burden people with my disease, as one person said,

"Drop the cancer bomb on them." On the other hand, I want to be the one who tells people, I don't want any of my friends to find out from someone else and think I was keeping something from them. I don't intend my disease to be a secret. On the other hand, I don't want it broadcast on the evening news either.

One of my friends has a blog, an online news report, which his wife writes. Anytime there is a change, she writes on it to tell whoever is interested what the change is and how he is feeling. It's a great idea. The most annoying part of cancer is having to repeat the same information over and over to people. I have to keep telling myself that it may be the twelfth time I've told it, but it is the first time they have heard it.

I decided to tell anyone who was going to find out anyway. I told my church because I am on the prayer list. If I didn't tell them, they might make up something worse. I told my family. I told my wife Elaine's family. I told our neighbors. Not only what kind of cancer I had, but what I was doing about it, and the side effects of the treatments. I also gave the people around me permission to talk about my cancer to others. I don't care who knows. But you might.

If you think this news is going to affect your life adversely, don't tell anybody. But realize that keeping a secret, especially one this big, is hard work. It takes a lot of energy that you might use to recover. Sometimes it's better to talk about cancer, get it out in the open, and let people think what they want. They are going to think what they want anyway.

The members of my group, who are called the "participants," are all cancer patients, although, in my group, our facilitator is a clinical psychologist. My support group is a place where I can be completely open, where I don't have to worry about looking foolish or being ridiculed for what I say. These are people I can trust to listen to me and keep my secrets. We are all at different stages of our treatment. But our group is not about pity.

Sympathy sometimes, but specifically not pity. My group is not particularly sympathetic to pity of any kind. Most of us don't want to receive it and we don't give it out. Each of us understands that we are probably going through one of the most stressful time of our lives. A cancer diagnosis from out of the blue, and most of them are out of the blue (nobody plans on having cancer) is impactful. It's like being hit in the back of the head with a shovel. It hurts. I don't need them to say, "Poor you. We feel so bad. Why is the world treating you this way?" There's enough of that already. All of us are going through the same sort of thing. Poor us. Why is the world picking on us?"

No. Not poor us. We have a disease, it does not have us. We can get through this one way or another. That's what my support group reinforces for me every time I go there. There is an end and I am not alone. I don't live alone, and when I die, I won't die alone. (Although I will be the only one dying. It is a contradiction.)

In my support group I can say almost anything and the people around me will have had, or are about to have, a similar experience. Nobody is obligated to agree with me, and many times they don't. In fact some of the best conversations we have had are when there is a difference of opinion about a specific subject. Support does not mean agreeing with. But most of the people in my cancer support groups have gone through or will be going through a similar experience. Some are just starting, some are in the middle, and some are finishing treatment. All of us share this common experience. All of us have similar anger, fears, and doubts.

My wife is also in a support group for care providers. My group has always assumed that providing care for someone with cancer is harder than actually having the disease. At least we, the participants, are doing something actively to get rid of the cancer. All my wife can do is transport me to and from, listen to the doctor, and wait. Her job is much harder than mine.

The supporters' group meets at the same time my group meets, but they meet in another room. (Actually they meet in the next room. Sometimes we can hear them laughing and we wonder who they are laughing at.) I don't know exactly what they say there, but I imagine they talk about us the same way we talk about them.

In addition to improving confidence, overall well-being, quality of life, and relieving stress, cancer support groups are actually being studied for their effect on improving the long-term survival rates of the survivors who attend them. (A survivor is anyone who has been diagnosed with cancer and is not dead. If you have a cancer diagnosis and you are reading this book, congratulations, you are a survivor. Good. Keep it that way.)

Most cancer patients I have met feel, in some ways, isolated. We are not as engaged as we once were with our jobs, our friends, or our families. Although some people can work through their treatment, most of us cannot. We must take disability leave or quit our jobs in order to treat the cancer. Our families want to help us. My wife and I had a big fight during my treatment. She wanted to help me and I didn't want any help. "I'm sick," I shouted, "Not disabled." She was trying to help, but she didn't know what to do. The isolation can be debilitating.

Talking about how you feel helps. Talking with people who understand the isolation, people who are experiencing it themselves is liberating. Letting whatever comes out, come out without worrying about the consequences is amazing. That is what my support group does for me.

There is a new field of study called Psycho-Neuro-Immunology sometimes referred to on the net as Psycho-Oncology. These two are not exactly the same, but they are close enough for those of us who are not health care professionals can think of them as the same. Although there seems to be a great deal of debate among doctors about this, the idea that having a good attitude, not being in pain or stressed out all the time, directly effects the immune system seems reasonable to me. The Wellness Community, the organization that hosts my cancer support groups, is set up specifically along the lines suggested by Psycho-Neuro-Immunology.

The issue of mind-immune system links is still up in the air. There are medical professionals, good people and I assume good doctors as well, who have opinions on both sides of the issue. For me there is no question, belonging to a group has made a difference in my attitude toward treatment, my quality of life, and my overall wellbeing. My wife, Elaine, also seems less stressed by my cancer and what it might mean to her. The groups are of value to us.

But there are still people who will not consider joining a group. "I can do this alone," they will think, or "I don't want or need anybody's support." It is not possible to do a cancer treatment without anyone's help or support, not if you plan to survive it. Even the best oncologist will have to have some help. I just can't see a doctor trying to do everything involved in a cancer treatment himself. If he doesn't, why should you? You didn't create this situation. It is what it is. Yield to the situation.

Lao Tze says: "Water is the softest and most yielding substance on earth. But nothing is better than water for overcoming the hard and rigid, because nothing can hold it contained forever. Everyone knows this; the soft and yielding overcomes the rigid and hard. But most people aren't able to put this knowledge into practice.

Therefore the Master says: "Only the one who is the lowest servant is worthy of becoming its ruler. The one who is willing to take on the most unpleasant jobs is the best ruler in the world.

True things often seem paradoxical."

(Tao Te Ching Chapter 78)

Chapter Fourteen

Quality of Life

This chapter deals with the quality of life and death. You may not be ready to think about death. That's OK. Just skip this chapter for now and go somewhere else in the book. If you are really not ready to think about death, take a nap or go for a walk. Do something you really enjoy. It is never necessary to think about death, but some planning will help those you leave behind.

The truth is this: everybody dies.

Death is one of the issues that comes up constantly in my support group, at least partially because we lose people from our group. Being born is a terminal disease, nobody gets out alive. But most people don't want to think about dying, even though it is something we will all do. "But not right now. Some time in the future," they say. "I'll think about it when I'm old."

Being diagnosed with cancer brought the idea of death right up into my face. I couldn't escape it, I couldn't hide from it. Nobody that I know wants to die, I surely don't, and so I didn't want to think about it. But there it was.

There was a letter to God written by a young boy. "Dear God," it said, "What is it like when you die? I don't want to do it, I just want to know. Sincerely, Bobby." There it is. We all want to know, but none of us wants to go through it.

Ron, the facilitator of my support group, once asked, "Suppose I told you exactly when, where and under what circumstances you would die. Would you really want to know? What would you do differently?"

I had to think about this for a long time. If I knew I was going to die, would I start doing the things I've always wanted to do or would I decide to skip those things which are unimportant and concentrate on important things I want to get done, like finishing this book? Would I spend more time with my family and friends or travel more? Would I eat more? Look for exotic foods that I've always wanted to try? Bungy jump? Sky dive? Go crab fishing in Alaska? Drive my car fast on the freeway? (Well, faster anyway.)

I asked my group this question. That's what a group is for, to ask questions that don't have exact answers. Several people volunteered their thoughts. Most of us would concentrate on important things and leave the unimportant things undone. "But if you know that you are going to die sometime, why would you do any unimportant things at all? Everyone knows he or she is going to die, but we spend our time on trivial things anyway. Why is that?" Ron sometimes asks hard questions.

I don't know the answer. I wish I did. There's a sign in my favorite wine store, "Life's too short to drink bad wine." I always thought it was funny, but now I'm starting to think it's true. If we are all really going to die, why are there so many bad television shows being watched, so many bad movies being viewed, so many bad video games being played? Why do we waste so much time on meaningless things, things that don't even make us happy? Why not concentrate our lives on the necessary things and let go of the trivial?

I've always wanted to know how to play the electric bass guitar. Not just plunk on the strings but really play it. And I got one, as a gift from my brother, for Christmas. So, instead of watching meaningless television in the evening I practice the guitar. I'm not sure I will ever be ready to play in a group or in public. (Although my guitar-playing friend Will seems to have other plans. Sometimes support is a swift kick in the butt, remember?) But practicing the guitar makes me happy. On the Internet are sessions with Eric Clapton, Bon Jovi, and other people I want to play with. It's great.

When St. Francis was asked what he would do if he knew he was going to die tomorrow, he is supposed to have said, "Continue hoeing my garden." That's always seemed a strange answer. He'd continue doing something that wouldn't yield any results in the immediate future. And yet if that's what made him the happiest, why not?

If I knew I was going to die, would I have done all the things I wanted to do in this lifetime? Probably not. Someone once said, "When you die there will still be things in your in-box." It's true. There's nothing I can do about it. (Except live forever, of course. This is a wonderful alternative and makes things much simpler.)

If jumping out of a perfectly good airplane and falling toward the earth held up only by a flimsy piece of nylon would make you happy, why not try it? If riding a motorcycle to Montana makes you the happiest you have ever been, why not do that? You could get killed, but you have cancer, so you know that you will die eventually anyway. The cancer survivors I know seem to waste less time than some of the other people I know. If they walk, they walk purposefully. If they eat, they enjoy eating.

Now I'm not recommending the taking of stupid risks or do anything life changing just for the sake of taking risks. And I'm not recommending abandoning your family or your responsibilities. Think about what you are doing. Don't jump out of a plane without a parachute. Don't drive your motorcycle excessively fast if your brakes aren't working. Don't start your skiing lessons on the master hill; start on the beginner's slope like everybody else. I'm not saying go out and kill yourself just because you are dying anyway, that would be stupid. Remember that somebody survived or there wouldn't be any odds of survival at all. And although I firmly believe that there is an afterlife after this life, there's always this nagging thought that I have been wrong before.

What this all leads to is this; either you have cancer or cancer has you. Most of the time during my treatment I had cancer, and I had a life. I tried not to let the cancer interfere with my life. But there were times when it didn't feel like I had a life. Then cancer had me. Then the thoughts would descend on my mind like the fog on a dark night.

What is it like to die? And when will I die? Under what conditions?

I don't think most people are really afraid of dying. Some are. For some people the word "dying" is as loaded as the word "cancer." But it's not the actual dying that scares me. Dying a prolonged, painful death scares me. And dying with all these things unfinished doesn't sit well with me either. I can't imagine what people with small children must go through.

One of the people in our group suggested that people fear dying without being known. That his children might only remember him as a father and not a person. Someone else suggested that dying without ever having the chance to make amends for bad actions was the real fear.

When will I die? And under what conditions? Who knows? Not me, that's for sure, especially in the middle of the night.   I'm not sure I want to know exactly when I am going to die. It upsets me when medical people say things like, "You have six months." How do they know? Are doctors God? They gave my friend Scott ten months to live, that was a year ago and he's still alive now. His tumor has shrunken and he's enjoying his family on vacation as I write this chapter. I hope he will be for many years to come, but I can't know that he will.

My friend Bill Clarkson has mouth cancer. He also has kind of a dark sense of humor. When we ran into each other at the at the Wellness Community he asked, "How do you know that you are not going to die of cancer?"

"I don't know. How?" I asked.

"When you die of something else."

It's true. Just because you and I are going through the cancer "experience" doesn't exempt us from being hit by a bus, or falling off a roof. We are the same as everyone else, we could die at any time. There's nothing special about dying, everybody does it. Living is something else entirely. There's an old saying, "Dying is easy, living is hard."

There is also a difference between being alive and living. Bacteria are alive; they breathe and eat, excrete, and try to reproduce. That's all there is to life. Microbes do it, chickens do it, and in the deepest sea there are creatures that exist on the hot water flowing out of vents in the ocean bottom. These creatures are alive. People are alive and we live. We have expectations, make plans, and have dreams. We want more. I want more. I want more life.

But suppose my quality of life takes a turn for the worst? Is there a time when I might want to bail out? Yes, for me there is. I have no desire to be hooked to a machine, unable to eat or breathe or excrete by myself. That could be called life, but it's not living. If I were locked in a small room and kept alive solely for the purpose of continuing to exist, I'm not sure I would want to continue to live. Being locked in my brain without being able to communicate, for me, is Hell.

There might also be other cases for discontinuing life. My mother died of ovarian cancer. She had done the chemotherapy treatments for nearly three years and had seen no positive results. After her last treatment she called us all into her hospital room and said, "I've had enough. I'm going home. This is not negotiable. I am not going to feel sick for six months so that I can feel good for three days. It's not worth it." And she packed her bag and went home. It was a very brave thing to do, and we, her children, (for the most part) respected her wishes. We didn't argue with her.

She died a week after leaving the hospital. She waited for my brother in Washington D.C. to fly out so she could say good-by to him, and then she went to sleep and didn't wake up. It was a brave decision and one I hope I will not have to make. But I could. And I have thought about it.

This is not an issue to think about when you are depressed. I say that, knowing that it is exactly the kind of idea I came up with in the middle of my chemotherapy. I had no way of knowing if the chemotherapy was working, it was making me sick, I couldn't go outside in the sun because of the chemicals, I wasn't eating regularly, and I was depressed. This is when I thought most about my death.

What is the purpose of living? What do I want out of life? And how do I want to exit this life? What things can I do without and what things do I have to have in order to continue living? At one time I thought I had to have my health. This turned out not to be true. I don't need to be as healthy and active as I was at twenty, which is a good thing, because I'm not twenty anymore. I thought food was important, but I lived without the pleasure of food for several months during the chemotherapy treatments. I ate, but there wasn't much taste to the food.

Chemotherapy wasn't, for me, a pleasurable experience, but I survived. I guess I will have to make choices about the future in the future, on a case by case basis.

During my vacation to celebrate the end of my chemotherapy treatments, I saw this on the dining room wall at the home of a friend of mine. (Craig rides motorcycles in his retirement. He and I talk bikes once and a while.)

The sign said: Life is not a journey to the grave with the intention of arriving safely in a pretty and well preserved body, but rather to skid in broadside, thoroughly used up, totally wrung out, and proclaiming "Wow, what a ride!"

I agree. Sitting around mourning your lack of life is killing what life you have left. What a waste.

Lao Tze asks, "Esteem or honor, which is more important to you? Money or happiness, which is more valuable? Success or failure, is one more destructive that the other?

If you look to other people for fulfillment, you can never truly be fulfilled. If your happiness depends on your possessions, no matter how much you have, you will never be happy.

Be content with what you have and enjoy life the way it is. When you realize there is nothing missing, the whole world belongs to you."

(Tao Te Ching, Chapter 44)

Chapter Fifteen

Health Care Crisis

I believe human beings may be the most arrogant creatures in the universe. "If you would just do as I say and believe what I tell you, your life would turn out so much better," we advise. Sometimes it sounds like this; "Here's what I would do." We tell everyone else; choose the government we believe in and choose it in the way we think is best. Eat what we think is the best food. Drink what we think is the best drink. Do what we tell you to do. (Not even "do as we do." Do what we tell you to do. We know better than you do how to live your life.)

When I began telling people I had cancer someone actually asked me, "Have you been saved?" I wanted to shout, "What the hell do you mean? What business is it of yours? Leave me alone, I have cancer. I have enough to worry about without your meddling in what I believe!"

But I didn't. It wouldn't have done either of us any good and there is a downside to that kind of response. Everyone I know, including myself, is arrogant. We all think our way of dealing with life is the best way. (If we didn't each believe we were living the best way we would change the way we live. Logical?) It's the best way to get through life.

I think the arrogance of adults starts in childhood. Adults tell children what to do without explanation. My father was slightly different. He told us, "If I yell get out of the street, I want you to get out of the street right now. If you want to know why I said it, come and ask me after you are out of the street." And he would usually explain that there was a truck coming or that he had seen something else dangerous that we hadn't seen. But at least he usually explained his decisions. "Just do it because I say so," isn't much of a reason.

What's this have to do with cancer, you ask? Our country (The United States of America) is in a health care crisis. I don't know how anyone would begin a cancer treatment without insurance. (47 million people did not have health coverage in 2006, up from 44.8 million in 2005. I have no idea what the current economy has done to these numbers, but it can't be good.)

I was fortunate. I am a member of Kaiser Permanente, one of the largest health maintenance organizations in the United States. I don't know what I would have done without them. Kaiser is one of the organizations that really wants someone to find a cure for cancer and every other major illness. They make their money by keeping their members healthy, not by providing expensive medical care. The perfect result for Kaiser would be for each of their members to pay for health care and for each of them to be well enough not to need it. I think most health care professionals would agree. It's easier to treat someone with a minor illness than it is to treat cancer.

As I say, I am fortunate. Everyone in this country isn't insured. In fact many people in this country are without insurance. And some people with insurance aren't covered for one of the most expensive treatments they will ever have because their organizations want to exclude "pre-existing conditions."

I happen to be part of a genetic study at a major university medical center. They are looking for a link between a specific gene and certain cancers. And they are careful because if they find a definite link between a cancer and a gene, the people with that gene might be excluded from health care coverage, employment, or other activities that they might want to participate in.

In the United States we have at least thought about genetic research and some of its consequences. Our government has passed, and the president has signed, a law that should make this kind of exclusion illegal. Unfortunately there have been laws against discrimination because of age, sex, marital status, and race for many years, and some people still discriminate. Will genetic discrimination happen? Probably. Some people just don't get it. Some people never will.

There's another issue I want you to think about. Heroin is the most effective painkiller ever invented for human beings. It is so good that it addicts almost everyone who uses it. So why would someone voluntarily use heroin? Could someone's life be so painful, seem so futile that they would need the most powerful painkiller ever invented just to get from one day to the next? They must feel some kind of pain; mental, physical, emotional, and want it to go away. They want to feel better. They want to escape. Who doesn't want to feel better sometimes?

Addiction is bad. But the idea that a seventy-nine year old man with end stage cancer can't use heroin because he might become an addict, get out of his bed, and steal my television set to support his habit it just ridiculous. This isn't a new thought. I have heard this from several knowledgeable people over the years, but nothing has been done to correct the situation. Our government is so afraid of heroin that it is on the "A" list, which prevents medical professionals from prescribing it or even testing it to see what medical benefits it might have. And this is not the only drug on that list.

Marijuana is also used to self-medicate pain and it is also illegal. Chris Rock is right, we are putting people in jail for getting high. We are spending millions of dollars for prisons and guards that could better be used for schools, fixing roads, perhaps even setting up treatment programs for people who's lives are so bad that they think they have to take a painkiller to survive life.

I grew up in the sixties near Berkeley California, so I have seen the results of recreational drug use. Friends have died either directly or indirectly from drug use. It's a tragedy, but it should not be a reason to prevent a doctor and a patient from using these drugs as an effective treatment, if the doctor and the patient agree to do so. Heroin and marijuana are effective. If they didn't work people wouldn't want to use them, there wouldn't be a law against their use, and there wouldn't be a problem. There's no law against smoking crabgrass. It won't accomplish anything, so nobody does it.

In California we have a law which allows the use of marijuana for relief of certain symptoms, especially cancer and glaucoma. If you've ever smoked marijuana or been around someone who has you will realize two things. First, for most people it is calming. You won't worry much while you're under its effects. And secondly you will be hungry while you are under the influence and for a time after.

The most dramatic effects of chemotherapy and radiation are usually loss of sleep, nausea, and weight loss. Marijuana will definitely help you sleep. There are pills for nausea, but if you are throwing up you can't keep the pills down to halt the throwing up. Taking the active ingredient in marijuana, THC, in pill form doesn't always work either. It's still a pill and your stomach is still rejecting anything that comes into it. But marijuana cigarettes are inhaled. The active chemicals enter your blood stream through your lungs, so your stomach doesn't have to cope with anything to get the benefits.

There are side effects to marijuana. I don't care what the Humboldt County growers say, anything you inhale will damage your lungs eventually. Smoke can cause cancer in your lungs. Any smoke. Cigarette or cigar smoke, smoke from air pollution, smoke in the air at your place of work, any smoke. For most people this alone should be enough to keep them from using marijuana. But I already have cancer. While I certainly don't want any other cancer starting, I want to use the most effective treatment available to get rid of this one, even if it makes me nauseous.

And if I were to go into a hospice program, I would want the most powerful pain and nausea relievers I could get, with the least amount of side effects. The Ninth Amendment says I should be able, with a doctor's oversight, to put whatever I want into my own body. "The enumeration in the Constitution, of certain rights, shall not be construed to deny or disparage others retained by the people."

(United States Constitution – Ninth Amendment)

This should include experimental medications, apricot pits, things that have not been approved by the Food and Drug Administration, Holistic medications, herbs, shark cartilage, beetles, yak dung, whatever. If I were dying I should be considered to be in a special class of people who are allowed to do whatever they think will work to relieve the pain or cure the illness, and hang the consequences.

There's the rub. The laws of the United States don't allow for a special class of people. This is called discrimination. If end stage cancer patients can use drugs to ease pain, why shouldn't people who live in constant pain, say people who can't walk because of a back or hip injury? What about people in psychological pain? What about people who have mental pain from stress at their jobs? If one "special group" can use marijuana or heroin why shouldn't all other special groups? And why limit its use to special groups? Why not everybody?

The National Organization for the Reform of Marijuana Laws insists that everybody should be able to smoke marijuana. Their mission statement says: "NORML's mission is to move public opinion sufficiently to achieve the repeal of marijuana prohibition so that the responsible use of cannabis by adults is no longer subject to penalty."

(Adopted by the NORML Board of Directors,
February 27, 1999)

There is evidence that regular smoking of marijuana kills brain cells and may cause mental aberrations, so I don't believe it should be legalized, just decriminalized. So what's my solution?

Suppose a person who was arrested for possession of a controlled substance (Heroin, Cocaine, Marijuana, etc.) was brought before a board of a police officer, a judge, and a psychiatrist. These are people who would be directly connected to the legal system specializing in use and sale of illegal drugs. These would be the most likely people to judge the facts of the presentations. Suppose while at this board the person who wanted the drugs had to prove, to the board's satisfaction, that his life was so painful it didn't matter what the law was, he was going to use drugs.

If he could prove this, the panel would issue him a prescription for his drugs, which he would fill at the local drug store just like any other prescription. The government could provide these drugs to the pharmacy at a slight profit to make money to support treatment programs for addicts.

What might the consequences of this be? The price of what are now illicit drugs would go down because obtaining things illegally costs more than obtaining things legally. Those who are addicted to these drugs wouldn't have to commit crimes in order to support their habits. They could get jobs like regular people. They couldn't do some jobs;

drive trains or taxis, work as healthcare professionals, or join the army. But a heroin addict can work as a waitress or a cook. Alcoholic addicts do these jobs all the time, usually without incident, and usually unnoticed.

This isn't a panacea. The Swiss, who are more tolerant than almost anybody in Europe except possibly the Dutch, decriminalized Heroin by agreement. They didn't change the laws; they just looked the other way. And there is now a park that, again by agreement, is a place where junkies would go to get and inject drugs. Every week the park becomes unusable by the average citizen. There was human filth, needles, cotton, and other drug paraphernalia scattered on the ground. The Swiss are reconsidering the policy.

The Swiss, as a people, tend to be very conscious of their living space and the idea of this kind of filth offends the average citizen. It would offend me. A park is not a place to do drugs. If we were to decriminalize drug use, there ought to be heavy fines for public intoxication and heavier fines for littering. Or we could establish a place where drugs are injected and charge a licensing fee as part of the price of the drugs.

In addition, the addicts would have to have regular monitoring to make sure that they were using all the drugs they were buying. This is not a program to increase the number of people addicted to drugs; it is an idea on decreasing the numbers of addicts and the number of people that we are paying to keep in prisons.

Now, if this were to go into effect, someone who robs you is a robber and should go to jail. The person who beats up other people is a thug. A person who steals is a thief. The person who kills is a murderer. They should all go to jail. No more excuse about having to support a three hundred-dollar a day heroin habit.

In addition, the gang problem should go away. If what were illicit drugs are sold at a drug store for a fixed price, there's no money to be made selling drugs on the street. When's the last time you heard about street dealers selling Exlax or Claritin? No drug money, no drug gangs.

And there wouldn't be any reason for an addict to hang around a schoolyard and sell drugs to children. What would be the point? There wouldn't be any money in recruiting new addicts. The drugs would be available to those who are addicted, but not to everyone, so someday the society might become drug free or at least the rate of drug addiction should eventually go down.

There might even be money in our government's budget to find out why someone's life is so bad that they have to use a powerful anesthetic to escape from it. We might be able to treat the problems in the society instead of trying to convert junkies to a new habit. "Do as I say and you will feel better" is not a solution to life problems.

End stage cancer patients who are in real pain should finally get whatever effective drugs they want and need. The prison population should go down. Drug gangs might go away, both here and in the supplying countries. Violence should go down as the need to support a thousand-dollar a day habit ended. And drugs would be seen for what they are; not sheik, not party material, and just an unfortunate habit that takes away the pain of life. All of these would be good things so it will probably never happen. Government doesn't seem to understand its place in a civilized society.

Lao Tze says: "When you use the Tao to conquer the world, all life's demons will lose their power to hurt you. Not that they lose their powers, but that they will lose the power to hurt anyone. Because they can not hurt anyone, you won't be able to hurt anyone either. When neither you nor your demons hurt anyone, not even yourself, you will be at peace.

(Tao Te Ching, Chapter 60)

And about government interventions Lao Tze says: "When taxes are too high many children go hungry. When the government is too intrusive the people will lose their vitality. Any government should act for the people's benefit. Trust the people: leave them alone."

(Tao Te Ching, chapter 75)

Chapter Sixteen

What Works?

Once a Tao master and his students stopped for their daily meal. As soon as they had all quieted, the master stood up, faced the north and clicked his chopsticks together three times. He repeated this action to the west, south, and east. Then he sat down.

"Master?" one of the students asked, "Why do you do that? You have never done it before."

"It is to keep tigers away," he answered. "The people in this village do this each time they eat a meal."

"But Master, there have never been tigers in this village. There aren't even any tigers in this province."

"See how well it works?" The master smiled and began to eat his rice.

"But Master, aren't the villagers just superstitious fools? This action won't keep away tigers. Even if it did, there aren't any tigers. Why would you do this?"

"If you do something to keep away tigers and no tigers appear, how do you know it doesn't work?"

My oncologist is not a big fan of vitamin pills and supplements. He says Americans have the most expensive urine of any people on the planet. He has said that if we would eat healthy foods we wouldn't need all the pills. He is probably right. But vitamin pills seem to keep away tigers, so who knows.

There are people who have recommended all sorts of Homeopathic and herbal nutritional supplements and rubs to me. Most of them smell bad, but most seem harmless and might help. Some are more expensive and don't seem to work for me at all. Maybe it is just me. These things must work for a number of people or the manufacturers would eventually stop making them. For some people homeopathic medicine keeps the tigers away.

There are people who recommended acupuncture for the treatment of my neuropathy. The cancer chemicals (Folfox 6) caused my fingers and toes to become numb and hypersensitive at the same time. If you don't have neuropathy this description makes no sense at all. If you have it I don't have to explain. My fingers and toes are not just numb, but tingling and painful too. It is difficult to explain

223

this to anyone who has not had the sensation, even my doctor. I had a hard time walking because I couldn't tell exactly where my feet were landing. I couldn't drive because I had no brake feel. I couldn't tell if I had picked up one pill or two pills without looking at my fingers. I loaded two CDs into my player most of the time because I couldn't feel the difference between one CD and two.

Someone in one of my groups suggested acupuncture. Fortunately my HMO is very progressive and has an acupuncture clinic, so I went. By the final treatment I certainly felt the needles in my fingertips and toes. The treatment took six weeks and I will never know if the results came from the needles or the six weeks. I don't really care. I can feel with my fingertips again. I still have troubles with my toes sometimes, but I can drive.

One of the people I know had a stem cell transplant. Her neuropathy was so bad that she dropped an iron on her foot and didn't feel it at all. Her toes swell up and turned dark blue and black, so she had to go to the hospital for several days to have her foot treated. Would acupuncture have helped her? I have no idea. But I recommended it to her because there aren't any tigers anywhere near my feet.

One of my friends gave me a sample of colloidal minerals. These are minerals dissolved in a solution, which is supposed to make them more accessible to a human digestive system. They also contain some rare minerals, like gold, which aren't usually available in multivitamin tablets. He said it helped him feel better after the chemotherapy. He told me that the trace minerals are usually washed out of our systems by the massive amounts of liquids we use to wash out the chemotherapy chemicals. I know that good things are washed out by the large quantities of water I was drinking after chemotherapy, so I took his suggestion and, as time passed, I felt better. Did the trace minerals help? I don't really know. Would I recommend you try colloidal minerals? Absolutely.

I also began taking glucosimine, MSM, and condroitin for my joints. One of the side effects of chemotherapy for me was a lack of energy. I knew that I should exercise, walk, move, but I just didn't want to. My joints hurt, along with almost everything else. And I couldn't take most painkillers because of the blood thinners I was taking.

There are scientific studies that support glucosimine and condroitin for joint health, and I felt better taking the pills than I did when I wasn't taking them. Does it work for everybody? No. Would I recommend it to you? Sure. As my oncologist says, if it can't hurt you, and it might make you feel better, try it.

There are many kinds of treatments, remedies, and procedures out there. Some of them have been tested in clinical trials but many have not. Some seem reasonable and some sound outright stupid. At one time people were taking shark cartilage because the rumor was that sharks didn't get cancer. I don't know if sharks get cancer or not, but the shark cartilage craze came and went. I can't find a report of anyone dying because of it. I also can't find anyone who was cured by it. Apparently it made some people feel better.

There are clinical studies underway all over the country testing out new cancer treatments. The main purpose of these clinical trials is to find a better way to prevent or treat cancer. Clinical trials are one part of a long, careful research process. People who participate in a clinical trial usually receive a drug or procedure that already has been researched in successful laboratory and/or animal studies. Most clinical trials study new drugs or procedures, but some study existing drugs to use in a new way. People who participate in clinical trials are volunteers, and they can choose to stop their participation in a clinical trial at any time. Most of today's standard cancer treatments, treatments that are accepted and widely used by medical experts, are based on the results of previous clinical trials. The information about clinical trials is usually available on the Internet. Your oncologist may also have information about clinical trials. Most of these trials have specific requirements; specific cancers in specific stages and locations. But there are so many of them that might work, you might want to find one and sign up.

But what about totally untested treatments?

When Steve McQueen developed cancer in the lining of his lungs, the doctors in the United States told him there wasn't anything they could do about it. So he went to Mexico, to a clinic that had a radical treatment which was not approved in this country. It didn't work for him, he died of the cancer, but he had the right to try it. If your doctors are telling you there's nothing they can do, what do you have to lose? Try something radical if it sounds to you like it might work.

Now this is NOT a recommendation that you start out your treatment with an unapproved and untested procedure. Medical science has come a long way in the treatment of cancers since the time of "Doc" Holiday, and with every passing week there are more and different treatments in clinical trial. Statistically your chances of living with cancer are higher than anyone in the past has ever had. Unfortunately, statistics don't apply to individuals. This is your life and it's your treatment. Don't let anyone tell you that there is NOTHING you can do. There are always choices. Some of the choices aren't as good as others, but there are always choices.

You can even choose not to know, although reading this book has rather ruined that option. But you may know someone who is ignoring his or her disease. You can do this too, if that is the way you want your life to be. Ignore it, live your life, and hope it will go away. I don't think this is the best choice, it's really a form of self-delusion, but it is a choice. Some people think self-delusion is bad. Self-delusion is a defense mechanism our brain has developed. It keeps some of us from going insane in an overwhelmingly bad situation. Psychologist Ronald David Laing, who specialized in schizophrenia, said "Insanity sometimes is the sane response to a mad society; insanity need not always be a breakdown; it can also be a breakthrough!" Psychiatrist James Hillman may have said, "Insanity is a sane response to an insane situation."

In whatever situation you will face remember that the objective of all of this treatment is to live as normal a life as possible. Why go through all the effort and expense of treatment, radiation, chemotherapy, hospitalizations, surgeries, and the massive loss of time if you aren't going to have a quality of life? I would hate to die the day before the cure for cancer is discovered. What a waste that would be. I know, this seems like advice, but it is really just information.

The great sage Lao Tze says:

"The brightest path seems dimly lit. Moving forward seems like going backward. The easiest way seems like the hardest. Real power seems, looks, and acts like weakness. Real purity appears tattered. The most consistent things seem to flip-flop. The strongest men look weak. Reality seems unreal. The perfect square has no corners. The greatest talents don't arrive until late in life. The highest notes are the hardest to hear. The most solid form has no shape.

This way of being (Tao) is hidden and without a name, but it alone brings everything to satisfaction."

(Tao Te Ching , Chapter 41)

Chapter 17

So What Now?

Lao Tze says: "The wisest man listens to this Way of Being (Tao) and practices it diligently. The average man hears this Tao and thinks about it now and again. The foolish man hears this Tao and laughs out loud. But if there were no laughter the Tao wouldn't be what it is."

(Tao Te Ching, Chapter 41)

My friend David Zollars died while I was writing this last chapter. He was one of the true gentlemen I have had the pleasure of meeting in my lifetime. He was a great golfer, had a wonderful bass-baritone voice, and always had a twinkle in his eye and a joke in mind. He had colon cancer that went undetected until a month before he died. I will miss him.

But there is a lesson in everything. David had what he thought was constipation and stomach problems for several months before he decided to go and have something done. If you know of someone who should be tested for something; colonoscopy, mammogram, pap smear, prostate exam, a mole on the skin which grows and changes color, or anything else which is irregular, tell them to go and have it checked! David is not the first person who I know that died of cancer, nor will he be the last, unfortunately. There are people dying out there who don't have to. But they won't go and have the tests. It is inconvenient, time consuming, or they just don't want to do it. I'm tired of people around me dying unnecessarily. It is a waste.

Not that I am necessarily saying we should all live forever. That is unrealistic. When I was in the middle of chemotherapy, my friend Will McGarvey came to see me. At one point he asked, "Are you afraid of dying?" I had to think about this for a moment. The verse that I had just been reading says this:

"If you can empty your mind of all thoughts your heart will be at peace. Look at the struggles of beings and consider the return of each thing to its source. Every creature in the universe returns to the point where each began. Returning to this source brings serenity.

Returning to serenity is called being consistent. Knowing consistence is called "enlightenment." Not being consistent is the source of evil deeds because we have no roots.

Knowing consistence we can accept things as they are. By accepting things as they are, we become unbiased. By being unbiased we become like Heaven. Being like Heaven, we become one with Tao. Being one with Tao we are no longer concerned about dying because we know the Tao is forever and we are one with Tao."

(Tao Te Ching Chapter 16)

Cancer treatments for me has, most of all, been a series of internal questions. The question I asked most was, "What am I supposed to do now?" I asked this when the doctor said I had cancer. I asked it when I started chemotherapy and again when chemotherapy ended. I asked this same question as I "recovered" from the chemotherapy, when I felt well enough to go back to work. "What am I supposed to do now?"

The truth is, I have never been afraid of dying. Death is easy, life is hard. But there are several things I am afraid of which are connected with dying. You may or may not have thought about these things.

I have a fear of leaving things undone. The thought of leaving nephews and nieces who will not remember me hurts me. I can't imagine what it must be like for someone with small children. Or, perhaps, small grandchildren. No matter when we die there will always be someone left behind. I can leave pictures, momentos, and other items for them, but I won't be here. That makes me sad.

I also fear a long, lingering death. If I am going, I want to go quickly and painlessly if possible. I definitely don't want to be trapped inside my brain, in a hospital bed, being kept alive by tubes and wires for no good purpose. So what can I do about it?

This is one thing. I am making this feeling known to everyone who knows me (and even some people who don't know me). I want to stay here on this earth as long as there is a purpose for my life and when that purpose is gone, I want to go too. I've written this out and given a copy to my HMO, so they will know, and talked about it with my family, so that they will understand.

As for leaving people behind, all I can do is the best I can do. I am as open with everyone as I can be. I really try to let them in on who I am and what I feel. Especially the youngest of them.

And now I go on with my life, a day at a time. Since I started writing this book several people have died and many new people have come into my life. I mourn the loss of those who are no longer here; they are a loss to me except as memories. I rejoice in those who are still here and live my life the best I can.

Lao Tze says: "Nature uses few words. When the gale blows, it does not last long. When the hard rains come they last a short time. Why is this? Heaven and Earth.

Why do we humans go on endlessly about such little things when nature does so much in such a short time?

If you open yourself to the Tao, you and Tao become the same thing.

If you open yourself to Virtue then you can become virtuous.

If you open yourself to loss then you will become lost.

If you open yourself to the Tao, it will welcome you.

If you open yourself to virtue, virtue will become a part of you.

If you open yourself to loss, the lost will be glad to see you.

"When you do not trust people, people will become untrustworthy."

(Tao Te Ching Chapter 23)

There are too many people for me to thank and to do it effectively. I know I will forget many people who have helped in the making of this book and in saving my life and sanity. Know that, if I have left you out I didn't mean anything by it, and I am truly sorry.

My wife Elaine saved me through all this. She listened for the things I couldn't hear and was patient when I wasn't.

The Wellness Community was a big part of my survival. If there is one near you, you might investigate it. The Taoist Center in Santa Cruz was also helpful. Writing books is not putting ones self in the lowest position, this I know. But Lao Tze hadn't written Tao Te Ching, where would we all be now? Sometimes one must choose between two goods.

For Betsy S. and Ann C. who did some of the editing, as did Jay M. and Sandy B. And for Ron, Jay, Mickey, Scott, Bernadette, Barbara, and all the other people in my various groups, Pastor Will, Ed and Lauren, Bill and Susan, Vic and Vickie, Mike and Sue. Thank you all. And last but not least, Dr. Butani, my sister-in-law Carol referred him to me, and the staff at Kaiser Permanente in Walnut Creek and Antioch. This is an amazing group of people. Thank you all.

Dale Grothmann

May 2010